Lots To Do In Line: Walt Disney World®

Lots To Do In Line: Walt Disney World®
1st Edition, Second Printing

Published by
The Intrepid Traveler
P.O. Box 531
Branford, CT 06405
http://www.intrepidtraveler.com

Copyright ©2013 by Meredith Lyn Pierce
First Edition
Printed in the United States of America
Cover Design by George Foster
Cover Photo by Naheed Choudhry
Interior Design by Tim Foster, tgfDesign
Library of Congress Control Number: 2012946440
ISBN13: 978-1-937011-25-3

About The Author

Meredith Lyn Pierce was born in England but grew up in Orange County, California, Disneyland's vast backyard. She was introduced to Disney magic at a very young age and enjoyed regular visits to the park as a child, teenager, and adult. Like millions of people, Meredith fell in love with the Disney magic the moment she first encountered it. The creativity, attention to detail, and positive environment of Disneyland kept her returning year after year.

In due time, Meredith graduated from The College of Communications at California State University Fullerton and spent the next 15 years working to improve the lives of children and adults with developmental disabilities and mental illness. Her jobs varied from helping people find and keep meaningful employment to finding ways for them to live independently with appropriate assistance. She was also responsible for creating a large portion of the staff training curriculum used by North Carolina's biggest provider of services for individuals with these challenges.

The inspiration for *Lots To Do In Line* came to her during her first trip to Disneyland with her own daughter, then age seven. Looking at the park in the role of Mommy made her notice things she had failed to register before. The lines were a wonderland of things to see and do, and they were going unnoticed and underappreciated. One year later, *Lots To Do In Line: Disneyland* was born. Encouraged by rave reviews from fans and frequently expressed hopes that a *Lots To Do In Line: Walt Disney World* was in the works, Meredith headed to WDW just in time to catch the opening of the Magic Kingdom's New Fantasyland. This guide is the result. Enjoy!

Dedication

To Lisa Book, my immeasurably wonderful friend,
and to Walt Disney, whose incredible imagination
inspired me to use mine.

Photo by Carol Curtis

Acknowledgments

No one writes a book of any kind without the help of many generous people. Thank you to my wonderful family. Thank you to my husband Ken the computer whisperer, who is also great at talking me down from the ledge. I love you. Thank you to my daughter Camille. No one should be without a daughter like you, but I am the lucky one who gets to benefit from your boundless enthusiasm and desire to help me. Thank you to my mother, who has helped me in the parks and on the book. You're the best mother ever, no doubt about it. Thank you to my Grandfather Nero Roy for your generous birthday gift that helped me complete my travels for this book. I am happy to make you proud.

A great big thanks to all of my friends, who have listened to my constant obsession with standing in line. I know it is odd and you are kind not to say so.

Thanks to Shuchi Sharma, for the gift of your time looking over my contract and all of your advice. You helped me feel safe as I started this journey.

Thank you to Ricky Brigante for your website "Inside the Magic." It is unendingly useful for checking facts and making discoveries. Ricky Brigante and Michelle Moss are responsible for having decoded the hidden message in the Haunted Mansion queue. Your cyphering skills are epic.

Thank you to The Intrepid Traveler and Kelly Monaghan, for standing in line with me again. Thank you to Sally Scanlon; I could not have asked for a more supportive editor. Thank you also to George Foster for your cover design and Tim Foster for making all my words fit so beautifully.

Thanks so very much to the Hall Salloom family, Kevin, Joanne, Lindsey, and Alana, for opening your home to Camille while I traveled. Thank you for the peace of mind.

Thanks to Michelle Dodds for the beautiful web page art. You did an incredible job.

Finally thank you to The Walt Disney Company for filling so many of the Walt Disney World® Resort's lines with amazing treasures and hidden treats.

Table of Contents

Enjoy the Fun Before the Ride

Welcome to "the happiest place on earth." You are in for a wonderful time. If you are a child, or a child at heart, the fun is everywhere. Many guidebooks have been written about the Walt Disney World Resort (WDW) and I have no intention of writing "just another guidebook." I wrote *Lots To Do In Line: Walt Disney World* to celebrate the fun that most people overlook on their visit to WDW's magical kingdoms – the lines. That's right, the lines. Puzzled? Read on.

As you are doubtless aware, lines at the theme parks tend to be daunting much of the year. No one likes to stand and wait. But happily, you don't have to just stand and wait at the WDW parks. Disney's Imagineers have packed a wealth of detail and delight in just about every queue in each of the four WDW theme parks. All you need to do is open your eyes and your imagination. With this book as your guide, a writing implement in hand, and a child (or a child at heart) by your side ready to play, you'll be all set to make your time in line some of the happiest memories of your visit. Disney provides all the rest, with occasional help from your fellow guests.

How Do I Use This Book?

Lots To Do In Line turns your wait time into fun time by using the wealth of visual (and sometimes audio) detail Disney builds into its parks and most of its ride queues to create games for rides in the Magic Kingdom, Epcot, Disney's Hollywood Studios, Disney's Animal Kingdom, and each show that tends to have a waiting queue. The rides and shows are grouped alphabetically in the "lands" and "areas" found in the official park Guidemaps (see the *Index* in the back of this book for specific page numbers).

As you join a new queue, open your book to the appropriate ride or show. You'll find challenging questions and treasure hunts that turn your time in line into an amusing game. You don't need any prior knowledge to play these games. All the answers can be found just by looking around you, in the queue and beyond, for those clever details the Disney Imagineers and designers have provided. The questions are multiple-choice, meaning you never need to stop to fill in an answer, and the hunts ask you to circle or check the items you find, so again, you have nothing to write in.

Waiting times vary, of course, and some queues are less well detailed than others. To ensure that you have fun all the way up to the loading dock, you will sometimes be directed to build a "Collection." Collections are groups of things to look for that you'll find sprinkled all around the parks (weather vanes, for example) or things you can spot on your fellow guests, such as sparkling shoes and character T-shirts. You can hunt for Collection treasure anytime you choose, while in line or while walking around the parks. "Collection Suggestions," below, offers a list of things you might "collect" during your park visit, but feel free to use your imagination.

Earn Points

Let's face it, everything is more fun when you get points for it. You get 1 point for every question you answer correctly. You also get 1 point for every item you find when treasure hunting and 1 point every time you add an item to one of your Collections. In addition, at the end of the day, you get 5 bonus points for every Collection in which you've gathered more than 10 items. If you pay close attention, Collections will help you clean up on points. Remember, the more you get involved in having fun at Walt Disney World Resort, the more points you'll rack up.

What do you get for your points? You get the joy of achieving them, of course! It's a great feeling to know you're succeeding – and you'll have the extra enjoyment of seeing all the wonderful details that make the WDW parks so entertaining.

Three Ways To Play The Lots-To-Do Games

1) Team up with other members of your group to answer as many questions as possible. You've undoubtedly heard the saying "two minds are better than one." Well that is certainly true here. If everyone works together, your team can earn the most points and become experts in "line-ology." You can add up

your points for each queue – and declare a winning team for each one. Or you can add up all your points for the park at the end of the day to see how each team did overall. Or both.

2) Compete individually with other members of your group. Whoever answers the most questions correctly before you reach the end of the queue gets the most points and is declared the winner for that queue. (This method works best when each player has a copy of the book.)

3) Play the games without competing. You or your child may simply want to use this guide to enjoy all the special details found in the queues. Of course, players must be able to read on their own to investigate the queues independently. Younger players will require the assistance of an adult or an older friend or sibling.

However you decide to play, you will be spending time interacting with each other and the park you came to enjoy. A large portion of your day will pass waiting in the queues. That time can be a wonderful part of your memories or a lost opportunity. It is up to you.

Pop Quizzes

When you come to any place in the book marked **? POP QUIZ!**, you are about to play a memory game. I can sense you sweating it right now. Don't worry, there is no grade. This test is just for fun! The instructions will direct you to have a quick look at something before you get in line. Whatever it is will be very close at hand. After you look, join the queue and prepare to have some fun remembering what you saw.

Tip: Many of the pop quizzes involve the sign for the attraction, so always have a good look at it as you head for the queue.

Order Of The Questions

Where possible, questions are presented in the order you're likely to encounter the visuals or audio to answer them. In this way, the clues are sprinkled throughout the lines. Keep checking the next few questions ahead in case you pass something without noticing it. If you think you've passed by a clue, don't worry, it means you're getting closer to the ride.

By the way, while every effort has been made to present the questions in the order you will discover the clues, it is important to remember that queues are sometimes rearranged to accommodate larger crowds. In the event that the questions don't seem to match what you are seeing or hearing as you move through the queue, you can assume that the line has been rearranged – especially if you are visiting at a busy season, such as a holiday. Read ahead to find the questions applicable to the area you are currently in.

Using "Lots To Do" In Interactive Queues

Walt Disney World has a handful of queues that are enhanced with interactive activities to entertain you while you wait. These queues are full of Disney magic and there is no doubt that they are a blast – and the wave of the future. But you won't want to put your book away when you enter one because it is really easy to miss some of their cleverest parts. A guest enjoying the Haunted Mansion interactive queue in Magic Kingdom, for example, will definitely discover the musical instruments that can come to life at your touch and the books that pop from their shelves. But it is very easy to miss the murder mystery waiting quietly to be solved among the stone busts or the cryptogram hidden discreetly in the bookshelves. With *Lots To Do In Line* in hand, you'll be pointed to all the extra special things in the interactive queue. So be sure to consult it as you are entering the line.

Using "Lots To Do" In FASTPASS Lines

Most of the time when you're waiting for rides, you will be standing in what Disney calls the standby queues. These are the "regular" lines, the queues you simply walk into and move along until you reach the loading area for the ride. A few of the most popular rides offer FASTPASS options. These are special queues with shorter waits. (The Guidemap you are given when you enter the park tells you which rides offer FASTPASS and exactly how they work.)

When you are using a FASTPASS, you won't see everything that you would see from the standby line because you will bypass much of the queue. So when you use FASTPASS, look for the questions marked *FP*. The clues for these questions are visible from both the standby and FASTPASS queues unless otherwise noted. In most cases, though, the FASTPASS line will move so quickly that you will only be able to answer a few questions at most.

Scan the questions marked *FP* to find ones that correspond to your location in the FASTPASS queue.

A Special Note For Grown-ups

Most people, regardless of age, truly hate waiting in line. Children find it particularly daunting because the very nature of a child is to be active. They are learning, thinking, seeing, and doing beings. They are never sedentary. Children do not just "look and enjoy," they "do" things. So while everything you need to stay happy and entertained is right there for you in most of the queues, it's easy for children (and many older folk, as well) to miss them. That's where this book comes in.

Lots To Do In Line will help you and your child experience the WDW theme park queues actively, turning the wait into a game. Instead of asking kids to appreciate, say, an interesting prop when they come to it, it will have them hunting for that prop, trying to discover something about it, and earning points for their accomplishments. And let's face it, adults and teens enjoy that, too; this book is designed to keep the whole family interested and interacting.

The questions are intended to offer a challenge but not to be so hard that a child feels he or she is losing the game. To that end, the multiple-choice design provides hints as to where to look to find the answer successfully. WDW, after all, is designed to be "the happiest place on earth," not a place to lose. While children are focused on a quest, they can't be complaining of being bored, hot, or hungry.

Happy kids equal happy parents. Have a great time enjoying the challenges at WDW.

Meredith Pierce

P.S. The WDW parks are constantly changing – adding new attractions and renovating and replacing others. So it is likely that when you visit, a few of the clues will have changed. If you spot things that are no longer there – or new things that have been added, I hope your will let me know care of my website, LotsToDoInLine.com. Sharing what you know will make these games even more fun for everyone.

Collection Suggestions

Lines aren't limited to rides and shows. From time to time, you'll find yourself waiting to meet a character, buy an item, or get a snack or meal. When that happens, you may want to pass the time – and rack up more points – by building a Collection or adding to one you've already started. Choose a Collection or two that you think will work well for the area you are in. For example, if you are in Fantasyland, a Collection of girls dressed like princesses should serve you well. If you are in Adventureland, you will probably find a Collection of pirate flags more useful.

Some things, such as Mickey Mouse ears, are useful absolutely everywhere.

When you come to a ride that calls for Collections, choose several. Remember, you get 1 point for every item you add to a Collection and 5 bonus points at the end of the day for every Collection that includes more than 10 items.

1) Weather vanes. Many Disney rides have interesting weather vanes on top. If you look carefully you should find lots.

2) Hats. There are many funny hats for sale at WDW, and guests come with hats of their own. Earn 1 point for each different kind of hat you collect. For baseball caps, earn 1 point for each separate color you find.

3) Pin collectors. Many people visiting the parks will have collections of Disney Pins. These are fun to look at and easy to collect. Earn 1 point for each pin collector you spot.

4) Girls dressed as princesses. Young visitors sometimes like to get in the spirit by dressing as their favorite princess.

5) Crazy backpacks. There are all sorts of funny backpacks available at WDW. You can count ones you see in stores (only one of a kind, please) and ones people are wearing.

6) Pirate flags. It would appear that pirates have made their presence known at WDW. If you keep your eyes open, you can find some of the places they have been, marked with their flag.

7) Different Mickey Mouse ears. Mickey ears come in many varieties. How many can you spot today?

8) Sparkling shoes. Time to check out the feet of your

fellow guests. Some of them are glittery.

9) Shoes with no laces. As long as you are looking down already, see how many you can spot.

10) People wearing different Disney characters on their T-shirts. Many people like to wear Disney-character T-shirts while visiting the parks. How many different people wearing character T-shirts can you find?

11) T-shirts picturing animals – the non-cartoon kind. How many different animals can you spot on the T-shirts worn by your fellow guests. (Count each kind of animal only once please.)

12) Modes of transportation. WDW operates many kinds of vehicles. How many different kinds can you find?

13) Images of Disney characters that aren't on T-shirts. There are pictures and sculptures of characters from various movies all around the parks. How many can you collect?

14) People with balloons. You'll see lots of balloons in the WDW parks. How many people carrying a balloon can you spot? (If a person is carrying multiple balloons that only counts as one find.)

15) Disney characters in the park. At various times, you'll see Disney characters in the theme parks greeting guests.

16) Waterfalls. Keep your eyes and ears out for these. You get 2 points for each one you collect.

17) Clock faces. There are many beautiful clocks around the parks. See how many you can find.

18) Water fountains. People get thirsty. Keep your eyes open for the water fountains.

19) People with face paint. (Yes. You can count yourself if you have your face painted – but only once.)

20) People texting. We all love to stay in touch.

21) Kids dressed as pirates. Ahoy there, sailor.

22) People with lightsabers. May the Force be with you.

23) Disney staff from places other then Florida. Look at the name badges worn by Cast Members. They include the place the person is from. How many different places can you spot?

24) Something printed in the pavement. At times you'll find treasure beneath your feet.

Magic Kingdom

In this chapter, you'll find games for most of the park's ride queues as well as for shows that tend to have queues. They are organized by lands, in the order you will find them on your Guidemap, and then alphabetically within each land. Attractions that don't have queues are not included.

If you want to continue to play when you are walking around the park from one place to another, turn to the Magic Kingdom Scavenger Hunt at the end of this chapter.

Tip: You may want to read over the list now and then stay on the lookout. The treasures on the scavenger hunt list are scattered throughout the park. You get 1 point for every treasure you find.

Note: When you see *FP* next to a question or section, it means you can find the answer (or gather Treasure or Collection items) from both the FASTPASS and standby lines. A **?** in the margin is your signal to look hard at something (often the attraction's sign) before you enter the queue.

Scoring: Unless specified otherwise, give yourself 1 point for each correct answer, 1 point for each Treasure you find, 1 point for each item you add to a Collection, and 1 point for any similar finds you make when you are hunting for something rather than answering questions. Don't forget to add 5 bonus points for each of your Collections with more than 10 items in it at the end of the day. Good luck!

Main Street, U.S.A.

Walt Disney World Railroad Station

1. There is a white sign in the window telling you that you are at Main Street Station. What animal is pictured on this sign?
  a. A lion
  b. An eagle
  c. Mickey Mouse, naturally
  d. There is no animal. The picture is of a train.

2. Have a peek inside the station office. Which of these things is not in the office?
  a. A padlock
  b. A stack of tickets
  c. A toy train
  d. A cup
  e. They are all there.

3. There is a music box in the station house. What year was it manufactured?
  a. 1885
  b. 1899
  c. 1904
  d. 1927

4. What costs 10 cents?
  a. A chance to play ball
  b. A look at San Francisco
  c. A ticket from the railroad office
  d. Bubblegum

5. Railroads could not have spanned the continent without what?
- a. The steel industry's financial backing
- b. The dedication of Americans
- c. Wheels
- d. America's forests

6. Treasure Hunt Time! It is time for a quick treasure hunt. See how many of these treasures you can find before the conductor calls, "All aboard!"
- ❏ A headband
- ❏ A clamshell shape
- ❏ Two trains on a bridge
- ❏ Glasses
- ❏ A soup ladle
- ❏ Bad behavior
- ❏ A big fall
- ❏ A man on a ladder
- ❏ A U.S. flag
- ❏ Someone with no arms
- ❏ A man on a horse
- ❏ Ten wooden spheres
- ❏ A steamer trunk

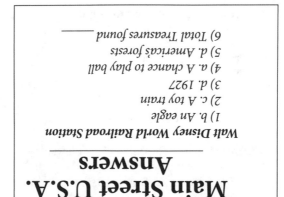

Main Street U.S.A.
Answers

Walt Disney World Railroad Station

1) b. An eagle
2) c. A toy train
3) d. 1927
4) a. A chance to play ball
5) d. America's forests
6) Total Treasures found _____

Adventureland

Jungle Cruise

? **POP QUIZ!** As you approach the queue, you'll pass a sign directing you to enter on the right for standby and on the left for FASTPASS. Have a good look at it, then join the queue.

FP **1. What animal was featured on that sign?**
> a. A snake
> b. A spider
> c. A lizard
> d. All of the above

FP **2. According to that sign, what has this tour company never done?**
> a. Become accredited
> b. Wasted valuable time on ship maintenance
> c. Lost a boat
> d. Remained captured by natives for more than one year

FP **3. Was there a boat pictured on the sign?**
> Yes / No

FP **4. Was there a globe pictured on the sign?**
> Yes / No

End of Pop Quiz

FP **5. You are near the live cargo holding area. What warning is offered here?**
> a. Keep your hands to yourself – if you want to keep them, that is!
> b. Have your ticket ready or prepare to be added to the live cargo holding enclosure!
> c. Smuggling live cargo onto the boat is punishable by being thrown overboard. (You have been warned!)

    d. Don't feed creatures in the live cargo holding
       enclosure – your fingers may become part of the
       menu!

FP 6. **Which of these things is not found in the live cargo holding enclosure?**
    a. A chain
    b. A boxed rat
    c. A bicycle
    d. A shipping tag for someone who lives in Florida
    e. All four are present.

7. **Which of the following can be found in the garden?**
    a. Three skull parts
    b. A lantern
    c. A hammer
    d. A metal teapot
    e. All of the above
    f. All but d

8. **Hey look, there is another kind of tour offered here. What kind of tour is advertised besides boat tours?**
    a. Single-engine airplane
    b. Walking
    c. Elephant
    d. Star

9. **Treasure Hunt Time!** See how many of these tropical treasures you can find before you get jungle fever.
- An old-time camera
- A broken jug
- A propeller
- A bamboo ladder
- A grass mat
- A notice
- An animal-drawn buggy
- A boat for ivory and spice dealers
- A diagram of ruins
- An elephant with something in its trunk
- A glass ball
- Khyber rifles
- A scale
- A metal teacup
- A lifesaver
- A rope ladder
- A pith helmet

FP 10. There is a chalkboard with a list of everything that has gone missing. Maybe we can help. What is missing?

    a. Luggage. Why do they always lose luggage?

    b. People! Maybe we should rethink using this jungle expedition company.

    c. Whole boats. Yup, definitely rethinking this.

    d. All of the above. Is this place accredited?

    e. All but a

FP 11. Which of these poor unfortunate people is listed as missing?

    a. U.N. Lucky

    b. B.N. Eaton

    c. Ilene Dover

    d. Ann Fellen

    e. They are all missing, poor dears.

    f. All but "a" are missing; lucky break for U.N. Lucky.

FP 12. There are some boats that will not be an option for travel today due to their… er… missing status. Which of these boats is not missing?

    a. Sunken Sonya

    b. Fateless Fiona

    c. Burning Bianca

    d. Missing Mele

    e. Sadly all these boats are, shall we say, not currently afloat.

13. **Treasure Hunt Time!** There are a few more treasures hidden deep in this jungle. Well, not the jungle exactly, but they are hidden deep in this queue. See how many you can unearth.

    ❑ A lady's blue hat with a feather

    ❑ A bell

    ❑ A shield made by the local natives

    ❑ A single rifle

    ❑ A lantern

    ❑ A barrel

    ❑ A large burlap sack

FP 14. There is a house just across the river from here. Nice view! The occupants seem to be rather sloppy housekeepers. Listed below are a number of their possessions. Some are visible here at the house while others were lost in the jungle years ago. Check all the things that are here.

    a. Fishing equipment
    b. A pineapple
    c. A banana
    d. Apples
    e. A bell
    f. A sign indicating the occupants' greeting to visitors
    g. A coconut
    h. A dartboard
    i. A claw
    j. An animal pelt
    k. A crutch

? **POP QUIZ!** OK, before you are allowed out into the jungle, you must pass a test. You don't think we let just anyone out there, do you? Have a good look at the Jungle Cruise office. Then see how many of these questions you can answer from memory.

15. How did it appear that they wrote letters here at the office?
    a. By computer
    b. By typewriter
    c. By hand
    d. By dictating to a monkey with pen and pencil

16. Was there an open lunchbox?
Yes / No

17. Was there a bell to ring for service if no one was at the desk?
Yes / No

18. Was a large black spider on the wall?
Yes / No

19. Was there a telephone off the hook?
Yes / No

20. Was there a photo of a girl?
Yes / No

21. Was there a note on the desk indicating that the person who should be manning it had gone fishing?
    Yes / No

22. Was an elephant figurine on the desk?
    Yes / No

23. Was a native-statue sitting on the floor?
    Yes / No

24. Was there a rifle in the room?
    Yes / No

25. Was there a radio?
    Yes / No

26. Hey, was there a chair at that desk?
    Yes / No

27. Was there a certificate on the wall awarded to Skipper Dan for 10 years of distinguished service?
    Yes / No

28. There was a jar of pencils. Did it also include a ruler?
    Yes / No

29. Was there a collection of butterflies?
    Yes / No

End of Pop Quiz

30. There is a glass case on the wall. Which of these things is not sitting on top of it?
    a. A bowling pin
    b. An oar
    c. A mask
    d. An oilcan
    e. They were all up there.
    f. All but c. That would just be silly.

***FP* 31. What is being shipped to Stanleyville Research Facility?**
        a. A live tiger cub. DO NOT open crate!
        b. A crate of shrunken heads
        c. Venom samples
        d. Flesh-eating beetles

FP 32. There is a creature in a cage on the dock. Cool. What is it?
   a. A cobra
   b. A tarantula
   c. A rat
   d. A baby elephant. Hey, wait a minute, should they be taking him out of the jungle?

FP 33. What activity is strictly prohibited for skippers?
   a. Inviting customers to take a dip in Crocodile Lagoon; we can no longer afford the insurance.
   b. Operating the boats in a backwards fashion to add spice to life
   c. Maintaining a pet crocodile on board the boat
   d. Using boats to go over Schweitzer Falls

FP 34. Can you find a box containing mosquitoes?
   Yes (Now why would someone want that?)
   No

FP 35. There is a T-shirt that has seen better days. What happened to it?
   a. Baby tigers can be enthusiastic.
   b. It was used for a sail when a motor gave out. That was a very slow trip.
   c. A boat passenger did not think the "Do not feed wildlife" sign applied to him.
   d. It got put in a load that included a red sock. Enough said.

FP 36. What food tastes like chicken?
   a. Fricassee of Giant Stag Beetle
   b. Barbecued Three-Toed Skink
   c. Fillet of Rock Python
   d. All of the above. None for me; I'm full.

FP 37. Treasure Hunt Time! Soon you will be cruising on jungle rivers, enjoying the local animals up close and not in cages. See how many treasures you can find before we wish you bon voyage.
   ❏ A mug of beer
   ❏ Three masks
   ❏ A coil of rope
   ❏ A barrel with a handle on it
   ❏ A red gas can
   ❏ A plane that can land on water

- ❑ A shovel
- ❑ A crate in the sky
- ❑ A pulley
- ❑ An oar
- ❑ An opportunity

Pirates of the Caribbean

? **POP QUIZ!** If ye head right inside the building, matey, skip to Question 9. But if the line for this attraction be long enough to start outside the building, then it be time to play "Pirate Memory." Before ye enter the queue, have a look at the big sign for the attraction located just in front of the building's courtyard. Now see how good your memory is, you scalawag.

1. Someone was standing in the crow's-nest. Who?
   a. Caption Jack Sparrow (a pirate with dreadlocks)
   b. A skeleton
   c. Mickey Mouse dressed as a pirate
   d. It was just a random pirate.

2. The ride's name was written on a white sail.
   True or False?

3. How many holes had cannonballs made in the ship's sail?
   a. 3
   b. 4
   c. 5
   d. Is someone firing cannons?

4. The bottom of the ship's sail was tied to something. What was it tied to?
   a. An oar
   b. A long rifle
   c. A flagpole
   d. Just an ordinary long pole

5. OK, so there was a skeleton up in the crow's-nest. What did he have in his hands?
   a. A parrot
   b. A rifle; not sure what good it will do him now.
   c. A telescope

d. A treasure chest (Apparently, you can take it with you.)

6. What did the skeleton have on his head?
    a. A captain's hat   b. A scarf
    c. A parrot   d. Mickey Mouse ears

7. Our skeletal friend had a lantern with him.
    True or False?

8. The skeleton was fully dressed.
    a. True, in rags
    b. False, he wasn't even wearing his birthday suit.
Avast, ye bilge rat, the Pop Quiz is over.

Special Pirates Collection: If ye are still on the patio, now would be a good time to work on a Special Collection, matey. Oh, ye say, ye've not been told what it is? That be a likely excuse. The Special Collection for this queue is "lamps." See how many unique lamps, lanterns, and flashlights ye can find before ye be left in the dark. Award yourself 1 point for each lamp found.

Inside the Building: Right Queue
The treasure map charts two different paths ye can plunder, if ye be brave enough. If ye head RIGHT, then start here. But if ye prefer to seek fortune to the LEFT, advance to Question 16.

9. Ye have entered the building. What be its name?
    a. Fort Port Royal
    b. Castillo del Morro
    c. Safe Hold at Farthest Gate
    d. Castillo de la Muerta

10. Treasure Hunt Time! How many of these treasures can ye dig up, matey?
- ❑ A barrel with a cork in it
- ❑ Three glass balls
- ❑ A bucket
- ❑ Two bags
- ❑ Two pulleys
- ❑ A boat
- ❑ A nest
- ❑ A barrel with yellow markings
- ❑ A rusty chain

11. Down the hall a little bit you will find another room. What is stored in the red barrels?

    a. They should hold rum. But why is the rum gone?

    b. Cannonballs

    c. Explosives

    d. Lemons to prevent the scurvy, ye landlubber

12. What is displayed on the walls in the room with the red barrels?

    a. Tools for stuffing cannons full of explosives

    b. Shelves littered with empty bottles of rum

    c. A collection of rifles

    d. A recipe for "The Scurvy Dog's best lemonade/ rum mixer"

    e. Nothing

Avast! Don't forget to keep yur eyes open for me Special Collection of lamps. They be real beauties.

13. This be a prison for the worst bilge rats on the seven seas. Some of the prisoners seem to have died of boredom, instead of the plank. Why?

    a. They were singing the song about beer on the wall. You can only do that so long with no grog, matey.

    b. They were staring at the wall and it was providing very little entertainment value.

    c. They were looking at books with no pictures. Pirates can't read!

    d. They were playing a game of chess that appears to have had no end but their own.

14. Which of these fine pirate luxuries was not provided to the prisoners in this cell?

    a. A rat   b. A pitcher

    c. A key   d. A bandana

    e. Both a and c

15. Treasure Hunt Time! Well, blow me down, it be almost time for ye to prepare for boarding, matey. As ye pass through the remaining spaces, see how much more booty ye can collect.

    ❑ Three cannons

    ❑ Four red explosives barrels

    ❑ A basket with a sack inside

    ❑ A length of rope

- ❑ A wood plane (woodworking tool)
- ❑ A skeleton that is not human
- ❑ A wrapped package tied up with a rope
- ❑ An open crate
- ❑ A mallet
- ❑ A pyramid
- ❑ A stick with a hook on it
- ❑ A pickaxe
- ❑ The thing ye'd be happy to find at the "X"

Inside the Building: Left Queue
If you went left, matey, then this be "Start" for you.

16. Ye have entered the building. What be its name?
- a. Fort Port Royal
- b. Castillo del Morro
- c. Safe Hold at Farthest Gate
- d. Castillo de la Muerta

17. Treasure Hunt Time! See how many of these treasures ye can dig up quickly.
- ❑ A nest
- ❑ Four glass balls
- ❑ Two pulleys
- ❑ A barrel with yellow markings
- ❑ A frayed knot
- ❑ A fuse
- ❑ A skull
- ❑ A bucket containing a rusty chain
- ❑ A basket containing a burlap sack

18. You will come to the room where the hand weapons be locked up and stored. Are they all locked up?
Yes / No

19. There be a lock with a lot "O" heart to it. Can ye find it?
Yes / No

20. Arrrrr! It be time to search for more of me missing booty. Be quick. It be all in this room.
- ❑ A cannon on its nose
- ❑ Three handguns
- ❑ A bucket of balls
- ❑ A double pulley

❑ A warm heart
❑ Four brass levers

Avast! Don't forget to keep yur eyes open for me Special Collection of lamps. They be real beauties.

21. Treasure Hunt Time! Well, blow me down, it be almost time for ye to prepare for boarding. As ye pass through the remaining spaces, see how much more booty ye can add to yur treasure chest. Find it or prepare to walk the plank.

❑ A skeleton that is not human
❑ A mallet
❑ A rope handle
❑ A wrapped package tied up with a rope
❑ A wood plane (woodworking tool)
❑ A cannon all hung up
❑ Two cannons on their noses
❑ Four tools for loading cannons
❑ A pulley with a rusty hook
❑ A tied-up length of rope
❑ An old man spitting
❑ A basket in a fancy shape
❑ Two hanging plants

The Magic Carpets of Aladdin

1. As you entered the queue, there was a beautiful carpet announcing the ride. Who was looking over the top of the carpet?

a. A monkey   b. A parrot
c. A camel   d. A genie

2. Was there anything unusual about her?

a. Yes, she is gold.
b. Yes, she is bejeweled.
c. Yes, she is wearing a jaunty little hat.
d. All of the above
e. Nope, totally normal-looking

3. Someone is providing periodic serenades. Listen closely for them. Who is singing to you?
- a. A group of six tiki totems
- b. A lamp
- c. A parrot
- d. That kid over there; she knows a lot of Disney songs.

4. Something is tipped over in the sand. What is it?
- a. A chest of treasure
- b. An urn
- c. A magic lamp
- d. A tiki

5. Notice anything about the pillar tiki that is, well, repetitive?
- a. Too many heads – but I guess two heads are better than one.
- b. Too many hands – unless he is an octopus
- c. Too many feet for someone who does not move
- d. All of the above

6. This tiki is acting as a pillar. What is he holding up?
- a. A building's roof
- b. A building's floor
- c. A lamp
- d. The line. I wish he would move.

7. Somewhere there is a camel behaving rudely. What is she up to?
- a. She is burping – not very ladylike.
- b. She is spitting – time for etiquette school.
- c. She is blowing bubbles out her nose.
- d. Camels are very polite creatures. They would never engage in these activities.

8. There is a roof nearby with some very special adornments. What makes this roof fancy?
- a. It is made entirely out of colorful silk carpets.
- b. It is topped with a giant emerald.
- c. It is solid gold.
- d. It is covered with bulls' heads. I think I will "steer" clear of it.

9. Treasure Hunt Time! See how many of Aladdin's treasures you can find before you fly away.
- ❑ A dolphin

- ❑ A tiger
- ❑ A purple rug out to dry
- ❑ A monkey doing a handstand
- ❑ Aladdin's lamp
- ❑ Golden eyelashes
- ❑ A diamond
- ❑ A ruby
- ❑ A sapphire
- ❑ Two drainpipes
- ❑ A red vest
- ❑ A stained-glass lamp
- ❑ A tiki with a horn hat
- ❑ Four terracotta urns
- ❑ Cactus
- ❑ A rooftop face
- ❑ A guy holding a torch over his head
- ❑ Three skulls
- ❑ A mound riddled with holes
- ❑ The number 16

Walt Disney's Enchanted Tiki Room

Soon you will meet two birds named Claude and Clyde. They are going to tell you how the birds of the Tiki Room came to talk. Before they come out, let's see how good you are at making birdbrained predictions. Will your guesses be as clever as an owl, or would you be more of a feather-head like our friend the dodo? Look at the following questions and make your guesses. The player with the most correct guesses gets all 10 points.

1. What kind of birds do you guess Claude and Clyde will be?

a. Parrots   b. Cockatoos

c. Toucans   d. An owl and a dodo

2. What color will Claude and Clyde be?

a. Red and blue   b. Green and orange

c. White and pink   d. Brown and browner

3. What do you think Claude and Clyde will be perched on?

    a. A tiki   b. A tree

    c. A bird perch   d. A baby elephant

4. What will the magical place where birds discovered that they can talk be called?

    a. Feathered Grotto

    b. Cacophony Landing

    c. Sunshine Pavilion

    d. The Chatter Box

5. Claude and Clyde are birds of a feather. How do you think they are related to each other?

    a. They are brothers.

    b. They are cousins.

    c. Claude is Clyde's Dad.

    d. They are not related, they are just friends.

6. Clyde tends to be a bit confused and sometimes forgets his name. What do you think Clyde thinks his last name is?

    a. Featherhead   b. Twitterpate

    c. Pretty bird   d. Birdbrain

7. Claude and Clyde make their discovery while on a ride. What do you think they were riding?

    a. An explorer's barge

    b. An elephant

    c. An explorer's shoulder

    d. The breeze

8. Clyde does animal impressions but some leave room for improvement. Which of these animals do you think Clyde needs to work on a bit more?

    a. African lion   b. Elephant

    c. Outraged birds   d. Monkey

    e. Crocodile

9. What animal do you think charged the birds while they explored?

    a. Bull elephant

    b. Angry lion

    c. Hungry bear

    d. A villager trying to shoo them away from the fruit trees

10. What animal do you think really upsets Clyde?
   a. Elephants
   b. Snakes
   c. Monkeys
   d. Peacocks. "They think they're so special."

11. What will Claude describe the show as?
   a. A treat of the tweet
   b. A flight of fanciful song
   c. A real tropical serenade
   d. A cacophony

12. If you still have time to wait this would be a good time to work on your Collections.

Adventureland Answers

Jungle Cruise
   1) d. All of the above
   2) c. Lost a boat
   3) No
   4) Yes
   5) a. Keep your hands to yourself.
   6) b. A boxed rat
   7) f. All but d
   8) c. Elephant
   9) Total Treasures found _____
   10) e. All but a
   11) f. All but "a" are missing
   12) e. Sadly all these boats are not currently afloat.
   13) Total Treasures found _____
   14) a. Fishing Equipment, c. Banana, d. Apples, f. Occupants' greeting sign, h. Dartboard, i. Claw, k. Crutch
   15) b. By typewriter
   16) No
   17) Yes
   18) Yes
   19) No
   20) Yes
   21) No
   22) No
   23) Yes

24) Yes

25) Yes

26) Yes

27) No

28) Yes

29) Yes

30) e. They were all up there.

31) c. Venom samples

32) b. A tarantula

33) d. Using boats to go over Schweitzer Falls

34) Yes

35) a. Baby tigers can be enthusiastic.

36) d. All of the above

37) Total Treasures found _____

Pirates of the Caribbean

1) b. A skeleton

2) False

3) c. 5

4) a. An oar

5) c. A telescope

6) b. A scarf

7) True

8) True

Inside the Building: Right Queue

9) b. Castillo del Morro

10) Total Treasures found _____

11) c. Explosives

12) a. Tools for stuffing cannons full of explosives

13) d. They were playing a game of chess.

14) e. Both a and c

15) Total Treasures found _____

Inside the Building: Left Queue

16) b. Castillo del Morro

17) Total Treasures dug up _____

18) No

19) Yes

20) Missing booty found _____

21) Total Treasures found _____

22) Number of lamps collected _____

The Magic Carpets of Aladdin

1) c. A camel

2) d. All of the above

3) a. A group of six tiki totems

4) b. An urn
5) d. All of the above
6) a. A building's roof
7) b. She is spitting.
8) d. It is covered with bulls' heads.
9) Total Aladdin Treasures found _____

Walt Disney's Enchanted Tiki Room Answers
1) c. Toucans
2) b. Green and orange
3) a. A tiki
4) c. Sunshine Pavilion
5) b. They are cousins
6) d. Birdbrain
7) a. An explorer's barge
8) e. Crocodile
9) a. A bull elephant
10) b. Snakes
11) c. A real tropical serenade
12) Number of items collected _____

Frontierland

Big Thunder Mountain Railroad

1. It's time to play "Mother Lode."
Barnabas T. Bullion, is the founder of the Big Thunder Mining Company. I reckin' you are welcome here at his mine. That is unless you are a filthy claim-jumping varmint. It seems some snake is trying to put a spoke through the wheels of Big Thunder Mining Company by stealin' Bullion's gold and bilkin' him out of his gold mine! In fact, some dreadful big nuggets have gone missin' just since you ambled up, pardner.

Hear that! There may be a gold thief in your group! Here is how to play "Mother Lode": Your group picks one person to be the gold poacher. Everyone else plays sheriff. Your gold poacher selects a spot within view as the hiding place for the stolen gold. (*Tip:* The queue offers many great hidey holes, but be sure to choose a place that will remain visible as you move along in the queue or the game won't work. If at any point the hiding place is no longer visible, the poacher should pick a new hiding place and tell the sheriffs that the gold has been moved.)

It is the sheriffs' job to puzzle out where the poacher hid the gold. Taking turns, each sheriff asks a yes or no question about the hiding place. For example, "Is it hidden someplace on the ground?" The sheriffs keep taking turns asking questions until someone thinks they've reckoned out where the gold is stashed and says, "The jig is up." If the sheriff's guess is correct, that player gets 5 points. If the sheriff is wrong, the poacher takes the points and re-hides the gold. When the stash is found, the finder becomes the next poacher and the game starts over.

2. Iffin you tire of huntin down the lawless, this would be a good time to ponder on your Collections. Hats and backpacks would work well here.

Country Bear Jamboree

? **POP QUIZ!** Have a quick look at the sign for this attraction and then see if your memory is a "claws" for celebration or just something to "growl" about.

1. There were three bears playing instruments on the sign. Which of these instruments was among them?
    a. Washboard
    b. Banjo
    c. Jug
    d. Harmonica

2. How many of the bears were sporting a hat?
    a. 1
    b. 2
    c. All three; hats are very stylish.
    d. Now what would a bear be doing with a hat?

3. One of the bears was wearing a sharp-looking bandana. What color was it?

    a. Red   b. Blue

    c. Orange   d. Green with a mustard stain

4. One of the instruments featured a decoration. What was it?

    a. A bone   b. A tooth

    c. A claw   d. A sticker advertising "The Five Bear Rugs Band"

5. One of the bears had no claws except the one he used as a guitar pick.

    Yes / No

6. One of the bears had his teeth showing.

    Yes / No

End of Pop Quiz

7. What is the name of the building you are about to enter?

    a. Brown Bear Auditorium

    b. Grizzly Hall

    c. Golden Claw Theater

    d. That Place Down Yonder Where We Sing

8. When was it established?

    a. 1795   b. 1898

    c. 1912   d. Longer ago than you can remember

9. An auction is scheduled. What will be auctioned?

    a. Broken instruments

    b. Liver Lips McGrowl's favorite hat

    c. A kiss from Trixie. "Pucker up, boys."

    d. A horse

Inside Grizzly Hall

10. Treasure Hunt Time! It is time for a quick hunt, country style. Let's see if your hunting skills are "Grrrrreate" or just "clawful."

    ❑ A raccoon

    ❑ A glass of wine

    ❑ A stump

    ❑ Mickey Mouse

    ❑ A pine cone

- ❏ A bear with wings
- ❏ A parasol
- ❏ A hat with a hole
- ❏ A honey of a treat
- ❏ Very small doors
- ❏ Bear damage
- ❏ That bear has no hair! At least his head doesn't.
- ❏ The "date" 1848
- ❏ A teddy bear
- ❏ Makeup
- ❏ A way to really stretch your money
- ❏ A golden bird
- ❏ A look of alarm
- ❏ A reflection of light
- ❏ Blue polka dots

Raft to Tom Sawyer Island

1. Someone has stored some crates rather precariously. What is the problem?
  - a. They are stacked with the smallest one on the bottom.
  - b. They are hanging from a pulley on the side of the roof.
  - c. They are perched on a tilted ledge.
  - d. All of the above
  - e. Only b and c

2. Hanging on the building are two ocean buoys together. What colors are they?
  - a. Green, red, yellow, and black
  - b. Red, green, blue, white, and yellow
  - c. Yellow, blue, white, black, and green
  - d. All red

3. What does Butterfly Brand sell?
  - a. Bait
  - b. Boat Sails
  - c. Stringless Beans
  - d. Buoys

4. There was something special about the keyhole on the door here. What was it?
    a. It is an upside-down heart.
    b. It appears to be an open mouth.
    c. It's nowhere near the doorknob.
    d. Keys are sticking out of it.
    e. Both a and d

5. There was a tool company named for its city. What city's tools were on the dock?
    a. New Orleans   b. London
    c. Tell City   d. St. Petersburg

6. Who was wanted "dead or alive"?
    a. Tom Sawyer
    b. Huck Finn
    c. Billy the Kid
    d. Sam and Belle Starr

7. Who was offering some nice refreshments?
    a. Aunt Polly
    b. Becky Thatcher
    c. Widow Douglas
    d. That nice churro stand over there. Mmmmm churros!

8. Treasure Hunt Time! See how many of these treasures you can find before your raft floats away.
- ❏ A windmill
- ❏ A bent chimney pipe
- ❏ A way to get clean
- ❏ A building made of logs
- ❏ Three pulleys
- ❏ Two wagon wheels
- ❏ A good reason to cry
- ❏ An onion-shaped roof
- ❏ Salt
- ❏ Huck Finn
- ❏ A clock
- ❏ A metal milk jug
- ❏ Some maple syrup
- ❏ Corn on the cob
- ❏ Pickles
- ❏ A barrel that would leak
- ❏ A washboard
- ❏ Something from 1818

Splash Mountain

? **POP QUIZ!** As you walk up to the queue, have a good look all around you. There's going to be a pop quiz.

1. Brer Rabbit was peeking out of the wooden tower's window. What was he holding?
   a. A fishing rod with a fish dangling on the hook
   b. A polka-dot bindle (a kerchief tied on the end of a stick to carry belongings)
   c. A bucket on a rope with a pillow in it
   d. A picnic basket with a white napkin sticking out

2. Hanging on the post as you entered the queue were three things. What were they?
   a. Two buckets and a washboard
   b. A horseshoe, a bucket, and a hammer
   c. Three rusty pulleys connected with rope
   d. Two pie pans and a jug hanging from a rope

3. There was something directly over your head as you walked into this queue. What was overhead?
   a. A barn door. Looks like it's too late to close it.
   b. A crate marked "flammable"
   c. A rabbit hanging from a rope
   d. I believe it was a barn door with a crate marked "flammable" sitting precariously on it and a rabbit hanging from it.

4. Three critters were there to welcome you as you entered. Which of the following animals was not on the welcoming committee?
   a. Bear   b. Rabbit
   c. Fox   d. Raccoon

5. Two of the animals were showing their shiny white teeth. Which animal was not displaying his dental hygiene?
   a. Raccoon   b. Bear
   c. Rabbit   d. Fox

6. What were the bear and the fox holding?
- a. The fox has an apple, the bear has some honey.
- b. They are both holding their hats.
- c. The fox has an axe, the bear has a club.
- d. The fox has a rabbit, the bear has some honey.

7. The rabbit seemed to have tricked his way into a free ride. Silly rabbit, tricks are for kids. How was he traveling?
- a. On the bear's club
- b. On the fox's back. Now that doesn't seem like a safe mode of transportation.
- c. On a kite; he is parasailing.
- d. In the bear's pocket

8. Were all three critters wearing hats?
Yes / No

9. Were all three wearing clothes?
- a. Yes
- b. No, the bear was, well…bare.

10. Just above the three animal greeters, there was a building built on a bridge. It had a sign; that's useful. What was pictured on the sign?
- a. A waterfall
- b. A train
- c. A group of animals playing instruments
- d. A fox scratching his head

11. Something was being collected and stored on the ledges of that bridge. What?
- a. Crates
- b. Laughs
- c. Rainwater
- d. Buttons

12. There was something very special underneath the bridge. What was it?
- a. The village of Brer Frogs
- b. A wishin' well
- c. A briar patch
- d. Brer Rabbit's Laughin' Place

13. OK, so in this special place, what was perched on the rooftops?
- a. A weather vane
- b. A rabbit laughin' his head off

c. An even smaller house, maybe for Brer Bird?

d. A kid whose parents want her to get down

End of Pop Quiz

14. Look for an animal who always knows which way the wind is blowing. Which animal is wind savvy?

    a. Rabbit

    b. Fox

    c. Squirrel

    d. Bear

Outdoor Courtyard

The queue in this area changes depending on crowd size. Enjoy the following treasure hunt if you are queuing outdoors.

15. Treasure Hunt Time! See how many of these country treasures you can find before you go indoors.

❑ A paw print

❑ A wagon wheel

❑ A place to buy general goods

❑ A crown

❑ A rope ladder

❑ A pulley

❑ A signpost for Brer Fox

❑ A guitar

❑ A horse and buggy

❑ The letter "z"

❑ A place for coffee

❑ A triangular lamp

❑ A wheelbarrow

❑ A blue flowerpot

❑ A horseshoe

❑ A watering hole

❑ A way to get around

❑ A sunken trashcan

❑ An egg

❑ A red pitchfork

❑ A red, white, and blue mailbox

❑ A birdhouse with red trim around its door

❑ A log-cabin birdhouse with moss on its roof

❑ A birdhouse with yellow doors and a window box

❑ A skyscraper apartment for birds

❑ A round birdhouse

❑ A birdhouse made of stone

You are now at the doors preparing to go inside.

FP 16. There is a newspaper for you to peruse. What's its name?
- a. "Hares the News"
- b. "The Brer Times"
- c. "Long-Eared Gazette"
- d. "Rabbit Tales"

FP 17. The newspaper features a picture of someone riding Splash Mountain. Who is getting all wet?
- a. Brer Rabbit
- b. Brer Fox
- c. Brer Bear
- d. Me, I think
- e. All of the above
- f. All but d, well, not yet at least

FP 18. When you step inside, you will see a railing. What is hanging from it?
- a. A bell
- b. A rug
- c. A ladder
- d. Only a and b
- e. Only b and c

19. There is something here made by Sunnyland. What is it?
- a. A washboard
- b. A metal stove
- c. A crate
- d. A pitchfork

20. **Treasure Hunt Time!** It is time for a quick treasure hunt. See how many of these treasures you can find in the barn.
- ❏ A feed bag
- ❏ A pull cart
- ❏ Oats
- ❏ A white jug
- ❏ A butter churn
- ❏ A barrel with a hole
- ❏ A rake
- ❏ Footwear for a horse
- ❏ A duck
- ❏ Beans
- ❏ A hammer
- ❏ A saddle
- ❏ A mallet

❑ A watering can
❑ A collar for a horse's neck
❑ A scythe (Death's tool)
❑ A pitchfork
❑ Lots of peanuts
❑ A toolbox
❑ A cork

FP 21. As you go upstairs, have a look out the window at the people waiting below. Earn 1 point for each of the following you spot:

❑ A person wearing a protective rain poncho
❑ A kid on her parent's shoulders
❑ Someone eating something
❑ Someone drinking something
❑ Someone wearing yellow

FP 22. How many feet is the plunge ahead?
a. 20 feet   b. 50 feet
c. 100 feet   d. Plunge, you say?

FP 23. Soon you will come to someone's door. Whose door is it?
a. Brer Rabbit   b. Brer Fox
c. Brer Squirrel   d. Brer Frog

FP 24. Which of these things can be found in Brer Frog's abode?
a. A bandana
b. A lantern
c. A tiny house
d. A frog talking to himself
e. All of the above
f. Only a and d

FP 25. Why can't you run away from trouble?
a. "Trouble is faster than a rabbit, and faster than a squirrel, and faster than you, I reckon."
b. "Trouble knows where you live."
c. "Ain't no place that far."
d. "Because trouble has already found you"

FP 26. There is an opening to look at the ride. Give yourself 1 point for each soaked person you spot.

_____

FP 27. While you are looking outside, find a lamp that is shaped like something else. What is the lamp pretending it is?

    a. An acorn   b. A bell

    c. A crate   d. A wagon wheel

FP 28. Down below, there is a sign for a "last chance to exit." What picture appears on the sign?

    a. A soaked rabbit

    b. A camera dripping with water; now that's not good.

    c. An arrow

    d. A pointing hand; don't they know it is rude to point?

FP 29. Back inside there is a portrait of Brer Rabbit. What is he looking for?

    a. Trouble   b. Adventure

    c. His laughin' place d. A good nap

FP 30. Take a very quick look at Brer Goose's picture and then see what you remember. What was Brer Goose doing?

    a. Eating   b. Fishing

    c. Dressing   d. Being prepared for a snack; this poor goose is cooked.

FP 31. There was a box next to Brer Goose's picture. What did it contain?

    a. Lunch

    b. Treasure

    c. Bait

    d. I couldn't tell; it was closed.

FP 32. OK, so he was fishing. Did he catch anything?

    Yes / No

FP 33. What does Brer Fox have in his hands?

    a. An axe   b. A rabbit

    c. A club   d. His hat

FP 34. What is Brer Fox wearing?

    a. Only a shirt and hat

    b. Pants with suspenders but no shirt

    c. A shirt, pants, and vest – and, oh yes, a nice hat

    d. He is dressed as a sheep. No wait, that is a wolf, not a fox.

FP 35. There is someone in the picture with Brer Bear. Who is ready for a close-up?

a. Brer Frog b. Brer Rabbit
c. Brer Bee d. I only see a bear.

FP 36. What is Brer Bear doing anyway?

a. Hunting
b. Just lookin'
c. Laughing
d. The "bear" minimum

FP 37. There is a picture of the briar patch. What unique features does it have?

a. A door
b. A stovepipe
c. A broom
d. You mean besides the barbs and stickers?
e. All of the above
f. Only a and b

FP 38. Does the briar patch have a porch swing?

Yes / No

FP 39. Does the briar patch have a way to receive mail?

Yes / No

FP 40. What can be seen behind Brer Fox's lair?

a. A mountain with a waterfall
b. A rabbit tied to a tree
c. A cave marked "Brer Bear's Lair"
d. A path to the forest

FP 41. If you look on top of that mountain, what do you see?

a. A housetop
b. A dead tree stump
c. A forest
d. Brer Fox hiding

FP 42. In the Fishin' Place picture, who is out catching dinner?

a. Brer Fox
b. Brer Bear
c. Brer Rabbit
d. Brer Frog. Do frogs fish?
e. Both a and b
f. Both c and d

FP **43. What have they managed to catch?**
    a. Two fish
    b. An old boot
    c. The backs of their own shirts
    d. Nothing

FP **44. What are they using for bait?**
    a. Bits of a sandwich
    b. Worms
    c. Smaller fish
    d. The hooks are empty.

FP **45. There is a "last chance exit" ahead. Who is pointing the way out for those who might melt?**
    a. Brer Rabbit
    b. Brer Fox; I think it might be a trick.
    c. Brer Bear
    d. No one; it is too late!

Walt Disney World Railroad Station

1. What is significant about the number 55?
    a. It is the number of the train with the only engine named for an actual U.S. city.
    b. It is the number of the train with the San Francisco engine.
    c. It is the only listed engine number with more than one digit.
    d. All of the above
    e. Only b and c

2. A. C. Dietz Co. is offering a complete new line of something. What is it?
    a. Model trains   b. Saddles
    c. Corsets   d. Rifles

3. Are all the engines scheduled to stop here in Frontierland station running on time?
    Yes / No

4. Who committed armed stagecoach robbery?
   a. The Younger Brothers
   b. The Sundance Kid
   c. Curly McKay
   d. Donald Duck. I always thought that duck had a
      wily look in his eyes.

**5. Have a quick look at the Lost and Found, then
turn your back on it. Check off each lost item you
remember seeing there.**
   a. An old-fashioned wooden doll
   b. A cuckoo clock
   c. An animal horn
   d. A candlestick
   e. A fur hat
   f. Two hatboxes
   g. A mousetrap
   h. Two lamps
   i. A pair of lace-up shoes
   j. A framed picture of a lady

6. Treasure Hunt Time! See how many of these
traveling treasures you can spot before you hear "All
aboard."
   ❑ A wooden train
   ❑ A mustache
   ❑ An eagle
   ❑ A phone
   ❑ A way to earn $6,500
   ❑ A place to hang your coat
   ❑ Three brothers
   ❑ Leaves that are not on a plant
   ❑ Pickles
   ❑ A saddle
   ❑ Someone who is 5'9" with black eyes

Frontierland Answers

Big Thunder Mountain Railroad
1) Mother Lode points: Player 1 _____ Player 2 _____
   Player 3 _____ Player 4 _____
2) Number of items collected _____

Country Bear Jamboree
1) b. Banjo
2) c. All three
3) a. Red
4) a. A bone
5) No
6) Yes
7) b. Grizzly Hall
8) b. 1898
9) d. A horse
10) Total Grizzly Hall Treasures found _____

Raft to Tom Sawyer Island
1) e. Only b and c
2) b. Red, green, blue, white, and yellow
3) c. Stringless Beans
4) a. It is an upside-down heart.
5) c. Tell City
6) d. Sam and Belle Starr
7) a. Aunt Polly
8) Total Island Treasures found _____

Splash Mountain
1) b. A polka-dot bindle
2) a. Two buckets and a washboard
3) a. A barn door
4) d. Raccoon
5) b. Bear
6) c. The fox has an axe and the bear has a club.
7) a. On the bear's club
8) No
9) Yes
10) b. A train
11) c. Rainwater
12) d. Brer Rabbit's Laughin' Place

13) c. An even smaller house
14) a. Rabbit
15) Total Treasures found _____
16) d. "Rabbit Tales"
17) f. All but d
18) e. Only b and c
19) a. A washboard
20) Total Barn Treasures found _____
21) Number of points collected _____
22) b. 50 feet
23) d. Brer Frog
24) e. All of the above
25) c. "Ain't no place that far."
26) Number of soaked people spotted _____
27) a. An acorn
28) d. A pointing hand
29) b. Adventure
30) b. Fishing
31) c. Bait
32) Yes
33) a. An axe
34) c. A shirt, pants, vest – and a nice hat
35) c. Brer Bee
36) b. Just lookin'
37) e. All of the above
38) No
39) Yes
40) a. A mountain with a waterfall
41) b. A dead tree stump
42) f. Both c and d
43) d. Nothing
44) b. Worms
45) a. Brer Rabbit

Walt Disney World Railroad Station

1) b. It is the number of the train with the San Francisco engine
2) b. Saddles
3) Yes
4) c. Curly McKay
5) b. A cuckoo clock, c. An animal horn, f. Two hatboxes, h. Two lamps, i. A pair of lace-up shoes
6) Total Traveling Treasures found _____

Liberty Square

Haunted Mansion

Interactive Queue

Ready to solve a little murder mystery? The stone bust family was a wicked crew, to their untimely murders they've left you clues. Who killed whom and how was it done? Check the epitaphs closely for some sleuthing fun.

Note: You can line up in the non-interactive queue, but if you're looking for fun while you wait, you'll want to choose the interactive line.

1. Who helped Uncle Jacob discover that you can't take it with you?

    a. Uncle Jacob's headache went from bad to worse. Cousin Maude nailed him for digging through her purse.

    b. Bertie could mix quite an excellent drink, even filled with poison it never would stink.

    c. Buried in money, such a sad way to go. The twins launched an avalanche when he said "NO."

    d. "Does this hat make me look fat?" Oh dear, Jacob, you should have said "No." Aunt Flo's shot you in the spot where your own hat used to go.

2. How did Bertie step into the beyond and who gave him a little push to get him going?

    a. The twins were bored and asked Bertie to play. Sadly "Hangman" can go badly when it doesn't go their way.

    b. Near Bertie's doomed head his snake did slither. Maude took aim and left Bertie to wither.

    c. He died full of lead and that's the truth. Aunt Florence shot him but left little proof.

    d. Bertie was caught with his hands in the pie. Jacob closed the safe door and left him to die.

3. Aunt Florence has gone to seed. Who planted her?

    a. When the lock on Jacob's safe she tried to pick, her end came swiftly from a well-placed kick.

    b. One sniff of her posy brought an end to life's woes, the scent of Bertie's poison went straight up her nose.

    c. Tredding the garden Maude thought a sin. She taught Florence a lesson and smashed her point in.

    d. The twins were the culprits who did the dark deed because their dear birdie she failed to feed.

4. Who put the twins to bed but never got them up again?

    a. Cousin Maude sang a bedtime ballad, then put them straight to sleep with a heavy mallet.

    b. Bertie gave them some water when he bid them good night, then he added some poison and turned out the light.

    c. Uncle Jacob put the twins into their beds, then placed the pillows atop their heads.

    d. I think their canary got them.

5. Cousin Maude is no more. Why did she go toward the light?

    a. A flash of a gun and out went her light. She was shot while sleeping late at night.

    b. The match to this riddle should fill you with dread. The answer is snarly as the bun on her head.

    c. Maude was felled by her own greed. Now she and her fortune are pushing up weeds.

    d. Maude has earned a just reward. The drink she swallowed left her stiff as a board.

6. Which of these family members is not guilty of murder?

    a. Uncle Jacob   b. The twins
    c. Cousin Maude   d. Aunt Florence

7. Who was the last Dread family member standing; you know, before he/she was standing no more?

    a. Uncle Jacob   b. Bertie
    c. Cousin Maude   d. Aunt Florence
    e. The twins

? POP QUIZ! Here a composer lies in repose. He is touched by your human attention. Why not join his orchestra? Run your hands over each instrument to add your touch to the ghostly tune. Pay attention to your work because the maestro tells me there may be a pop quiz in music class.

8. Which of these instruments was not part of the orchestra?
 a. Bagpipes
 b. Drum
 c. Tambourine
 d. Trumpet
 e. All four instruments were there.

9. It appears the maestro had some rather odd pets. Which one of these animals was featured on his crypt?
 a. A rat with five tails
 b. A one-eyed cat
 c. An octopus that makes its home inside a horn
 d. A bat
 e. All of the above were creeping around this crypt.
 f. All but a. What would a rat do with five tails?

10. Did any of the instruments include candles built in?
 Yes / No

11. Were any of the instruments oozing slime?
 Yes / No

12. Did a skull figure into any of the instruments?
 Yes / No

13. There was a raven mounted on the top of the pipe organ. What was she nested on?
 a. Bones   b. A branch
 c. A dagger   d. A spider web

14. The bat-shaped instrument had an unusual tone. What did it sound like?
 a. Screaming   b. Breaking glass
 c. Bells   d. Humming

15. What was the brand of the pipe organ?
a. Raverstroli   b. Badland
c. Pipedreams   d. Rigorvarius

End of Pop Quiz

16. What was searched for but could not be carried?
a. A trunk   b. A fortune
c. A safe   d. A tune

17. How did brother Dave die?
a. He fell from the rooftop.
b. He chased a bear into a cave.
c. He was crushed by a falling piano.
d. He choked on his pie.

18. What was Master Gracey's final request?
a. No mourning
b. That you dance on his grave
c. Toast his name and leave him a drink.
d. Please speak up; it's hard to hear from the other side.

19. What would Captain Culpepper Clyne be likely to describe as his most fearsome foe?
a. The Kraken when it is in a cranky sort of mood
b. The ticktock sound emanating from his arch nemesis the crocodile
c. Sudsy water
d. His mother-in-law

20. I think the captain has a cold. Why?
a. There is a bottle of cold medicine on the edge of the tub.
b. There is a thermometer sticking out of his hand.
c. Could be that big, wet sneeze
d. He is dead; I am sure he is very cold.

21. There is something unusual about this tomb, it's leaking! Can you stop up the leak?
Yes / No

22. Look closely at the library. A message has been left for you from beyond – if you can decipher it. Each symbol represents a letter. Some symbols look a bit like the letters they represent, others don't. See if you can crack the code.

23. What was Campbell's postmortem claim to fame?
    a. A strong smell of chicken soup that lingers by his grave
    b. Best haunting skills in the small- to medium-size graveyard category
    c. Sticking the landing
    d. The ability to sing better after death than before

24. What brought a stop to the life of Prudence Pock?
    a. Chicken pox
    b. Planting poison ivy, imprudently
    c. A book fell on her head.
    d. Writer's block

25. Who holds the patent on the Spectrecom?
    a. E. M. Path   b. Claire Voyant
    c. R. H. Goff   d. Bea Yond

26. Prudence needs a muse. Give yourself 1 point for each correct answer you give her. _____

27. Why is Uncle Blaine resting in pieces?
    a. He was not very skilled with the chipper.
    b. He was hit by a train.
    c. He had one foot in the grave.
    d. Saying goodbye always made him go to pieces.

28. Whose glass overfloweth?
    a. Ken's   b. Brother Roland's
    c. Mister Free's   d. Yours

Liberty Square Riverboat

1. What is Louisiana besides a state?
    a. The name of a store visible in town
    b. The place where riverboats were first invented
    c. The name of a boat
    d. The name of the boathouse cat. "Here, kitty kitty."

2. What is inside the service room?
    a. White paint
    b. Tools and miscellaneous boat parts

    c. A nice place for the crew to kick up their feet and relax

    d. A fire extinguisher; great – unless the service room is on fire.

3. There is evidence that Tom and Huck have been in these parts. How do we know?

    a. Well, it could be the fact that they painted their names on a fence.

    b. There is a fence that has been partially whitewashed. Looks like their work.

    c. There is a plaque in their honor.

    d. Their faces are on wanted posters in the boathouse.

    e. All of the above

    f. Only a and b

4. How do we know Tom loves Becky?

    a. Becky is the name of Tom's boat.

    b. There is a carving in a tree that says "Tom + Becky."

    c. He painted a heart for her.

    d. Because he left her a box of spiders for a present

    e. Who is Becky?

5. What form of punishment is waiting for wrongdoers in these parts?

    a. The stocks

    b. The jailhouse

    c. A firing squad

    d. All wrongdoers must apologize and promise never to do wrong again.

6. What is significant about the number 71?

    a. It is the number of the boathouse you are waiting in.

    b. It is the weight of a crate of goods.

    c. It is the number of years the riverboat has been in service.

    d. It is the age Mark Twain was when he wrote the story of Tom Sawyer.

7. Treasure Hunt Time! See how many of these treasures you can find before your river cruise.

    ❑ A castle

    ❑ Something that is lucky and made of gold

- ❑ A building with columns
- ❑ Two small barrels sitting on a crate
- ❑ A black dog
- ❑ Two double chimneys
- ❑ A pipe
- ❑ Two rifles
- ❑ An eagle
- ❑ A star
- ❑ Two log cabins
- ❑ A yellow wagon wheel
- ❑ Four burlap sacks
- ❑ A tall building with many roofs, one on top of the other
- ❑ A diamond
- ❑ Red-and-white checkered curtains

The Hall of Presidents

1. Special Collection: Attention! There is a Special Collection of eagles for this queue. Earn 1 point for every eagle you find. _____

2. Queueseum Hunt: Welcome to the presidential "queueseum," my term for an area filled with the details that make Disney spaces so magical. Look around. This waiting room is chock full of treasure. See how much you can find before the next show begins.

- ❑ A pony
- ❑ A patriotic breakfast food
- ❑ A green flag
- ❑ A green wine glass
- ❑ A president taking his hat off
- ❑ A clown holding an umbrella
- ❑ A thermos
- ❑ A sword
- ❑ A seal featuring an oak leaf and an acorn
- ❑ A teddy bear
- ❑ A hat sitting upside down
- ❑ "We The People"
- ❑ A recreational item owned by Woodrow Wilson
- ❑ A man holding a book
- ❑ A baby

❑ A pair of glasses
❑ A clock
❑ Pearls
❑ A collection of arrows

Liberty Square Answers

Haunted Mansion Interactive Queue

1) b. Bertie did him in with poison.
2) c. Aunt Florence shot him.
3) d. The twins did it to avenge their canary.
4) a. Cousin Maude whacked them with a mallet.
5) b. She burned up in a fire.
6) a. Uncle Jacob
7) c. Cousin Maude
8) e. All four were there.
9) f. All but a
10) Yes
11) No
12) Yes
13) d. A spider web
14) b. Breaking glass
15) a. Raverstroli
16) d. A tune
17) b. He chased a bear into a cave.
18) a. No mourning
19) c. Sudsy water
20) c. A big, wet sneeze
21) No
22) The encrypted message is "Welcome home you foolish mortal, this mansion is your mystic portal, where eerie sights and spooky sounds, fill these happy haunting grounds."
23) c. Sticking the landing
24) d. Writer's block
25) c. R. H. Goff
26) Number of correct answers you gave to Prudence
_____
27) b. He was hit by a train.
28) d. Yours

Liberty Square Riverboat

1) c. The name of a boat
2) d. A fire extinguisher

3) f. Only a and b
4) c. He painted a heart for her.
5) a. The stocks
6) b. It is the weight of a crate of goods.
7) Total Treasures found _____

The Hall of Presidents
1) Number of eagles collected _____
2) Total Queueseum Treasures found _____

Fantasyland

"it's a small world"

? **POP QUIZ!** Before you get in line, take a look at the "it's a small world" sign. Give yourself a minute and then join the queue. It is time to play "it's a small memory."

1. There were a lot of children above the sign. What were they doing?
    a. Standing in a group holding a globe overhead
    b. Standing in line on a globe holding hands
    c. Sitting in a boat
    d. Standing in line; they want to go on the ride.

2. Did any of the children have curly red hair?
    Yes / No

3. There was a boy wearing a cowboy hat. What color was his hat?
    a. Blue, pink, and black
    b. Brown with silver trim
    c. White
    d. Black

4. Was anyone wearing feathers?
    Yes / No

5. Was there a child dressed as an Eskimo?
   Yes / No

6. Was there a boy with a bandana around his head?
   Yes / No

7. Was anyone waving?
   Yes / No

8. Was anyone wearing a pink hat?
   Yes / No

9. Were any of the children holding flags?
   Yes / No

10. Was there a girl with braids?
    Yes / No

11. Were any of the children wearing jewelry?
    Yes / No

12. So, the children were in a boat. What did it look like?
    a. It was an all-red boat.
    b. It was green on one side and blue on the other.
    c. The boat was white and there was a painting of a globe on it.
    d. The boat was rainbow colored.

13. What was the backdrop behind the children?
    a. The sun   b. The earth
    c. The sky   d. The ocean

14. There was something unusual about the words on this sign. What was it?
    a. There were no capital letters.
    b. They were all different pastel colors.
    c. The word "small" was, well, very small.
    d. Both a and c
    e. Looked like a normal sign to me.

End of Pop Quiz

15. "small world" features a giant clock. But there is a second method of tracking time displayed on the front of the building. Can you identify it?
    Yes / No

16. There are three famous towers hinted at on the front of "small world." Which one is not there?
- a. The Leaning Tower of Pisa (a tower leaning to the side).
- b. The Tower Bridge (two rectangular towers with a bridge connecting them)
- c. The Empire State Building (a thin, tall tower with a point on the top)
- d. The Eiffel Tower (arches on the bottom, crisscross railings going up.)

17. Look for the golden tulips. What is that sprouting out of the top of them?
- a. A gold bee
- b. A stick of gold balls
- c. A gold flag
- d. All of the above
- e. Only b and c

18. What color are the hands on the clock?
- a. Gold
- b. Baby blue
- c. Silver
- d. No hands; it's digital.

19. Look up high. There are some people who can watch you. What else are they doing?
- a. Eating a meal. Looks good.
- b. Shopping for gifts
- c. Getting face paint applied
- d. They're just peeking at me. I think they're spies.

20. Look for parts of "small world" that move. Give yourself 1 point for each moving object you find. _____

21. Treasure Hunt Time! See how many of these treasures from around the world you can find before your boat departs.
- ❑ A bell
- ❑ A dark blue flag
- ❑ A red flag
- ❑ A place for you to spy on boat passengers
- ❑ A gold flag
- ❑ A light blue flag
- ❑ A solid, sparkly gold circle
- ❑ Someone wearing a top hat
- ❑ Someone humming or singing, "It's a small world after all."

- ❑ 63
- ❑ A fleur-de-lis
- ❑ Two drums
- ❑ Someone with sunshine in their smile
- ❑ A building with columns and a triangular roof
- ❑ A roof shaped like an onion
- ❑ A triangle resting on its tip
- ❑ A gold circle containing six more gold circles
- ❑ Six clock gears
- ❑ "x" marks the spot, all in lights

Mad Tea Party

1. Teacup Race: Before the ride starts up, have a good look at the people who are in the teacups. Which cup full of people do you think will be the fastest spinner? Each member of your group should make a prediction. When the ride is over, your group should vote on whose cup was the winner. If your cup wins, give yourself 3 points. Run as many races as you desire. Racers place your bets!

2. How many teacups are at this tea party?
    a. 14   b. 16
    c. 18   d. 20

3. The Mad Tea Party opened in 1971. Is this ride older or younger than your dad?

4. Pick a teacup design that you like. Now look around. How many times can you find that same design on either another teacup or on something else? Give yourself 1 point each time you find "your design" on a teacup. Give yourself 2 points each time you spot "your design" on something else. Once you've finished finding one design, you can try another.

5. Treasure Hunt Time! Can you find all these treasures before it is time for tea?
- ❑ A top hat
- ❑ A dormouse
- ❑ A teacup that is two different shades of pink
- ❑ Someone who looks very dizzy

- ❑ A teacup where no one is trying to make it spin
- ❑ A polka-dot rim
- ❑ A teacup that is yellow with purple trim
- ❑ Purple-and-white stripes
- ❑ A blue frame
- ❑ Big purple leaves

6. If you are still waiting to go for a spin, work on a Collection or two. See page 16 if you need suggestions.

Mickey's PhilharMagic

? **POP QUIZ!** Take a quick look at the PhilharMagic sign and then join the queue.

1. What did Mickey have in his hand?
   a. Sheet music
   b. A flute
   c. A conductor's baton
   d. A sandwich

2. Was Mickey wearing anything on his head?
   a. A pointy blue wizard's hat
   b. A black top hat
   c. A singing bluebird was perched there.
   d. Nothing; it's rude to wear a hat at the symphony.

3. Were there any other members of the orchestra up there with Mickey?
   Yes / No

4. What was Mickey dressed in?
   a. Not much; he is a mouse.
   b. A magician's robe in blue and purple
   c. A red suit with gold trim on the collar
   d. A tux with tails

5. OK, so he was wearing a hat, and it had a shape on it. What shape was on Mickey's hat?
   a. A musical note
   b. A star
   c. A curlicue
   d. I still say he was not wearing a hat.

6. Mickey was standing on a sign featuring his own name. There was something out of the ordinary about his name. What was it?
    a. The apostrophe in "Mickey's" is a musical note.
    b. The letters are floating away like music that's already been played.
    c. His name is in lights; he is the star after all.
    d. His name appears to be in all capital letters.

7. Something appeared in gold all over the sign. What?
    a. The names of the musicians featured in today's performance
    b. Musical instruments
    c. Musical notation
    d. Stars

End of Pop Quiz

8. Have a look at the musical instruments on the wall. Nice orchestra. Which of these instruments is not in the picture?
    a. Violin (a small stringed instrument)
    b. Cello (a large violin-shaped instrument)
    c. Tuba (a large horn)
    d. Flute (a small wind instrument)
    e. They are all there.

9. As you walk inside the building, you will see a poster for Mickey's PhilharMagic. There is something this poster has that most posters do not offer. What's so special?
    a. It is painted on glass so you can see right through it.
    b. You can see Mickey's front side, and his back side, too.
    c. It is playing music from the show very softly. You can hear it if you put your ear close to the poster.
    d. It is posted upside down.

10. Nearby, there is a poster featuring Donald. What musical instruments appear on the poster with him?
    a. Maracas
    b. Drums
    c. Violin
    d. None; ducks are not very musically inclined.

11. What did Donald prove about his trumpeting abilities?

    a. When it comes to the trumpet, he is no quack.

    b. He is the monarch of the mariachi scene.

    c. He fit the bill.

    d. He has natural skill and wasn't just winging it.

12. What is the Wolf Gang Trio playing?

    a. "Brick House," a tribute

    b. "Straw, Sticks, and Bricks" in B-flat

    c. "Against the Wind"

    d. It never matters what they play; the audience is always blown away.

13. One little pig is playing a unique piano. What is its claim to fame?

    a. It is made of sticks.

    b. It is made of straw.

    c. It is made of bricks.

    d. It is constructed from all three.

    e. There is nothing special about it.

14. Willie The Whale is creating a problem on stage. What is it?

    a. He is crying so much that the audience is forced to take cover.

    b. His "wailing" is so loud that the audience is running away.

    c. He has flooded the audience and they are forced to swim.

    d. Willie is too big and has put a hole in the roof.

15. Willie has brought something onstage with him. What does he have?

    a. A handkerchief. Do whales need to dry their eyes?

    b. A glass of water

    c. A big old clown nose

    d. All of the above

    e. Only a and c

16. What description is given for Ariel's Coral Group?

    a. You'll leave "humming a tuna."

    b. A singing sensation that's never "floundered"

    c. A starfish is born.

    d. A "must sea"

17. Who made a splash in their second season?
    a. Ariel did while performing under the sea.
    b. Willie The Whale in a whale of a second season
    c. The audience at Hades' performance when the
       music hall caught on fire
    d. Genie did, though critics thought he was all wet.

18. What is Genie's claim to fame?
    a. Hey, cat, he is a smooth singer.
    b. He tickles the keyboard.
    c. He stays hip on the jazz bass.
    d. He bangs it out on the drums.
    e. He is a one-man band and can play all of those
       things.
    f. Only a, b, and c; the man can only do so much!

19. There is something cool about Genie's microphone. What makes it special?
    a. It matches his hair. Very sharp!
    b. It is his lamp. It also serves as a home and a cool
       pocketknife.
    c. It is made "from him." Now that's what I call
       singing solo.
    d. Looks like an ordinary microphone to me.

20. How is Genie's fifth-season performance described?
    a. "Leaves fans wishing for more"
    b. "Out of the bottle"
    c. "You've never seen a performer like Genie."
    d. "Genie may be blue, but you won't be too."

21. Wheezy has something in his mouth…er…um… beak that most singers do not. What is it?
    a. A fish
    b. A squeaker
    c. An ice cube
    d. A Green Army Man

22. What is "An Evening with Wheezy" now in?
    a. The spotlight
    b. Its final squeak
    c. The Toy Box
    d. A yard sale

23. Hades seems to be having technical difficulties. What is the problem?
    a. His microphone appears to be dead.
    b. His performance is on fire.
    c. His singing is so good it's sinful.
    d. All of the above
    e. All but c

24. How is Hades seventh season described?
    a. Smokin'   b. On fire
    c. Dead   d. Sizzling

Peter Pan's Flight

? **POP QUIZ!** Have a look at the sign for this ride and then join the queue. We will see if your memory is sharp as a hook, or your brain is already in Never Land.

FP 1. Who is not featured on the sign?
    a. Wendy (a girl in a nightgown)
    b. Her brothers (two boys in sleepwear)
    c. Tinker Bell
    d. Peter Pan
    e. They are all there.

FP 2. On the sign, the kids are flying. Pretty amazing! What are they flying around?
    a. An island known as Never Land
    b. The roofs of London
    c. A clock tower
    d. A pillow, I hope; they are beginners after all.

FP 3. Peter had something with him. What did he have?
    a. A shadow   b. A dagger
    c. A thimble   d. A bag of pixie dust

FP 4. What was the youngest boy, Michael, bringing with him on his first flight?
    a. A blanket
    b. A teddy bear
    c. A sword
    d. Nothing; he needed his hands free for flying.

FP 5. What was the oldest boy, John, bringing with him to Never Land?
 a. An umbrella
 b. A sword
 c. A book
 d. Nothing; he checked his baggage.

FP 6. What was the girl, Wendy, bringing with her on her first flight?
 a. A sewing kit
 b. A thimble
 c. A storybook
 d. Nothing; her hands were empty.

FP 7. What time did this flight take place?
 a. 7:30 p.m.
 b. 8:15 p.m.
 c. 9:00 p.m.
 d. Midnight

FP 8. What was Tinker Bell up to in this picture?
 a. She was standing on Peter's shoulder.
 b. She was sprinkling pixie dust on the kids.
 c. She was lighting up the "i" in the word "flight."
 d. She is up to no good; she is Tinker Bell after all.

FP 9. How many of the children were wearing hats?
 a. 1
 b. 2
 c. 3
 d. 0 – not too useful while you fly.
End of Pop Quiz

FP 10. What is holding the signs for the standby and FASTPASS lines?
 a. Nothing; they fly magically with pixie dust.
 b. A hook sticking out of the wall
 c. A sword stuck in the wall
 d. A trumpet blaring the way.

11. See if you can complete this shield Collection. You can never have too many shields, right?
 ❑ A blue shield with a white cross
 ❑ A shield with a cross made of four triangles
 ❑ A shield that is outlined in gold and white and has a solid color in the center.

❑ A red-and-white striped shield
❑ A checkerboard shield with four squares: two of plain gold and two white with a fleur-de-lis in the center.
❑ A shield with stripes at an angle
❑ A shield with four stripes: two gold and two white
❑ A shield with a cross that has three circles on each of its four tips

12. If you are still waiting to fly away, this would be a good time to work on another Collection or two.

Prince Charming Regal Carrousel

1. What story is featured on the carrousel?
   a. Sleeping Beauty
   b. Snow White
   c. The Little Mermaid
   d. Cinderella

2. Are there any animals on whose backs you may ride that are not white horses?
   Yes / No

3. There is a bird featured on this carrousel. What kind is it?
   a. An eagle in gold
   b. An owl in gold
   c. A sparrow in its natural colors
   d. A hummingbird in its natural colors
   e. Both a and d

4. Treasure Hunt Time! See how many of these "charming treasures" you can find before the clock strikes midnight.
   ❑ A bridge
   ❑ A ladder
   ❑ A clock
   ❑ A pumpkin that is on the move
   ❑ A couple dancing

❑ A magic wand
❑ A horse sitting down
❑ A mouse wearing clothes
❑ A shield with a red-and-gold checkered pattern
❑ Someone wearing a ring
❑ Helpful birds
❑ A cat
❑ A glass slipper
❑ A silver eagle
❑ A gold castle
❑ A soldier

It is time to check out the horse parade and then see how many of these questions you can answer.

5. Is there a lion's head holding a rope in its mouth under a saddle?
Yes / No

6. Is there a Pegasus (a winged horse) with silver feathery wings?
Yes / No

7. Is there a horse with a shield featuring a Native American chief?
Yes / No

8. Is there a horse with a shield featuring a full lion's body in silver?
Yes / No

9. Is there a horse with a gold crown on its head?
Yes / No

10. Is there a horse with green reins?
Yes / No

11. Is there a horse wearing the flag of the United Kingdom?
Yes / No

12. Is there a horse adorned with flowers in pink and yellow?
Yes / No

13. Is there a horse with feathers of blue, green, and red?
Yes / No

14. Is there an eagle in its natural colors anywhere on the carrousel?

    Yes / No

15. Is there a horse with three gold feathers on its head?

    Yes / No

16. Is there a horse with a gold star on it?

    Yes / No

17. Is there a horse with red, white, and blue ribbons in its tail?

    Yes / No

18. Is there a horse with a mace on the saddle?

    Yes / No

19. Can a silver buffalo be located on this ride?

    Yes / No

The Many Adventures of Winnie the Pooh

1. As you approach the queue, you'll see the standby wait time posted on something. What is it on?

    a. A sign in the tree

    b. A stack of honey pots dripping with honey. Mmmmmm, delicious!

    c. A sign in the treehouse window

    d. A ball held by Tigger.

2. Kids can enter this area through another, smaller door directly into the tree. What is written over this door?

    a. "Pooh's House"

    b. "Welcome"

    c. "Watch Your Head"

    d. "Mr. Sander"

3. Inside the little house something is sitting on the windowsill. What is it?

    a. A large jar or pot

   b. A bedtime story
   c. A plant with red flowers
   d. Nothing is on the sill.

4. There is a corner shelf. Which of these is not on it?

   a. A carrot
   b. Two books
   c. A candle
   d. A pot or jar
   e. They are all there.
   f. All but a

5. There is artwork in here, too. What art is featured on the wall of this house?

   a. A red balloon
   b. A still life of a honey pot
   c. A cute little bee
   d. I think it's the Mona Lisa.

6. Inside Pooh's house there is a submarine; yes, I said submarine. Can you find it? (It's hard to spot.)

   Yes / No

7. There is a vegetable garden nearby with a rather unwelcoming sign. Who or what is not wanted?

   a. Rabbits
   b. Tigger; he might bounce on the turnips.
   c. Gophers; but can they read?
   d. Anyone at all. This garden is the private
      property of Mr. McGregor. Wait…that's a
      different story, isn't it?

8. Treasure Hunt Time! Which of these treasures can you spot before they are eaten or disappear?

   ❑ A radish
   ❑ A big bag of seed
   ❑ A pumpkin
   ❑ A wheelbarrow
   ❑ A hive
   ❑ A place to leave a message
   ❑ A carrot with its greens still attached
   ❑ An uninvited guest
   ❑ Footprints
   ❑ Eeyore

9. Look! A map of the queue. Now that is useful, but the directions make no sense. There is no "N, S, E, W." Can you figure out what the new directional indicators mean?

Yes / No

10. Who is in Eeyore's Gloomy Spot?

a. No one. Who could be gloomy at Disney World?

b. Eeyore, of coarse

c. Several gophers are enjoying the shade.

d. You mean besides that kid there?

11. What is Eeyore's Gloomy Spot made of?

a. A miserable cave

b. A crummy, broken old crate

c. Some grumpy-looking sticks

d. A horrible hole in a tree

12. Hey, there is Piglet's house. What happens if you knock?

a. The door creaks open. If only I could fit!

b. Piglet answers. He is a pig with manners.

c. A bell rings. Now that is strange.

d. Nothing; it is just a sign after all.

13. In the picture, Piglet is growing something at his house. What is it?

a. A red flowering plant

b. Carrots

c. A cactus

d. Well, his house is a tree. Does that count?

e. Both a and d

f. Both b and d

? **POP QUIZ!** Go play in the garden. Later see if you saw everything or if you should eat more carrots to improve your eyesight.

14. If you pound a pumpkin, what happens?

a. Your hand gets sticky with pumpkin goo.

b. The pumpkin says, "Ouch"

c. Random noises play.

d. You get a great drumbeat going.

15. If you squish the vegetables by the pumpkins, what happens?

a. Bike horns honk.   b. Water oozes out.

c. They say ouch.   d. Absolutely nothing

16. If you want to summon a gopher, what must you do?
   a. Call out "I love gophers!"
   b. Knock.
   c. Step on the footprints.
   d. Provide a carrot.

17. Which of these things was never said by a gopher?
   a. "It's me again."
   b. "You rang?"
   c. "Hello there."
   d. "Here I am."
   e. Gophers have said all those things; they
      are very talkative.

18. Were any of the gophers upside down?
   a. Yes
   b. No
   c. They all were.

19. Were any of the gophers wearing any clothing?
   Yes / No

20. What happens if you spin the sunflowers?
   a. They grow taller or shorter.
   b. They make pretty bell-like noises.
   c. They make whoop sounds.
   d. You see a spinning rainbow of colors.

End of Pop Quiz

**21. Oh no! The honey pots have spilled and are
dripping down the walls! You might as well get your
hands in it. Try these things:**
   ❑ Draw Mickey Mouse in the honey.
   ❑ Write your name in the honey.
   ❑ What happens if you clear the honey away,
      anyway?

FP **22. Treasure Hunt Time!** Soon you will be on the ride,
but before you climb in your honey jar, see how many
of these treasures you can find.
   ❑ Lost mail
   ❑ Two balloons
   ❑ A double mailbox
   ❑ Holding hands
   ❑ A monocle

❑ Two watering cans
❑ A scarf
❑ A door with a circle on it
❑ A book on its side

Walt Disney World Railroad Station

? **POP QUIZ!**

1. What is the elevation of this railroad station?
    a. 87 feet   b. 102 feet
    c. 216 feet   d. 301 feet

2. As you walked in you may have spotted a weather vane atop this building. What was its shape?
    a. A train   b. A rooster
    c. A fleur-de-lis   d. Mouse ears

3. Where is the station located?
    a. Tinker Bell Plaza
    b. Fantasy Promenade
    c. Dream Way
    d. Carolwood Park

4. There was something mounted up high on the roof. What was it?
    a. An American flag
    b. A clock
    c. A bell
    d. A bird's nest

End of Pop Quiz

5. Treasure Hunt Time! See how many of these treasures you can find before the train leaves the station.
    ❑ A fire
    ❑ Rusty water
    ❑ A cannon
    ❑ A bell
    ❑ A bad landing

❑ Goggles
❑ A black feather
❑ A "hole body"
❑ A frightened fowl
❑ A trunk

Enchanted Forest

Enchanted Tales with Belle

1. Which of these things is not part of the sign for Enchanted Tales with Belle?
 a. A candlestick
 b. Two gears
 c. One wind wheel
 d. A whisk broom
 e. They are all there.

2. Look at Belle's lovely cottage. What shape is carved in the wood shutters?
 a. Heart   b. Diamond
 c. Gear   d. Curlique

3. Belle's father Maurice loves to create things out of odd parts. What did he use in making the light poles?
 a. Old broken wagon wheels
 b. Reclaimed clock hands
 c. Curled metal
 d. Broken pieces of stair railings
 e. All of the above
 f. Only a and c

4. Which of these things has Maurice used to repair his fence?
 a. A chair bottom   b. A chair back
 c. A wagon wheel   d. A shutter
 e. A saw   f. A stair spindle
 g. All but f   h. They were all there.

5. It appears Maurice is all about alternative energy sources. Which of these does he use to power his house?

    a. A steam generator built from rusted scrap metal

    b. A water wheel

    c. A windmill-like contraption

    d. A large black coal-burning furnace

    e. Both b and c

    f. He uses hamster-wheel power just like every one else.

6. Treasure Hunt Time! Maurice and Belle have many everyday items around their home, all waiting to be turned into unique treasures. Some are needed for Maurice's next invention. Can you spot them for him?

    ❏ A shovel blade

    ❏ A birdhouse

    ❏ A small bit of chain

    ❏ Two milk jugs

    ❏ A rain barrel

    ❏ A red heart

    ❏ A crank

    ❏ A high tower

    ❏ A gear

    ❏ A small barrel with a bag on top

7. Now that you've found all the parts Maurice requires, what do you think he will create with them?
3 points for a creative answer _____

Inside Belle's Cottage

8. On the wall, there is a beautiful painting of Belle and her mother reading a book. What book are they enjoying?

    a. Le Prince Charmant (Prince Charming)

    b. La Belle et la Bête (Beauty and the Beast)

    c. La Belle au Bois Dormant (Sleeping Beauty)

    d. It is a mystery because the book is untitled.

9. Belle's mother wears one special adornment in the painting. What is it?

    a. A cameo brooch

    b. A pearl necklace

    c. A rose

    d. Red earrings

10. Belle's family has been marking her growth on a wall of their home since she was very small, but they missed a few years. How old was she the first time they missed marking a year?

a. 2 years old   b. 11 years old

c. 13 years old   d. 15 years old

11. It appears Belle and her father were playing a game. What was it?

a. Checkers   b. Cards

c. Majong   d. Chess

12. Just before we got here, someone was working hard to keep this cottage neat and tidy. What chore was being done?

a. Dusting the shelves

b. Cleaning the dishes

c. Mopping the stairs

d. Baking bread

13. Oh look, Maurice left his plans for a new invention on the table. What do you think he was designing?

a. A horseless carriage run on steam

b. A flying contraption using bike pedals

c. A drill for digging deep holes in the earth

d. A new water-wheel system

14. There is a beautiful hand mirror lying on the dresser. What is painted on the back of the mirror?

a. Roses

b. A heart

c. A picture of Belle

d. A bow

15. Treasure Hunt Time!

❑ A blue umbrella

❑ A bridge

❑ Two teapots

❑ A pewter mug

❑ A rolling pin

❑ A basket of ideas

❑ A small bouquet of one red, one yellow, and one orange flower

❑ An iron

❑ This cottage – only small

❑ A washboard
❑ An acorn
❑ A cutting board

Under the Sea—Journey of the Little Mermaid

1. Oh a shipwreck, did you see it? Ariel has been carved as part of the boat, what an honor. What color are her eyes?

a. Blue   b. Green

c. Brown   d. Hazel

2. Wow! Look at the little room on the end of the long arched bridge. What is that holding it up?

a. Cement fish

b. Mermaid tails

c. Carved octopus-like arms

d. Crab claws aplenty

3. It is time to play "Scuttle Says." When Ariel finds new human treasures she takes them to her seagull friend Scuttle for identification. Scuttle fancies himself knowledgeable about all things human. When presented with a human item he makes up a crazy name for it. Then he tells what it is used for. He is always wrong. Today Ariel can't find Scuttle, so it is up to you to help her out. Here is a list of human treasures you may find on the guests in line with you. When you find one you must give it a name. For example, when presented with a fork, Scuttle called it a "dingulhopper". He went on to tell how humans use dingulhoppers to straighten their hair.

To earn your points you must find a human treasure, name it, and tell what it is used for. Earn 1 point for each treasure that you find, rename, and give a silly purpose to. Find:

❑ Cell phone
❑ Drink cup
❑ Book
❑ Glasses
❑ Headband
❑ Hat

- ❏ Purse
- ❏ Balloon
- ❏ Backpack
- ❏ Watch
- ❏ Bandana
- ❏ Toy
- ❏ Necklace
- ❏ Lanyard
- ❏ Brush or comb
- ❏ Camera
- ❏ Coat
- ❏ Pen
- ❏ Snack

In Ariel's Treasure Cave

4. Wow! Ariel's human-stuff collection is all mixed up. How did that happen?
    a. The crabs mixed it all up. Look no farther, they are the "claws".
    b. Ariel's father King Triton is not a fan of things from the human world. He blasted it with his trident.
    c. Everything was knocked asunder when an overly large shark chased Ariel into the cave.
    d. A storm caused the damage. I hope her insurance company didn't think that was too fishy.

5. Some people – and mermaids – have fancy signatures. What is special about Ariel's?
    a. The "i" is dotted with a clam shell.
    b. It has bubbles in it.
    c. It is in all capital letters.
    d. It is sparking gold.

6. Ariel has some crab friends helping her tidy up her collection. Where can you find these hard-working crustaceans?
    a. In a glass ball
    b. In a glass dome
    c. In a porthole
    d. In a cabinet
    e. Those helpful little guys are in all of those places.
    f. All but a

7. What do the blue crabs do if they want your attention?
>   a. They wave.
>   b. They jump up and down.
>   c. They click their claws – crabs do not like to be ignored.
>   d. They bang on the glass.

8. Treasure Hunt Time! See how many of these human treasures Ariel has gathered in her cave before they all float away.
>   ❑ A anchor
>   ❑ A collection of wooden spoons
>   ❑ A glass doorknob
>   ❑ A red glass bottle
>   ❑ A bell
>   ❑ A cameo
>   ❑ A collection of glass floats
>   ❑ A chain
>   ❑ A spyglass

You come to Scuttle's area next. Enjoy the show, and pick up *Lots To Do In Line* again when you leave the room.

Circular Waiting Area Past Scuttle's Room

9. Find the painting of sirens. They seem to think something is very funny. What are they laughing about?
>   a. An ominous-looking storm cloud
>   b. A lovesick sailor
>   c. A shipwreck
>   d. Scuttle, they think he is really quite funny.

10. Things are looking pretty bad for those sailors, but it seems their situation will get even worse. Why?
>   a. It might have something to do with the hungry-looking shark in the water.
>   b. The sirens' song is not all it is cracked up to be and appears to be off-key.
>   c. One of them is losing his pants – now that is embarrassing.
>   d. The mast they climbed up is just about to break in two; I hope they brought their swim trunks.

e. All of the above

f. Only a and b

11. There is a large fish about to have a snack. Which of these is not part of this fishy meal?

a. A king

b. A feather

c. A spyglass

d. A crate

e. They are all there. Now that's a whale of a meal.

12. Oh dear, it appears that the sea witch Ursula is attacking the ship. These sailors can't catch a break today. What has she captured?

a. The flag, perhaps she was just playing.

b. The king

c. King Triton's trident

d. Ariel

13. What are the men using as their means of escape from the sea witch?

a. A paddle boat

b. A broken plank of wood

c. A dolphin

d. Nothing, they are doomed.

14. Oh no, there is one more piece of bad fortune befalling the ship. What is it now?

a. The ship is caught up in a whirlpool.

b. The ship has been attacked by a parrot-beaked dragon in a bad mood.

c. A tidal wave is about to plunge the ship to the bottom of the ocean.

d. Lightning has struck the mast and the ship is on fire. Good thing there's so much water around really.

15. Treasure Hunt Time! There's time for a quick hunt. See how many of these treasures you can spot before the sirens' song calls you to sea.

❑ Bread

❑ A potato

❑ Peppers

❑ A cork

❑ A bell

❑ A yellow fish

- ❑ A teakettle
- ❑ A lock
- ❑ A globe
- ❑ A chest covered in netting
- ❑ A cement fish
- ❑ A boat's wheel
- ❑ A candlestick
- ❑ A crow's-nest
- ❑ A fishy end

Storybook Circus

Dumbo The Flying Elephant

Outside Queue

So you want to join the circus and fly an elephant? Well step right up. If you are waiting outside the tent try your luck with these questions.

FP 1. **Dumbo's first flight here at Walt Disney World was in 1971. Is this ride older or younger than the oldest person in your group?**

FP 2. **The circus tent has lots of pendants waving in the breeze. Are they all red?**

Yes / No

3. **The Tomorrowland Speedway cars are racing past you. See how many of the following drivers and passengers you can collect before you go inside.**
- ❑ A driver wearing glasses
- ❑ A driver with only one hand on the steering wheel
- ❑ A driver who is taller than the seat back
- ❑ A passenger who is doing the steering
- ❑ A driver or passenger wearing a hat
- ❑ A driver not watching the road
- ❑ A driver with a ponytail
- ❑ A driver or a passenger in a costume.
- ❑ A driver who is having a hard time making the car go.

4. As you enter the big top, you'll see circus banners. Who is the ringmaster pictured on them?
    a. Dumbo the elephant
    b. A mouse
    c. A clown
    d. A crow

5. What does Dumbo hold in his trunk?
    a. A feather   b. A hose
    c. A peanut   d. A ticket

6. The mouse is wearing a hat with a feather in it. What color is the feather?
    a. Black   b. Pink
    c. Red   d. White

7. The mouse is using something as a slide. What is it?
    a. A cannon   b. A trunk
    c. A hose   d. A feather

Elephants never forget but what about you? Take one more look at the banners and then look away and test your memory on Questions 8 to 14.

8. Can you remember what shape was always on top of the poles that hold the banners ?
    a. Feather   b. Peanut
    c. Star   d. Diamond

9. What part of the human body did you see in the banners?
    a. Foot   b. Eye
    c. Ear   d. Hand

10. What letter was at the bottom of each banner?
    a. D   b. C
    c. M   d. P

11. Were there gold tassels on the banners?
    Yes / No

12. Were the banners all purple?
    Yes / No

13. Did Dumbo wear a hat?
    Yes / No

14. What color were Dumbo's eyes?
    a. Brown   b. Blue
    c. Green   d. Black

After Your Pager Goes Off

FP **15. Treasure Hunt Time!** While you wait outside to board your elephant, see how many of these spinning treasures you can find before you fly an elephant.
- ❏ A gold peanut
- ❏ A parachute
- ❏ A gold feather
- ❏ A train
- ❏ A palm tree
- ❏ Four "special delivery"s
- ❏ A whip
- ❏ A gray baby elephant with no hat
- ❏ A pink hat
- ❏ A fire
- ❏ A green hat

The Barnstormer

? **POP QUIZ!** Have a look at the entry, then head in.

FP **1. It looks like some of Goofy's planes may have lost some of their parts. What plane part was part of the sign you just walked under?**
    a. Propeller
    b. Wing
    c. Wheels
    d. All of the above

FP **2. A good pilot needs to know what direction the wind is blowing. What kind of windsock was Goofy flying for that purpose?**
    a. Knitted, knee-high
    b. Pants
    c. A chicken feed bag
    d. Goofy is not a good pilot, so his airstrip has no windsock
    e. Only a and b

FP 3. At the entry, there was a ticket booth but no one was inside. Luckily, there was a sign.
What did it say?
 a. Don't Look Up!
 b. Duck!
 c. Out Flying!
 d. Closed for public safety

 There was a picture of Goofy the Barnstormer directly over the ticket booth. See what you remember about it.

FP **4. He was wearing a scarf. Was it red?**
 Yes / No

FP **5. He had a leather jacket.**
 Yes / No

FP **6. His two front teeth were showing.**
 Yes / No

FP **7. He wore a shiny blue crash helmet.**
 Yes / No

 8. He had goggles.
 Yes / No
End of Pop Quiz

 9. Treasure Hunt Time! If you are visiting Goofy on a particularly crowded day, the queue may take you around the outside stone wall for a while. See how many of these silly circus treasures you can find while you wind your way around. If the queue goes directly under the entry sign, skip this treasure hunt and proceed to Question 10.
 ❑ The number 7
 ❑ Five clothespins
 ❑ Three camels
 ❑ A mischievous monkey
 ❑ A Dumbo
 ❑ A big wet nose
 ❑ A rope
 ❑ A cowboy hat
 ❑ A green flag
 ❑ A yellow flag
 ❑ An unshelled snack

FP 10. Goofy left a pile of balls on the ground, very messy. What kind of balls are lying there?
- a. A bouncy ball with a star on it
- b. Cannonballs
- c. A bowling ball
- d. The world's biggest ball of rubber bands
- e. All of the above
- f. Only b and c

FP 11. What are the settings on Goofy's cannon?
- a. High – Very High – Very Very High
- b. Low – High – Highly Dangerous
- c. High – Very High – Chicken
- d. Low – High – To The Moon

FP 12. To light the cannon, Goofy uses some rather large matches. Is there anything unusual about his match collection?
- a. One match is bent and rubbery.
- b. One is broken and hooked together with tape.
- c. One match is all burned up.
- d. One is lit!

? POP QUIZ! Oh dear! The Great Goofini seems to have crashed his rocket. Take a quick look at it and then turn away. Let's see how many details you remember.

FP 13. What did the Great Goofini use to mount himself to the rocket?
- a. A saddle and reins
- b. Duct tape
- c. Super glue
- d. Rope

FP 14. What was the name of his rocket?
- a. Betsy
- b. Shooting Star
- c. Old Paint
- d. Dolores

FP 15. Goofy traveled on the rocket with a companion. Who?
- a. A chicken
- b. A monkey
- c. A bear
- d. No one is goofy enough to get on that thing with him.

FP 16. Was the rocket dented?
Yes / No

FP 17. Were there stars on the rocket?
　　　Yes / No

FP 18. Was lightning painted on the side?
　　　Yes / No

FP 19. Was a large Band-aid covering a hole in the side?
　　　Yes / No

FP 20. Was there a buckle on it?
　　　Yes / No

End of Pop Quiz

21. The Great Goofini seemed to have tried his luck on the Wheel of Peril. What happened to him there?
　　　a. He was pelted with eggs while spinning.
　　　b. Tomatoes were tossed at him.
　　　c. Knives were thrown at him while he spun.
　　　d. He was spun really fast and then had to walk a tightrope.

22. In the poster Goofini has not yet been hit. How many near misses have there been?
　　　a. 7　　　　　　　b. 11
　　　c. 17　　　　　　d. 18

23. Goofini's clothing seemed to have suffered some serious damage in this act. What part of his wardrobe is beyond repair?
　　　a. Hat　　　　　　b. Tie
　　　c. Shoe　　　　　d. Tails
　　　e. Both a and b　f. Both a and d

24. **Treasure Hunt Time!** Soon you will be flying with Goofy and good luck to you. See how many of these treasures you can find before you take flight.
　　　❏ A peak that's out of this world
　　　❏ Tracks
　　　❏ A whole hand
　　　❏ A well-hit bull's-eye
　　　❏ A star within a star
　　　❏ A checkerboard pattern
　　　❏ A propeller
　　　❏ A barn door
　　　❏ A buckle
　　　❏ The back side of peril
　　　❏ Water

❑ The Great Goofini's initials
❑ A broken water ski
❑ Goggles
❑ A poorly placed helmet

Fantasyland Answers

"it's a small world"
1) c. Sitting in a boat
2) No
3) a. Blue, pink, and black
4) Yes
5) Yes
6) Yes
7) No
8) Yes
9) No
10) Yes
11) Yes
12) b. It was green on one side and blue on the other.
13) a. The sun
14) a. There were no capital letters.
15) Yes, it's an hourglass.
16) c. The Empire State Building
17) e. Only b and c
18) c. Silver
19) a. Eating a meal
20) Number of moving objects found _____
21) Total Treasures found _____

Mad Tea Party
1) Teacup race points: Player 1 _____ Player 2 _____
   Player 3 _____ Player 4_____
2) c. 18
3) The answer depends on your family _____
4) Teacup design-matching points:
   a. Number of matching teacups found (1 point
   each): Player 1 _____ Player 2 _____
      Player 3 _____ Player 4_____
   b. Number of other things found (2 points each):
      Player 1 _____ Player 2 _____
      Player 3 _____ Player 4_____
5) Total Treasures found _____
6) Number of items collected _____

Mickey's PhilharMagic

1) c. A conductor's baton
2) a. A pointy blue wizard's hat
3) No
4) d. A tux with tails
5) b. A star
6) a. The apostrophe in "Mickey's" is a musical note.
7) c. Musical notation
8) e. They are all there.
9) b. You can see Mickey's front side, and his back side, too.
10) a. Maracas
11) c. He fit the bill.
12) b. "Straw, Sticks, and Bricks" in B-flat
13) c. It is made of bricks.
14) a. He is crying so much that the audience is forced to take cover.
15) e. Only a and c
16) d. A "must sea"
17) b. Willie The Whale
18) e. He is a one-man band.
19) c. It is made "from him."
20) a. "Leaves fans wishing for more"
21) b. A squeaker
22) b. Its final squeak
23) e. All but c
24) d. Sizzling

Peter Pan's Flight

1) e. They are all there.
2) c. A clock tower
3) b. A dagger
4) b. A teddy bear
5) a. An umbrella
6) d. Nothing.
7) b. 8:15 p.m.
8) c. She was lighting up the "i" in the word "flight."
9) b. 2
10) d. A trumpet blaring the way
11) Number of shields found _____
12) Number of items collected _____

Prince Charming Regal Carrousel

1) d. Cinderella
2) No

3) a. An eagle in gold
4) Total Treasures found _____
5) Yes
6) No
7) Yes
8) Yes
9) No
10) Yes
11) No
12) Yes
13) Yes
14) Yes
15) No
16) Yes
17) No
18) Yes
19) Yes

The Many Adventures of Winnie the Pooh

1) b. A stack of honey pots dripping with honey
2) d. "Mr. Sander"
3) a. A large jar or pot
4) f. All but a
5) c. A cute little bee
6) Yes
7) c. Gophers
8) Total Treasures found _____
9) Yes, the letters spell out POOH – silly old bear.
10) a. No one
11) c. Some grumpy-looking sticks
12) b. Piglet answers
13) a. A red flowering plant
14) d. You get a great drumbeat going.
15) a. Bike horns honk.
16) c. Step on the footprints.
17) e. Gophers have said all those things.
18) a. Yes
19) No
20) b. They make pretty bell-like noises.
21) Number of activities you tried (1 point each)
_____
22) Total Treasures found _____

Walt Disney World Railroad Station
1) b. 102 feet
2) a. A train
3) d. Carolwood Park
4) b. A clock
5) Total Treasures found _____

Enchanted Forest
Enchanted Tales with Belle
1) d. A whisk broom
2) a. Heart
3) f. Only a and c
4) h. They were all there.
5) e. Both b and c
6) Total Everyday Treasures found _____
7) 3 points for a creative answer _____
8) d. The book is untitled.
9) c. A rose
10) b. 11 years old
11) a. Checkers
12) c. Mopping the stairs
13) d. A new water-wheel system
14) a. Roses
15) Total Cottage Treasures found _____

Under the Sea—Journey of the Little Mermaid
1) a. Blue
2) c. Carved octopus-like arms
3) Number of human treasures found, renamed, and given a purpose _____
4) d. A storm caused the damage.
5) b. It has bubbles in it.
6) e. Those helpful little guys are in all of those places.
7) a. They wave.
8) Total Human Treasures found _____
9) c. A shipwreck
10) d. The mast they climbed up is just about to break.
11) c. A spyglass
12) a. The flag
13) b. A broken plank of wood
14) b. The ship has been attacked by a parrot-beaked dragon.
15) Total Treasures found _____

Storybook Circus
Dumbo The Flying Elephant
1) The answer depends on your family
2) No
3) Number of drivers and passengers collected_____
4) b. A mouse
5) a. A feather
6) d. White
7) c. A hose
8) c. Star
9) d. Hand
10) a. D
11) Yes
12) No
13) Yes
14) b. Blue
15) Total Treasures found _____

The Barnstormer
1) a. Propeller
2) e. Only a and b
3) c. Out Flying!
4) No
5) Yes
6) Yes
7) No
8) Yes
9) Total Circus Treasures found _____
10) f. Only b and c
11) d. Low – High – To The Moon
12) c. One match is all burned up.
13) a. A saddle and reins
14) d. Dolores
15) b. A monkey
16) Yes
17) Yes
18) No
19) No
20) Yes
21) c. Knives were thrown at him while he spun.
22) b. 11
23) f. Both a and d
24) Total Treasures found _____

Tomorrowland

Astro Orbiter

? **POP QUIZ!** Just to the side, there is a resident of Tomorrowland doing his job. He is a robot. Take a quick look at him and then join the queue. It is time to see if you have a memory like a robot.

1. Our robot friend was busy doing his job. What line of work is he in?

    a. He is a galactic police officer.

    b. He is a paperboy.

    c. He is a fortune-teller; being from the future he knows all about it.

    d. He is a waiter.

    e. I don't know, perhaps he is a hobo robot.

2. Something was embedded right in the center of his robot chest that was important to his work. What is it?

    a. An Astro Blaster 2000

    b. A typewriter

    c. A crystal ball

    d. A menu with push buttons for ordering – very convenient!

    e. A slot for you to insert spare change

3. What was this robot's claim to fame?

    a. His papers are printed "While-U-Wait."

    b. He can blast bad guys into the next galaxy.

    c. He shares the future with absolute precision because he has already been there.

    d. He carries every flavor of astronaut ice cream.

4. What was the top article featured in today's "Galaxy Gazette"?
   a. Robot Elected to Congress. (Finally equal representation for robotic man!)
   b. Milky Way Leaks!
   c. Stitch Escapes!
   d. Disney Opens "Planet Disney!" (a new theme park on Mars!)

5. Did the robot have a place to plug in to be rejuiced?
   Yes / No

6. How many different newspaper titles were visible?
   a. 1
   b. 2
   c. 3
   d. 0 (I tell you he is a cop!)

7. How many fingers did he have?
   a. Four fingers and one thumb on each hand.
   b. Two fingers and two thumbs on each hand.
   c. No fingers, he had pincers.
   d. I thought it rude to stare.

End of Pop Quiz

8. There is something made of metal that would normally be made of something else. What is it?
   a. A hamburger
   b. A cat
   c. A flowerpot
   d. A palm tree

9. There are a number of Little Green Men looking at you. They have a symbol on their chests. What is it?
   a. A spotted planet with a ring around it
   b. A rocket ship with wings
   c. Three eyes
   d. A sun

10. Astro Orbiter opened in its first form in 1974 as the Star Jets. Is this attraction older or younger than your mother? _____

11. Is it older or younger than your grandfather? _____

12. Treasure Hunt Time! See how many of these galactic treasures you can discover before you blast off.

- ❏ A rocket ship shaped like a cola bottle
- ❏ A place to make calls around the galaxy
- ❏ A shop that is out of this world
- ❏ A silver triangle with circles in it
- ❏ The number 29
- ❏ A flying saucer
- ❏ A wet granite ball
- ❏ A yellow gear that knows the year
- ❏ A hot dog
- ❏ A clock
- ❏ Green circles that will split if you "go up"
- ❏ A blue metal hat

Buzz Lightyear's Space Ranger Spin

The following questions are for outside, Space Ranger. Stay alert!

1. What is Star Command's symbol?
- a. A planet with a ring and spots
- b. A planet with a ring, a rocket, and wings
- c. A rocket with a star on it and fire coming out the back
- d. That changes daily, Cadet. Check your bulletins.

2. What is unusual about the word "spin" on the sign for the ride?
- a. It has two rings around it.
- b. It is spinning.
- c. It is in the shape of a rocket ship.
- d. It is upside down.

3. There is an informational sign outside the entrance. What is the sign sitting on top of?
- a. A rocket
- b. A stack of stars
- c. A Buzz Lightyear still in his original box; very collectible!
- d. Two C-cell batteries

4. In the sign for the attraction, there is a bad guy. Which of these things is true about Zurg?
- a. He has a helmet with horns.
- b. He wears a snazzy looking cape fastened with a "Z."
- c. He has really big teeth.
- d. All of the above are true, and more. He is a terrifying adversary, Space Ranger!
- e. Well a and c are true, but no bad guy worth his salt would don a cape.

5. This is a very busy place in the universe, Cadets. See how many rocket ships you can find here in port while you wait. Earn 1 point for each rocket ship you spot. _____

6. Treasure Hunt Time! See how many of these space treasures you can find before you go into orbit.
- ❏ A blue planet
- ❏ A blue planet with a yellow ring
- ❏ A large yellow antenna
- ❏ A spaceship with four neon-green rings
- ❏ A microphone
- ❏ A clear orb
- ❏ A star
- ❏ The Galactic Federation Prisoner Transport Center
- ❏ Someone green with one eye
- ❏ Someone green with two eyes
- ❏ Two red arrows

7. There is a space collectibles convention coming! Who can you meet there?
- a. Buzz Lightyear
- b. R2-D2 and C-3PO
- c. Famous celebrity aliens
- d. People who like to keep their toys in the original packaging

8. The collectibles convention will feature asteroid art. Cool! What asteroid creation do they show?
- a. The "Mona Lisa" made entirely from asteroids
- b. Mickey Mouse's head
- c. A statue of Buzz himself
- d. A great big "Z"

9. What is the "Martian Princess"?
   a. The name of Buzz's rocket cruiser
   b. The restaurant at the end of the galaxy
   c. The name of the fair space-maiden–in-distress whom Buzz must rescue
   d. A space yacht

The rest of the questions will be best answered inside the building, Cadets. At ease.

FP 10. Who appears to make up the Universe Protection Unit?
   a. All Space Rangers
   b. Little Green Men
   c. Buzz Lightyear
   d. Zurg
   e. Just b and c

FP 11. There is a Green Man plugging his ears. Why?
   a. A rocket is blasting off.
   b. There was an explosion. Look out, Space Rangers!
   c. All of the Green Men are shouting.
   d. He just likes to keep his fingers in his ears.

FP 12. What can be found in sector 5?
   a. A planet with rings around it
   b. A square planet
   c. Batteries floating in space
   d. Robotic space crabs

FP 13. Where is Star Command located?
   a. On a blue planet with a yellow ring around it
   b. On a purple planet with many craters. Watch your step, please.
   c. Hidden deep in the Molbekk Nebula
   d. That is an uncharted location, Cadet.

FP 14. What can be found at the Star Command Power Center?
   a. A power-sucking space aardvark. Look out! The power is dangerously low!
   b. A Green Man and a plug
   c. A bunch of computer screens all flashing, "Alert, low power!"
   d. Six DD batteries

FP 15. There is a power gauge. What is the arrow pointing to?
> a. The red
> b. The green
> c. The line between red and white
> d. The "insert batteries now" message

FP 16. Oh no! There is a robot attack in progress! What are the robots doing?
> a. Stealing batteries, alkaline too. That's the best kind. Those monsters!
> b. Blowing up star craft
> c. Kidnapping Buzz
> d. Smashing the city; robots never clean up their mess.

FP 17. What is an XP-37?
> a. A high-power space blaster good for blasting anything with a "Z" on it
> b. A space cruiser for Jr. Cadet Training
> c. The designation of a planet in sector 7 that has been getting a bit uppity
> d. How did you find that number? That is Top Secret information, Cadet!

FP 18. What unknown object was detected in sector 9?
> a. A robot hurtling through space towards us at this very moment
> b. Some sort of star cruiser with the letter "Z" clearly visible on its side
> c. A spider-like space beastie
> d. It is unknown. If I knew what is was it would be known wouldn't it?

FP 19. Hey, look, there's Buzz! What enormous toy is he standing next to?
> a. A View-Master, and he is putting it to good use
> b. An Etch A Sketch
> c. A toy rocket ship
> d. A giant blaster; hope that doesn't go off.

FP 20. What is the job of Green Squadron?
> a. To lead the mission
> b. To find Zurg
> c. To blast robots to infinity and beyond
> d. To retrieve the power cells

FP 21. What is the job of everyone not in Green Squadron?
- a. To find Zurg
- b. To concentrate on the robots
- c. To retrieve power cells
- d. To bring justice to the universe

FP 22. Where is our rendezvous point?
- a. Planet "Z"
- b. Back at Star Command Headquarters
- c. In the toy box
- d. I'm still not clear on those directions. Could we ask someone?

Monsters, Inc. Laugh Floor

1. OK, as you walk in you will see a green monster named Mike. What is unique about him?
- a. He is furry.
- b. He has only one eye and it is a lovely blue color.
- c. He has horns.
- d. He has vampire teeth.
- e. Only b and c

2. Check the lovely view behind our friend Mike. Is there anything special about his view?
- a. He is in front of New York City.
- b. The city is filled with buildings that are, well, monstrous.
- c. The buildings are being eaten by a large, hungry-looking monster with multiple mouths.
- d. The city is upside down.

3. What is the future of energy?
- a. A laugh
- b. A scream
- c. A joke
- d. A hoot

4. What can you do to help power Monstropolis?
- a. Text in a joke.
- b. Tickle you brother until your Mom yells at you.
- c. Don't hold it in.
- d. Laugh your head off, but don't forget to take it with you.

5. Treasure Hunt Time! See how many of these monstrous treasures you can catch before the curtain goes up.

- ❏ An "M" with an eye in it
- ❏ Horn-rimmed glasses
- ❏ A green star
- ❏ Purple horns
- ❏ A banana peel
- ❏ Someone holding up a finger
- ❏ A telephone
- ❏ Some scary writing
- ❏ The fine print
- ❏ A "beauty" spot???
- ❏ A child's screaming face
- ❏ A car with teeth
- ❏ A scary view
- ❏ A trashy piece of equipment
- ❏ Gears
- ❏ The number 17 in a circle

6. Mike has his own dressing room, how nice. What is the room's other function?

- a. Everyone else's dressing room
- b. Kitchen door
- c. Garbage shoot
- d. Maintenance closet

7. In the Laugh Systems Diagram, what are the humans doing?

- a. Screaming
- b. Smiling
- c. Singing
- d. Scaring

8. What is significant about the number 432?

- a. It is the capacity of the theater you are about to enter.
- b. It is the office of B. Brute.
- c. It is Mike's employee number.
- d. Well, it is composed of descending numbers. Do you consider that significant?

9. Hey, I'm hungry. Which of these snacks can I get from the vending machine?

    a. Blort

    b. Sugar, Salt, and Fat

    c. Polyvinyl Chloride

    d. Chocolate-covered Boogers

    e. All of the above

    f. All but d; boogers taste terrible with chocolate.

10. What are the critics saying about Monsters, Inc. Laugh Floor?

    a. "Two claws, way up"

    b. "3½ spikes"

    c. "These monsters are so funny it's scary."

    d. "I laughed. I cried. Then I laughed again. Then I cried one more time. Then I sighed. Then I coughed. Then I had a lozenge."

    e. All of the above

11. Oh no, a monster lost a body part at the show. What part went missing?

    a. The head; it was laughed off.

    b. A tentacle, but it will grow back eventually.

    c. Ten of the monster's feet ran away compelling it to remain for the next show.

    d. The poor beast lost its belly button, but who needs a belly button?

12. What is the slug/frog-like bookkeeper Roz's hobby?

    a. Collecting puce-colored forms that have not been filled in right

    b. Hiding in the closets of co-workers who deserve it

    c. Scaring Mike Wazowski

    d. Screaming; Roz is old school.

13. Why do the monsters invite you into their world?

    a. To laugh

    b. To cry

    c. To scream

    d. To stay as dinner

Space Mountain

Outside the Building

Attention: If you go directly inside, skip to Question 5.

1. Tick Tock, the clock has something special about it. What is it?

    a. The clock hands are bolts of lightning.

    b. It is a digital clock with neon numbers that flash.

    c. It is an entirely audio clock announcing the progression of time on Earth and Mars every five minutes.

    d. The face is made of gears. I guess that makes it a gear head.

    e. Both a and d

    f. Nothing; time means nothing in space.

2. The building the clock decorates seems to serve an important purpose. What is it?

    a. It is the ticketing office for all space travel from this spaceport.

    b. It is an arcade. You can't get enough of those in space.

    c. It is the Light and Power Company.

    d. It is the best place to get a meal that is "Out Of This World" here on Earth.

    e. All except a

    f. Only b and c

3. Oh no, something is happening to an itsy-bitsy building! What is the problem?

    a. It's about to be hit by a star ship.

    b. It's being sucked into a flying saucer.

    c. Lightning is striking its top.

    d. All of the above. It's a very bad day for mini buildings.

    e. Only a and c

4. Treasure Hunt Time! See how many of these treasures you can unearth before you go inside.

- ❑ A large spaceship
- ❑ A glowing blue circle
- ❑ A green gear
- ❑ A castle tower
- ❑ Three flags of three different colors
- ❑ Three squares of see-through green
- ❑ The number 9
- ❑ A "Bright New Tomorrow"
- ❑ A Coke bottle rocket

Inside the Building

FP **5. What is very significant about the number SEVEN – FIVE?**
- a. It is the number of this starport.
- b. It is the number of galactic destinations that can be reached from here.
- c. It is the model number of the space vehicle you will be boarding here today.
- d. It is the badge number of the admiral in charge of this port.

FP **6. Which of these is not a connecting point from Alpha Centauri B?**
- a. 14 Herculis
- b. Mu Arae
- c. Altair
- d. Galaxy M39
- e. You can connect to all of the above from Alpha Centauri B.
- f. You can only connect to b and c.

FP **7. Which of these are active Earth stations?**
- a. Tomorrowland Station MK-1
- d. Discovery Landing Station–Paris
- c. Ashita Base–Tokyo
- d. TL Space Station 77
- e. All of the above
- f. All but d

FP 8. What is this Starport?
  a. Your Gateway to the Galaxies
  b. A wretched hive of scum and villainy
  c. A lovely place for a burger
  d. The oldest functioning port in the known universe

FP 9. Can you find an airlock?
  Yes / No

FP 10. In what sector can an intrepid traveler find a Disney resort?
  a. Outer System–Ice Dwarf Sector
  b. Titan Stations–Sector Two
  c. Triton Stations–Sector Three
  d. Nebula Warp Gates
  e. Sorry, there are not yet any Disney resorts in space because those mouse ears won't stay on at zero-g.

FP 11. Pluto has fewer connections to and from it than any other location in the Outer System–Ice Dwarf Sector.
  True or False?

FP 12. There is a dwarf galaxy named "Boots Dwarf Galaxy"
  True or False?

FP 13. What nebula is named for an animal?
  a. Horsehead Nebula
  b. Cat's Eye Nebula
  c. Crab Nebula
  d. Eagle Nebula
  e. All of the above
  f. None of the above; space is no place for animals.

Attention: You have arrived at a game console. If you play, it should be a blast! When you are done playing see how many of these questions you can answer.

14. What shapes were the buttons you just used?
  a. One square, one triangle, and one circle
  b. Three squares – two upright and one tilted
  c. Three circles
  d. Four rocket shapes

15. There are two different directions indicated on the wall. What are they?
 a. Right and Left
 b. Alpha and Beta
 c. Alpha and Omega
 d. Boarding or Last-Chance Exit

FP **16. Treasure Hunt Time!** See how many of these you can spot before you embark on your flight.
 ❑ Planets _____
 ❑ Ride-vehicles going by _____
 ❑ The control tower _____
 ❑ A warning _____

FP **17. It is time to play "Space Wars."**
 Divide yourselves into two teams, the Earthlings and the Aliens. Your battle is over the other passengers in this spaceport, and your team's mission is to find two passengers who fit each of the descriptions below before the other team can spot them. You will proceed description by description, starting with "passengers wearing something on their heads." The first team, Earthlings or Aliens, to find two passengers who fit that description gets 5 points; the other team gets nothing. Then both teams advance to the next description. The war is over when you've gone through all the descriptions or reach the ride loading dock. The team with the most points wins.
 Note: If the players wish to skip a description, they may.
 ❑ Passengers wearing something on their heads: hats, headbands, mouse ears, etc.
 ❑ Passengers carrying a shopping bag
 ❑ Passengers wearing stripes
 ❑ Passengers with backpacks or purses
 ❑ Passengers wearing shorts
 ❑ Passengers wearing a necklace
 ❑ Passengers looking at or talking on cell phones
 ❑ Passengers wearing or carrying a sweatshirt
 ❑ Passengers wearing a Disney shirt
 ❑ Passengers with red pants
 ❑ Passengers with braided hair
 ❑ Passengers wearing neon
 ❑ Passengers wearing yellow T-shirts
 ❑ Passengers with ponytails

Stitch's Great Escape!

? **POP QUIZ!** We are going to play "It's All Alien to Me." Before you get in line, take a look at the sign for this attraction. Also look at the sign for the attraction across the street, Monsters, Inc. Laugh Floor. Now get in line and see what you remember about the strange dudes on the signs.

1. What was Stitch wearing? (Stitch is the creature on the sign for the attraction you are entering now.)
   a. An astronaut's suit complete with head bubble
   b. A silver jacket, just right for those nippy days in outer space
   c. An orange jump suit; not too flattering, really
   d. Nothing, he is an alien after all.

2. What about Mike, the creature on the Monsters, Inc. sign. What was he wearing?
   a. An orange jump suit
   b. A green pair of pants with suspenders
   c. A tux
   d. Nothing. He was naked as a jaybird.

3. One of these creatures appeared to have better dental hygiene than the other. Who has been brushing?
   a. Stitch   b. Mike
   c. Both   d. Neither

4. Who had four hands?
   a. Stitch   b. Mike
   c. Both   d. Neither

5. Who had one eye?
   a. Stitch   b. Mike
   c. Both   d. Neither

6. Who sported long lashes?
   a. Stitch   b. Mike
   c. Both   d. Neither

7. Whose skin was blue?
- a. Stitch
- b. Mike
- c. Both
- d. Neither

8. Whose complexion was a bit green?
- a. Stitch
- b. Mike
- c. Both
- d. Neither

9. Who had horns?
- a. Stitch
- b. Mike
- c. Both
- d. Neither

10. Who had claws?
- a. Stitch
- b. Mike
- c. Both
- d. Neither

11. Who was adorned with a fancy back frill?
- a. Stitch
- b. Mike
- c. Both
- d. Neither

12. Who was missing a nose?
- a. Stitch
- b. Mike
- c. Both
- d. Neither

13. Who was hanging upside down?
- a. Stitch
- b. Mike
- c. Both
- d. Neither

14. Who had a single gold tooth?
- a. Stitch
- b. Mike
- c. Both
- d. Neither

15. Who had antennae?
- a. Stitch
- b. Mike
- c. Both
- d. Neither

16. Who had something in his hand?
- a. Stitch
- b. Mike
- c. Both
- d. Neither

17. Who had no ears?
- a. Stitch
- b. Mike
- c. Both
- d. Neither

End of Pop Quiz

18. If I were to combine an alien and monster like Stitch and Mike, which of these descriptions would best fit the creature I would create?

    a. The Stike: An aqua-colored critter with three eyes, six hands, and four legs. He would have horns and antennae and, most certainly, a big mouth.

    b. The Mitch: A round creature with blue and green spots. He would have long nails on his many hands and a kicky frill sticking off his back.

    c. The Stitmik: A round green little kid with koala-type ears and long antennae. He would wear a jumpsuit and have just one eye, most of the time.

    d. Movie history has proven that it is best not to mix monsters and aliens.

19. Alien vs. Monster Collection Battle!

It is time for the aliens and the monsters to engage in epic combat! Divide into two teams, "Aliens" and "Monsters." Your goal is to complete your Collection before the other team does. The first team done, or the team with the most points when you enter the attraction, wins. Here is how you play: Look at your fellow guests as they pass by. Any guests wearing green have become monsters, while any sporting blue are aliens. (No, blue jeans do not count.) Try to collect a monster or an alien for each of the categories below. For example, if the category is "wearing something furry" and you are on the Alien team, you will want to find someone wearing something blue who is also wearing something furry. Guests who are wearing both blue and green are alien-monster mutants and count for the team that spots them first.

Note: The number in parentheses after of each category is the number of points you get for collecting that monster or alien.

    ❑ Wearing a pair of mouse ears (1)
    ❑ Carrying a purse (1)
    ❑ Carrying a toy (2)
    ❑ In flip-flops (1)
    ❑ Eating something (1)
    ❑ Wearing a backpack (2)
    ❑ Looking at a map (3)

- ❑ Wearing a "Mickey Mouse" on some part of their clothing (2)
- ❑ Having a drink (1)
- ❑ Holding or sucking on a bottle or a pacifier (3)
- ❑ In shorts (1)
- ❑ In a dress or skirt (2)
- ❑ Wearing a white hat (1)
- ❑ Wearing a hat that is not white and not a baseball cap (1)
- ❑ Wearing a lanyard of pins (3)
- ❑ Wearing a ponytail (2)
- ❑ Wearing the name of a sports team (2)
- ❑ With glasses (1)
- ❑ With a sweater or sweatshirt (2)
- ❑ With stripes (1)
- ❑ Pushing a stroller (1)
- ❑ Wearing a Hawaiian print shirt (3)
- ❑ Holding a shopping bag (2)
- ❑ Talking on the phone or texting (2)
- ❑ Holding hands (1)

Tomorrowland Speedway

1. Speedway Special Collection: Here at the Speedway there are lots of black-and-white checkered flags. If you want more points, collect every flag you see, whether it is a real flag or a painted one. You get 1 point for each checkered flag you collect. _____

? **POP QUIZ!** Before you enter the queue, take a quick look at the sign for Tomorrowland Speedway. Then get in line and play "Speedway Memory."

2. What color were the letters in the words "Tomorrowland Speedway"?
- a. Black
- b. White
- c. Blue
- d. Red
- e. Both a and b
- f. Both b and c

3. There was a little indicator device telling how long your wait in line would be. What was on both sides?
    a. Cars
    b. Black-and-white checkered flags
    c. Wheels
    d. Flashing lights

4. There were some flags on the sign. Let's see what you remember about them. How many green flags were there?
    a. 1   b. 2
    c. 3   d. 0

5. How many black-and-white checkered flags were there?
    a. 1   b. 2
    c. 3   d. 0

6. How many flags had a design on them?
    a. 1   b. 2
    c. 3   d. 4

7. Was there a black flag?
    Yes / No

8. Was there an orange flag?
    Yes / No

9. Did one flag have a cross on it?
    Yes / No

10. Was there a flag with a single diagonal line on it?
    Yes / No

11. How many flags festooned the top of the sign?
    a. 6   b. 7
    c. 8   d. 9
    e. Are you sure there were flags?
End of Pop Quiz

12. How tall must you be to drive a Speedway car?
    a. 54 inches
    b. 49 inches
    c. 40 inches
    d. 8 oil cans tall
    e. Both a and d
    f. There is no height restriction here.

13. Treasure Hunt Time! See how many of these racing treasures you can find before you speed away.

- ❏ A red triangle
- ❏ A strange parking space
- ❏ Half a blue star
- ❏ Old Glory
- ❏ A sign for Interstate 4 that Mickey should like
- ❏ A racing-themed umbrella
- ❏ A red circle containing a Coke bottle
- ❏ A topiary
- ❏ A large dark sphere
- ❏ A small yellow sphere
- ❏ 210 mph
- ❏ A Goodyear tire
- ❏ A blue-and-yellow flag
- ❏ Blue gears
- ❏ Mickey Mouse in goggles
- ❏ A helmet
- ❏ An all-white flag
- ❏ North, South, East, and West
- ❏ Pit Row
- ❏ A teapot
- ❏ Someone with both hands over his head
- ❏ Hong Kong's track
- ❏ A red spinning light
- ❏ The lap number
- ❏ Crossed checkered flags

14. What is significant about the number 50?

 a. It is the number of years this ride has been in the park.

 b. It's the number of the car in the victory circle.

 c. It's the speed limit on the track.

 d. It's the number of cars available to drive.

15. How many turns are on this track?

 a. 3   b. 4

 c. 5   d. 6

16. There are a lot of cars on the track. See if you can spot these as they go by.

- ❏ A yellow car with a black-and-white " V" on its hood
- ❏ Car 64
- ❏ An orange car with red lightning on its hood
- ❏ Car 10

- ❑ Car 36
- ❑ A blue car with black lines on its hood
- ❑ Car 20
- ❑ A green car
- ❑ An orange car with blue stripes on its hood
- ❑ Car 33
- ❑ A blue car with a green-and-white "V" on its hood

Walt Disney's Carousel of Progress

Treasure Hunt Time! See how many of these treasures you can find before it is tomorrow.

- ❑ A yellow gear with a purple and green center
- ❑ A solid blue gear
- ❑ A dog
- ❑ A purple gear with Mickey Mouse heads in it
- ❑ A solid yellow gear that is connected to a green gear
- ❑ Visitors from outer space
- ❑ A door featuring five green circles
- ❑ A creature with yellow teeth. Time to see the dentist!
- ❑ A circle that is half white and half gray
- ❑ A yellow hexagon
- ❑ A scale model of the Carousel of Progress
- ❑ A globe

Tomorrowland Answers

Astro Orbiter
1) *b. He is a paperboy.*
2) *b. A typewriter*
3) *a. His papers are printed "While-U-Wait."*
4) *c. Stitch Escapes!*
5) *Yes*
6) *b. 2*
7) *c. No fingers, he had pincers.*
8) *d. A palm tree*
9) *a. A spotted planet with a ring around it*

10-11) The answers depend on your family.
12) Total Galactic Treasures found _____

Buzz Lightyear's Space Ranger Spin

1) b. A planet with a ring, a rocket, and wings
2) a. It has two rings around it.
3) d. Two C-cell batteries
4) d. All of the above are true, and more.
5) Number of rocket ships spotted _____
6) Total Space Treasures found _____
7) c. Famous celebrity aliens
8) b. Mickey Mouse's head
9) d. A space yacht
10) e. Just b and c
11) a. A rocket is blasting off.
12) b. A square planet
13) a. On a blue planet with a yellow ring around it
14) d. Six DD batteries
15) c. The line between red and white
16) a. Stealing batteries
17) b. A space cruiser for Jr. Cadet Training
18) c. A spider-like space beastie
19) a. A View-Master
20) d. To retrieve the power cells
21) b. To concentrate on the robots
22) a. Planet "Z"

Monsters, Inc. Laugh Floor

1) e. Only b and c
2) b. The city is filled with buildings that are, well, monstrous.
3) c. A joke
4) a. Text in a joke.
5) Total Monstrous Treasures found _____
6) d. Maintenance closet
7) b. Smiling
8) b. It is the office of B. Brute.
9) f. All but d
10) e. All of the above
11) a. The head
12) c. Scaring Mike Wazowski
13) a. To laugh

Space Mountain

1) e. Both a and d

2) f. Only b and c
3) c. Lightning is striking its top.
4) Total Treasures unearthed _____
5) a. It is the number of this starport.
6) b. Mu Arae
7) e. All of the above
8) a. Your Gateway to the Galaxies
9) Yes
10) b. Titan Stations–Sector Two
11) False
12) True
13) e. All of the above
14) b. Three squares – two upright and one tilted
15) c. Alpha and Omega
16) Total Treasures found _____
17) Total Points:
     Earthling Team _____
     Alien Team _____

Stitch's Great Escape!
1) c. An orange jump suit
2) d. Nothing
3) b. Mike
4) a. Stitch
5) b. Mike
6) d. Neither
7) a. Stitch
8) b. Mike
9) b. Mike
10) c. Both
11) a. Stitch
12) b. Mike
13) a. Stitch
14) d. Neither
15) a. Stitch
16) b. Mike
17) b. Mike
18) a, b, c, and d. All are right because it's your
     imagination at work.
19) Total Points:
     Team Monster _____
     Team Alien _____

Tomorrowland Speedway
1) Number of flags collected _____

2) f. Both b and c
3) b. Black-and-white checkered flags
4) a. 1
5) b. 2
6) c. 3
7) Yes
8) No
9) No
10) Yes
11) c. 8
12) e. Both a and d
13) Total Racing Treasures found _____
14) b. It's the number of the car in the victory circle.
15) c. 5
16) Number of cars spotted _____

Walt Disney's Carousel of Progress
Total Treasures found _____

Magic Kingdom Scavenger Hunt

You can hunt for the treasure below as you walk from attraction to attraction. Or if you prefer you can devote part of a day to finding these treasures. Either way, keep your eyes open to rack up the points.

❑ A large barrel of rum
❑ A glass ceiling
❑ A collection of yarn
❑ Three skulls on bamboo poles
❑ A talking trashcan (if you are very lucky)
❑ A choir with very wooden voices
❑ An elephant wearing a necklace
❑ A crow in its nest
❑ A flag with a heart on it
❑ A log mailbox
❑ A street sign hanging from a shovel
❑ A windmill
❑ A native American chief
❑ A horse auction
❑ Mounted antlers
❑ A golden horseshoe
❑ A waterwheel

- ❑ A "timeout" place from the olden days
- ❑ A cauldron
- ❑ A sled
- ❑ An old, rusty anchor
- ❑ A golden rooster
- ❑ A crocodile holding a lantern
- ❑ A puppet with a slice of cake
- ❑ A mural squirrel
- ❑ A sneaky cat at a watering hole
- ❑ Alice looking positively green
- ❑ A granite sphere
- ❑ A purple planet
- ❑ A sailmaker
- ❑ Really hot glass
- ❑ Mickey and a ship's wheel
- ❑ A large collection of patches
- ❑ A big pink hatbox

Magic Kingdom Scavenger Hunt Tally

Total Treasures found _____

Epcot

In this chapter, you'll find games for most of Epcot's ride queues as well as for film queues that often necessitate a wait. They are organized into three sections, Future World East, Future World West, and World Showcase and then by pavilion in each section in the order you'll find them on your Guidemap. Attractions within the same pavilion are listed alphabetically.

Note: Pavilions that don't offer rides or films aren't included in this book. But that doesn't mean you'll want to skip them. There's lots of interest in every one.

If you want to continue to play while you are walking around the park from one place to another, turn to the Epcot Scavenger Hunt at the end of this chapter. *Tip:* You may want to read over the list now and then stay on the lookout. The treasures on the scavenger hunt list are scattered throughout World Showcase. You get 1 point for every treasure you find.

Note: When you see *FP* next to a question or section, it means you can find the answer (or gather Treasure or Collection items) from both the FASTPASS and standby lines. A **?** in the margin is your signal to look hard at something (often the attraction's sign) before you enter the queue.

Scoring: Unless specified otherwise, give yourself 1 point for each correct answer, 1 point for each Treasure you find, 1 point for each item you add to a Collection, and 1 point for any similar finds you make when you are hunting for something rather than answering questions. Don't forget to add 5 bonus points for each of your Collections with more than 10 items in it at the end of the day. Good luck!

Future World East

Spaceship Earth

1. Extraterrestrial Hunt

Space is big, I mean really BIG, and sometimes so is this line. Epcot gets visitors from a lot of unique places. While you wait, see just how good you can be at recognizing visitors from other planets. Have a look around; you might see Extraterrestrials!!! Of course, you need to know what to look for. Martians (people from Mars) will be wearing green on some part of their bodies. Venusians (people from Venus) will be wearing something red. It could be clothing, face paint, or a tattoo. Both will be doing their evil best to blend in and look like your average Earthling. Your job is to find them before they can infiltrate Earth.

Divide into two teams. One will look for Martians and the other will hunt Venusians. If a person is wearing both colors, he may have lived on both planets and who knows where else. The first team to spot such an ET gets the points.

To make it more fun, instead of just counting the number of people wearing green and red, you must find people wearing the color but also matching the descriptions found below. Each description can be used only once, by one team or the other. For example, if the Martian-hunting team finds a person with a hat who is also wearing green, then "An ET wearing a brimmed hat" goes to the Martian hunters.

❑ An ET wearing a brimmed hat
❑ An ET with a tote bag
❑ An ET with a camera bag
❑ An ET carrying a plastic bag

- ❑ An ET carrying a Disney character
- ❑ An ET wearing crocs
- ❑ An ET wearing Mickey Mouse ears
- ❑ An ET walking alone
- ❑ An ET listening to music
- ❑ An ET with earrings
- ❑ An ET with a headband
- ❑ An ET with boots
- ❑ An ET with a child on their back
- ❑ An ET eating something
- ❑ An ET drinking something
- ❑ An ET in flip-flops
- ❑ An ET with a vest
- ❑ An ET wearing an animal print
- ❑ An ET in a jersey
- ❑ An ET jumping
- ❑ An ET looking at a map
- ❑ An ET texting
- ❑ An ET with a baby stroller
- ❑ An ET with a camera

2. Still waiting? Try working on a Collection or two.
Or play the ET hunting game again, this time searching
for Martians wearing yellow and Venusians in blue.

Universe of Energy: Ellen's Energy Adventure

1. Treasure Hunt Time!

On this ride we are going to do a very different kind
of treasure hunt. We will be hunting treasure that
shines and sparkles. Look closely at the building you
are next to. It is covered in tiny mirrors that obscure
almost everything they reflect. That's where your
treasure is hidden!

The treasure you're hunting is your fellow guests.
Choose any one person and take a really good look at
what they are wearing. Now check out the mirrored
wall in front of you and try to find your target person
among all the tiny reflective squares. Once you spot
your person, pick another guest and start again. Then
see how many people you can locate before it is time to
go inside.

Tip: To make your hunt even more challenging, you can look at the person and then close your eyes and have someone spin you around before you try to find the guest in the mirrors. Or have someone in your group describe a person for you while you have your back to the other guests and then try to locate that person in the mirrors.

2. If you run out of people to find in the mirrors, make two special Collections. There are a large number of circles and spheres in this area. Some are big and some small, and you can spot them both nearby and in the distance. Give yourself 1 point for every circle you discover and 2 points for every sphere.

Mission: SPACE

? **POP QUIZ!** You just walked into line past some pretty cool decorations. Turn your back on them now and let's see how good your memory is.

1. There were three big planets.
Yes / No

2. One of the planets appeared to be Earth. It was the smallest.
Yes / No

3. There was a ring of light around the Earth. It went all the way around the planet.
Yes / No

4. The light ring was blue.
Yes / No

5. The light had a space vehicle on the end of it that appeared to be blasting off.
Yes / No

6. Resting on top of the light ring were the words "Blast Into Tomorrow."
Yes / No

7. There was a large rocket ship on the ground as you walked in.

Yes / No

8. The name of the ride, Mission: SPACE, appeared on the largest planet.

Yes / No

9. It was possible to go inside the largest planet.

Yes / No

10. There were clouds around only one planet.

Yes / No

End of Pop Quiz

11. Who said, "We shall not cease our explorations"?

a. An astronaut   b. A president
c. Mickey Mouse   d. A poet

12. What is the "only way of discovering the limits of the possible"?

a. "To believe that everything is possible if we only persevere"
b. "To know all is possible"
c. "To venture a little way past them into the impossible"
d. "To boldly go where no man has gone before"

13. According to astronaut Frank Borman, what is the essence of the human spirit?

a. Exploration
b. Determination
c. Childlike wonder
d. Some pink gooey stuff that looks a lot like cotton candy

14. Who said, "Dare to dream"?

a. An actor
b. A U.S. astronaut
c. A Russian astronaut
d. OK, this one really was Mickey Mouse, right?

15. Soon you will be asked to join a team, orange or green. Which team should you join if spinning is not your thing?

a. Team Orange
b. Team Green

16. There is a blue door. Who can use it?
    a. Flight crew only
    b. Trainees only
    c. Teachers; it is their private lounge.
    d. Maintenance

17. There is a sign announcing the number of years of human space flight as of the building of this facility. How many years are we celebrating?
    a. 50 years   b. 75 years
    c. 90 years   d. 100 years; I'd better send a
                                   card.

FP 18. Treasure Hunt Time! Can you spot these?
    ❏ A nice place for a snack if you are a bat
    ❏ A satellite dish
    ❏ Four blasters
    ❏ A place for a long walk
    ❏ ISTC
    ❏ A camera
    ❏ A hatch
    ❏ The moon's surface

FP 19. What must all personnel do before they conduct any training at the Gravity Wheel Training Center?
    a. Suit up
    b. Pass a health screening
    c. Check in
    d. Certify they haven't eaten in the last eight hours

FP 20. The Aerospike Engine used in the X-2 Deep Space Shuttle is really something special. What is used to power it?
    a. A mix of hydrogen and oxygen
    b. Solid hydrogen does the trick.
    c. Nuclear fusion power
    d. Hamsters on a wheel; it is remarkable how fast
       they can go.

FP 21. Which of these features is not part of the X-2 Deep Space Shuttle?
    a. Buckytubes
    b. Extending Wing
    c. Aerobrakes
    d. Anti-Asteroid Super Alloy Siding
    e. All are included; it is super deluxe.

FP 22. **The X-2 is lighter than earlier space shuttle modules, but by how much?**
    a. 100 pounds
    b. Exactly 549 pounds
    c. Over a million pounds
    d. Lighter? No, actually it is heavier.

FP 23. **Where can you find the number 42?**
    a. It is on a large door.
    b. It is the number of the Lunar Roving Vehicle.
    c. It is the number of hours people spend in simulated antigravity space training.
    d. It can be found on the side of the long cylindrical piece of equipment hanging overhead.

FP 24. **Are the tires on the Lunar Roving Vehicle made by Goodyear?**
    Yes / No

FP 25. **There is something unusual about the tires on the Lunar Roving Vehicle. What is it?**
    a. They are flat.
    b. There are only two; now how does that work?
    c. They are spiked.
    d. They are metal. That's going to be bad for potholes.

FP 26. **What is the Lunar Roving Vehicle space car's top speed?**
    a. 8.7 mph
    b. 15 mph
    c. 50 mph
    d. 1000 mph; now that's what I call "zoom zoom!"

FP 27. **What is the power source for the Lunar Roving Vehicle?**
    a. Solar   b. Battery
    c. Water   d. Petroleum

FP 28. **What does ISTC stand for anyway?**
    a. Interconnected Spinning Terrain Capsule
    b. Individual Simulation Tolerance Capacity
    c. International Space Training Center
    d. Indigestion Stimulating Torture Chamber

FP 29. According to the posted training schedule, what is the Orange team doing at 0400?

    a. They are learning to launch.

    b. They are practicing landing.

    c. They are in the mess hall.

    d. They are increasing their weightlessness tolerance.

    e. That is classified.

FP 30. Where is Hypersleep practiced?

    a. SSMT   b. A-T Lab

    c. Your bunk   d. Fixed Base Sim

FP 31. Who was the first American in orbit?

    a. John Glenn

    b. Philip Crawford

    c. Neil Armstrong

    d. Michael Collins

FP 32. What happened on February 7, 1984?

    a. The first man walked on the moon.

    b. The first untethered space walk

    c. The first woman went into space.

    d. The first space shuttle flight

FP 33. Which plaque includes both people wearing helmets and people without them?

    a. First space shuttle flight

    b. First family in space

    c. First men on Mir

    d. First space rendezvous

FP 34. What year did the first family go into space?

    a. 6/1/3022   b. 12/1/2018

    c. 9/1/2030   d. 1/1/3011

FP 35. Did the first family in space include a space pet?

    a. Yes, a fluffy Persian cat

    b. Yes, a chimp, naturally

    c. Yes, a Dalmatian

    d. No, litter boxes are simply ineffective in zero gravity. Yuck!

FP 36. Was there a woman on the first deep-space mission?

    Yes / No

Test Track

FP 1. What is the name of the silver concept sports car?
    a. Sliver   b. Dream
    c. Quicksilver   d. Miray

FP 2. This car seems to be missing something important. What does not come standard?
    a. Steering wheel
    b. Doors
    c. Mirrors
    d. Headlights
    e. What are you talking about, that car's got everything!

3. What normal car feature is not to be found on the car designed to deal with extreme weather?
    a. Wheels
    b. Windshield
    c. Tail lights
    d. The Chevrolet symbol

4. What number of wheels is on the car that is best for handling turns?
    a. 0   b. 2
    c. 3   d. 4

5. Which car is best for the environment?
    a. Capability   b. Efficiency
    c. Power   d. Responsiveness

6. Which car has no visible doors?
    a. Responsiveness
    b. Efficiency
    c. Power
    d. Capability
    e. Hey wait a minute; none of those cars has doors I can see.

7. Which car features a cool neon green glow?
    a. Responsiveness   b. Efficiency
    c. Power   d. Capability

8. You are coming upon an ultra-cool two-wheel vehicle. What is it called?

    a. ME4000   b. zip-e

    c. en-v   d. NEON

9. How is this car steered?

    a. It is programed to drive itself. Now that's what I call convenient.

    b. It has a steering wheel.

    c. It has a moving steering panel/stick.

    d. You control it with your brainwaves, giving you ultimate responsiveness.

    e. Only a and c

    f. Whatever. But how many cup holders come standard?

10. The en-v video shows an interesting and space-saving new parking solution. What is it?

    a. Cars will stack like blocks.

    b. Cars will fold up on themselves, making them roughly the size of a shoebox.

    c. Cars will park inside giant rolling wheels.

    d. Car doors will be on the roof so that the vehicles may be parked right next to one another.

11. So how is the car going to drive itself exactly?

    a. An underground network of magnets allows for firm control.

    b. The en-vs are hooked up in a train-like fashion for all freeway driving.

    c. It will be controlled by a robotic driver dubbed "RX-24 or REX for short."

    d. It will be controlled by what appears to be an overhead grid. Oh no, I'm on the grid.

12. How is the en-v powered?

    a. It is electrical.

    b. It is a hybrid.

    c. It has its own solar panel.

    d. 200 hamster-wheel powered, need I say more?

13. According to the video, what special feature will buildings of the future have to best accommodate your en-v?

    a. Self-steering parking bays

    b. Exterior car elevators

c. Instant tune-up stations

d. Car-wash tunnels

14. You will see a large overhead sign for Chevrolet Design Studio. Look beneath it at the lit-up design images to gather a Special Collection. See how many Chevrolet symbols you can spot within these pictures. You get 1 point for each one you find. _____

Next you will find a white car that is constantly changing. There is a video with it. See if you can spot the answers to these questions in the video.

15. There are some children discussing their perfect car. A girl tells how her car would be powered. What is her perfect power source?

a. Solar

b. Garbage burning

c. Hydro electric

d. Double A batteries

16. Which of these features did the kids suggest for the perfect vehicle?

a. Self-driving so you can take a nap

b. Flying so you can skip the traffic

c. Hovering so that it can drive on water

d. Gravity adjusted so it can climb walls

17. At one point, the morphing car takes on the texture of a ball. What kind of ball is it?

a. Football   b. Tennis

c. Soccer   d. Basketball

18. Which of these coverings is never on the imagined car?

a. Stamps

b. Feathers

c. Wooden doors

d. Red, white, and blue with stars

19. A young man is asked what kind of instrument his car would be. Which is it?

a. Tuba   b. Contra

c. Guitar   d. Piano

e. Both a and b

20. A girl choses an animal to base her imagined car on. What animal is it?
    a. Alligator   b. Bunny
    c. Panda bear   d. Peacock

21. Another girl uses an imaginary animal as her inspiration. What pretend creature is it?
    a. A unicorn. You won't drive too slowly in front of a car with a sharp horn.
    b. A phoenix. A flying car – need I say more?
    c. A Pegasus. Flying and with a soft plush interior. Nice!
    d. A dragon. A dragon! I swear I drove a dragon!

You are about to walk down a short hall of touch screens. It is time to play with the shape and performance of imagined cars. Enjoy the screens. The questions will pick up at the end of the hall.

22. According to the video, what does the shape of your vehicle affect?
    a. Maneuverability and balance
    b. Power and capability
    c. Efficiency and responsiveness
    d. Cuteness and estimated cost
    e. Both a and c
    f. Both b and c

23. Touching the optimize button will improve your attributes?
    True or False?

24. Every person must have his own design station.
    True or False?

25. The red car has a lightning bolt on it.
    True or False?

26. There is a driver in the car that you will manipulate on the screen.
    True or False?

27. The symbol in the center of the efficiency circle on the screen is a leaf.
    True or False?

Once you exit the design studio, it is time to play "Spotted on the Highway."

FP 28. **Have a look at the traffic, er… I mean people, around you.** You are trying to find the things listed below that are associated with cars. Earn 1 point for each one found. And remember, even cars hate to be pointed at.

- ❑ Racing Stripes (a person wearing stripes)
- ❑ "Child On Board" sign (a child being carried by a parent)
- ❑ Lowrider (a person jumping up and down)
- ❑ Gas guzzler (a person who is drinking)
- ❑ Tinted windows (a person wearing sunglasses)
- ❑ Convertible (a person wearing a hoodie)
- ❑ Visor (a person with a sun visor)
- ❑ Gray sedan (two people who are dressed alike)
- ❑ Tail fin (a person with a ponytail)
- ❑ VW beetle (a person wearing neon)
- ❑ Forklift (a person eating)
- ❑ High clearance (a person taller than your dad)
- ❑ Ticket bait (a person talking on a cellphone)
- ❑ Junk in the trunk (a person wearing a pouch)
- ❑ Car wax (a person wearing sparkly clothes)
- ❑ New paint job (a person with painted toenails)
- ❑ Doing donuts (a person spinning)
- ❑ A jack (a person wearing heels)
- ❑ Seat cover (a person wearing fur)
- ❑ New tires (a person wearing boots)
- ❑ Peeling paint (a person wearing multiple shirts)
- ❑ Race flag (a person wearing black and white)
- ❑ Fuzzy dice (a person wearing spots)
- ❑ Air conditioning (a person fanning themselves)
- ❑ Bumper sticker (a person whose clothing features a brand name)

Future World East Answers

Spaceship Earth
1. *Extraterrestrial Hunt:*
   Total points for Martian hunters _____
   Total points for Venusian hunters _____
2. *Number of items collected* _____

Universe of Energy
Ellen's Energy Adventure
1) *Number of Guest Treasures found* _____
2) *Number of circles collected (1 point each)* _____
   Number of spheres collected (2 points each) _____

Mission: SPACE
1) *Yes*
2) *Yes*
3) *No*
4) *No*
5) *Yes*
6) *No*
7) *No*
8) *No*
9) *Yes*
10) *No*
11) *d. A poet*
12) *c. "To venture a little way past them into the impossible"*
13) *a. Exploration*
14) *b. A U.S. astronaut*
15) *b. Team Green*
16) *a. Flight crew only*
17) *b. 75 years*
18) *Total Treasures found* _____
19) *c. Check in*
20) *b. Solid hydrogen does the trick.*
21) *d. Anti-Asteroid Super Alloy Siding*
22) *c. Over a million pounds*
23) *a. It is on a large door.*
24) *No*
25) *d. They are metal.*

26) a. 8.7 mph
27) b. Battery
28) c. International Space Training Center
29) b. They are practicing landing.
30) d. Fixed Base Sim
31) a. John Glenn
32) b. The first untethered space walk
33) d. First space rendezvous
34) c. 9/1/2030
35) c. Yes, a Dalmatian
36) Yes

Test Track

1) d. Miray
2) c. Mirrors
3) b. Windshield
4) c. 3
5) b. Efficiency
6) e. None of those cars has doors.
7) b. Efficiency
8) c. en-v
9) e. Only a and c
10) c. Cars will park inside giant rolling wheels.
11) d. It will be controlled by what appears to be an overhead grid.
12) a. It is electrical.
13) b. Exterior car elevators
14) Number of Chevrolet symbols found _____
15) d. Double A batteries
16) a. Self-driving
17) c. Soccer
18) b. Feathers
19) e. Both a and b
20) a. Alligator
21) d. A dragon
22) f. Both b and c
23) True
24) False
25) False
26) True
27) True
28) Number of people spotted on the highway _____

Future World West

The Seas with Nemo & Friends

The Seas with Nemo & Friends attraction

1. As you walked in someone was sounding just a bit greedy. Who was it?
    a. A little girl holding Nemo in a bag
    b. A small flock of self-centered seagulls
    c. Bruce the shark
    d. Some kid who wants his parents to buy an ice
       cream cone for him

? POP QUIZ! If the line stretches outside the building, take a minute to look at the fish mural on the wall. Then turn your back on it. No peeking. See what you can remember about the picture before you head inside.

2. Were there any striped fish?
    Yes / No

3. Were there any sparkly fish?
    Yes / No

4. Were any fish showing their teeth?
    Yes / No

5. Were gills visible on any fish?
    Yes / No

6. **Were there any creatures in the picture that were not fish? What were they?**
   a. Coral and snake
   b. Turtle and diver
   c. Octopus and turtle
   d. They were in the water, right? Fish all of them.

7. **There were a lot of fish moving in schools. Did any of the schools include fish of different colors?**
   Yes / No

8. **Was a blowfish swimming around in this picture?**
   Yes / No

9. **There was a sea turtle out for a swim in this group. He was a parent. How many children did he have to look after?**
   a. 1
   b. 2
   c. 3
   d. I don't know where you get this parent stuff; he was on his own.

10. **Which of these creatures was not in the picture?**
   a. Seahorse
   b. Ray
   c. Octopus
   d. Shark
   e. It's a big ocean. They were all there.

11. **What color was the largest school of fish that were all the same color?**
   a. Blue   b. Pink
   c. Green   d. Yellow

12. **Speaking of color, what color was the seahorse?**
   a. Yellow   b. Blue
   c. Pink   d. Green

End of Pop Quiz

13. **When you walk inside you will find yourself at a beach. What is the name of this place?**
   a. Sydney Tide Pools
   b. Mickey's Cove
   c. Wallaby Way Cove
   d. Coral Caves

14. There are creatures you are not supposed to feed. Who are they?
    a. Fish
    b. Koalas, mate; they're everywhere.
    c. Seagulls
    d. Yourself, there is no eating on this beach.

15. What are the hours of operation for this beach?
    a. 5 a.m. to 11 p.m.
    b. 8 a.m. to dusk
    c. 9 a.m. to 7 p.m.
    d. It's a beach; there are no hours of operation, silly.

16. What things are beachgoers advised of?
    a. Jellyfish
    b. Sharks
    c. Strong currents
    d. All of the above

17. Tanks A Lot Dive Shop has a fish mascot. What is their fish wearing?
    a. A life preserver and a scuba tank
    b. A fishing hat – and he has a pole
    c. A life jacket and a snorkel
    d. A sun hat and sunglasses

18. What animal are we told nests here at Coral Cove?
    a. Pelicans
    b. Seagulls
    c. Turtles
    d. None of the above

19. What animals can be seen on signs posted at this beach?
    a. Hammerhead sharks
    b. Pelicans
    c. Seagulls
    d. People. Yes, we count as animals too.
    e. All of the above

20. What are the surf conditions today?
    a. Mild
    b. Just swell
    c. Choppy
    d. Well, there is surf, mate

21. Who has no reef funds?
 a. Darla's Beach Rentals
 b. Tanks A Lot Dive Shop
 c. Marlin's Fishing Supply and Bait Shop
 d. Coral Cove is completely funded by your
    donations, and we are not giving them back.

22. What creature has a name that reminds you of a meal?
 a. The omelet flounder
 b. The flapjack octopus
 c. The fried egg fish
 d. Oh, I am so hungry. I think I want seafood now.

23. Treasure Hunt Time! See how many of these fishy treasures you can spot before it is time to sail away.
 ❏ The letter "e" partially formed using a fish body
 ❏ 5A
 ❏ A rope frame
 ❏ Two things you are asked not to do at this beach
 ❏ Coral
 ❏ "Fish are friends"
 ❏ Two sea stars
 ❏ A butterfly that belongs on the water
 ❏ Two boards for saving your life
 ❏ A sun
 ❏ A small ladder

24. It is now time for you to dive in. As you swim around under the pier you will see something formed from rusty metal. What is it?
 a. A shark   b. An octopus
 c. A turtle   d. A fish

25. "Fishy Artists" Game
 There is a school of really good performing moonfish swimming by to entertain you while you wait. Watch them move around. When they decide to form a picture they will form it in pieces, a little bit at a time. See if you can guess what these fishy artists are creating before the picture is fully formed. "Wat'er" you waiting for? Give it a try. You get 1 point for each correct guess you make.

26. Underwater Treasure Hunt. Before you set off to find Nemo – that boy is always going missing – see how many of these soggy items you can dredge up.

❑ Sea life that is just hanging around
❑ Several large rusty "X"s
❑ An anchor
❑ A propeller
❑ A fish swimming near the surface
❑ Seaweed

Add 1 bonus point if you hear someone say, "Just keep swimming," as you wait _____

Turtle Talk With Crush

While you wait for your chat with a sea turtle, take a look around. Lots of Crush's friends are trying to get your attention. If you run out of creatures to check out, see if you can answer some of these very wet questions.

1. What creature in this aquarium has a history of space travel?
    a. A ray, she might be related to Mr. Ray, the teacher; he looks pretty smug about it.
    b. It was a little Blue Tang; sadly she doesn't remember a thing.
    c. The moon jelly, of course; traveled aboard the Space Shuttle Columbia.
    d. Fish in space, come on!

2. Jellyfish are 94% to 98% a clear jelly-like substance. That is how they get their name.
    True or False?

3. A jellyfish can still sting even after it is dead.
    True or False?

4. Plastic bags are often mistaken for prey by sea creatures hungry for a delicious snack of jellyfish.
    True or False?

5. A balloonfish fills itself with air to inflate whenever it feels threatened.
    True or False?

6. Royal Grammas do which of the following things

when they must retreat?
- a. Squirt ink
- b. Hang upside-down in caves
- c. Blow bubbles to obscure their path
- d. Shrink to one-tenth their normal size
- e. Royal Grammas are royal; they have someone to do that stuff for them.

7. Why are green sea turtles so named?
- a. They eat so much algae and sea grass that their body fat turns green. I knew there was a reason I avoid broccoli.
- b. They are from the East Indian Green Sea.
- c. They are most prevalent wherever the water has a greenish hue.
- d. They were named by Dr. Joseph Green. In fact, their color is closer to brown than green.

8. Somewhere in this aquarium, there is a creature with no brain, bones or heart. What creature here could fill in for the Scarecrow and the Tin Man any day?
- a. The shark; wish he were toothless.
- b. The sea turtle
- c. The shrimp
- d. The jellyfish; he is all squishy.

9. What makes turtles cry?
- a. Turtles are very emotional creatures; they cry when they are sad.
- b. They are shedding excess salt from their eyes.
- c. Turtles cry when they are hungry; much like some people I know.
- d. I don't know why they cry; it never seemed polite to ask them.

10. Treasure Hunt Time! See how many of these ocean treasures you can net before you start talking to turtles.
- ❏ Someone with a really gross diet
- ❏ A live Blue Tang (a blue fish with a yellow tail)
- ❏ Brain coral
- ❏ A solid yellow fish
- ❏ A fish with black-and-white stripes and a yellow tail
- ❏ Starfish; 1 point for each one you find _____
- ❏ Something hiding in the sand
- ❏ Something you should look at but never touch

❑ A hammerhead
❑ A ray
❑ A turtle in a bubble
❑ An orange fish with a black mask
❑ Another ray
❑ A creature with spots

The Land

Circle of Life

? **POP QUIZ!** Before you enter the waiting area for this show, have a quick look at the four pieces of art featuring *Lion King* characters posted on the wall just outside. Also look at the sign over the entrance area. After you check them all out, join the queue and test your memory with this quiz. Good luck.

1. On the entrance sign, what was Simba the lion standing on?
   a. He was on top of the world.
   b. He was on a rocky ledge.
   c. He was on the back of a warthog.
   d. He stands where he pleases; he is a lion.

2. According to that sign, what are you about to see?
   a. An environmental tale
   b. An environmental celebration
   c. An environmental musical
   d. An environmental fable

3. Simba was enjoying a great view of Earth. What landmasses were partially visible?
   a. North, South, and Central America
   b. Africa, Europe, and part of South America
   c. Asia and Oceana
   d. I don't know, it was spinning a bit fast.

4. There were three animals visible in the sign. Which ones were smiling?
   a. Simba the lion, Pumbaa the warthog, but not Timon the meerkat

    b. Pumbaa the warthog and Timon the meerkat
       had big cheeky grins, but not Simba the lion.
    c. All three had welcoming smiles.
    d. All three looked sad.

5. In the series of four signs leading up to the entry door, someone was very busy. Who was hard at work?
    a. Simba was hard at work.
    b. Pumbaa and Timon were being industrious.
    c. All three were working hard.
    d. All three were hardly working.
    e. Four signs, you say?

6. What were the worker or workers so busy doing?
    a. They were making signs to direct us to the Circle
       of Life.
    b. They were building a fort that said "No Girls
       Allowed!" How rude!
    c. They were making drinks for visitors with
       umbrellas and fancy straws and everything.
    d. They were building a stage for their upcoming
       starring roles in the Circle of Life.

7. In the art farthest from the door, Timon was putting a great deal of effort into something. What was he up to?
    a. He was finding the best place for a window.
    b. He was squeezing a lemon into a glass; hard
       work for a little guy.
    c. He was hammering a sign into the ground.
    d. He was industriously sewing curtains for the
       theater.

8. Was Timon using a mallet?
    Yes / No

9. Was Pumbaa holding nails with his tail?
    Yes / No

10. Pumbaa was grinning. In his mouth he had one white tooth showing.
    True or False?

11. Pumbaa had two enormous tusks.
    True or False?

12. The four signs leading to the entrance told you environmental facts.
    True or False?

13. In one of the signs, Timon was holding something in his hands and looking very pleased. What was he holding?
    a. A star
    b. A saw
    c. A paintbrush
    d. A crayon
    e. Both a and b

14. What had Timon done to be so pleased with himself?
    a. He had put his name down as the star of the show.
    b. He had cut the sign down to the proper size.
    c. He had decorated a star to put on the sign.
    d. Oh, meerkats are like that, always so darn happy.

15. In one of the Circle of Life pictures Pumbaa held something in his mouth. What was it?
    a. Food, naturally
    b. A paintbrush
    c. Timon
    d. A hammer

16. Pumbaa had done something naughty. What did he do exactly?
    a. He stuffed a great big pile of food into his mouth leaving none for Timon.
    b. He painted over Timon's name on the sign and replaced it with his own.
    c. He was pretending to have Timon for a snack.
    d. I don't know, but that pig is always up to no good.

17. Pumbaa was getting something on the ground, what was it?
    a. Food crumbs
    b. Drool
    c. Fur; he needs a good brush
    d. Paint drippings on the grass

End of Pop Quiz

Living with the Land

If some of the players in your group are not old enough to read the quotations on the wall of this queue, it may be more fun to tackle this one in teams. This would also be a great place to work on Collections.

1. What author said, "The secret powers of nature are generally discovered unsolicited"?
  a. William Shakespeare
  b. J. K. Rowling
  c. Hans Christian Anderson
  d. Steve Barrett said it right after he spotted a melon that looked like Mickey.

2. What can one person do?
  a. Save the Earth.
  b. Change the mind of another person, well except my father, no point trying to change that.
  c. Reduce, reuse, recycle.
  d. Be the one person who makes a difference.

3. What former president has a remark on this wall?
  a. Bill Clinton   b. George H.W. Bush
  c. Jimmy Carter   d. George Washington

4. What have we changed the environment quicker than?
  a. Than the Earth can compensate
  b. Than we have changed ourselves
  c. Than nature can keep up
  d. Than the speed of the cars on Test Track

5. According to Francis Bacon, "who is not governed except by obeying her"?
  a. Nature   b. The Earth
  c. The universe   d. Life

6. Why is this planet called Mother Earth according to a very insightful 10-year-old?
  a. Because all life grows right here from her
  b. Because she loves us even if we hurt her
  c. Because you get punished if you make a mess
  d. All three reasons are true.

7. What does a 6th grade girl compare the environment to?

a. A patchwork quilt
b. A game of chess
c. A river
d. A child

8. Rousseau says "nature never" does something. What does nature never do?

a. Hurt us
b. Deceive us
c. Give up on us
d. Take a day off; rough schedule

9. According to a 15-year-old from New Jersey, what would be required for a masterpiece?

a. For society and the environment to work together
b. For the residents of planet Earth to open their eyes, because the masterpiece is all around them
c. For people to love Mother Earth as much as she loves them
d. Some paints and a brush or two should do it.

10. What have we borrowed from our children?

a. Their video games, and it's time to give them back
b. The future
c. The environment
d. The world

11. In nature, there are neither _____ nor _____.

a. Gifts nor payments
b. Debts nor debtors
c. Rewards nor punishments
d. Blues nor chartreuses

12. What is the age of the youngest person to be quoted on these walls?

a. 5   b. 8
c. 10   d. 11

13.What will we not get another of?

a. Life
b. A moment, like this one, to make a difference

c. The Earth

d. A giant lollypop; one is more than enough

14. Living with the Land opened in 1993. How many members of your group are older than this ride?

_____

Soarin'

? POP QUIZ! STOP! Before you enter this queue, take a look at the hot air balloons soarin' outside the ride in The Land pavilion. After you've had a good look, head inside and play a memory game to see if your head is filled with memories or just hot air.

FP **1. How many hot air balloons were there in all?**
    a. Four, that's easy.
    b. No, there weren't. I saw five!
    c. There weren't any balloons; I think they flew away.

FP **2. Each of the balloons represented something. What did they stand for?**
    a. The weather
    b. The seasons
    c. Things that fly
    d. Balloons don't "stand" for anything exactly, they fly.

FP **3. There were several animals in this balloon display. What were they?**
    a. Butterflies and white owls
    b. White owls and seagulls
    c. Seagulls and butterflies
    d. Seagulls, and white owls, and butterflies, oh my!

FP **4. There was a bit of weather happening under the balloons. Yes under. What was the under-balloon forecast?**
    a. Rain   b. Snow
    c. Ice   d. All of the above
    e. None of the above

FP 5. The balloons each represented a season. What was the picture on the balloon for the fall?

    a. A leaf

    b. A tree losing its leaves

    c. Wind

    d. Both a and c

    e. Both b and c

FP 6. What picture was painted on the winter balloon?

    a. A snowstorm   b. A snowflake

    c. A snowman   d. A snow pea

FP 7. Think about the summer balloon. What represented summer?

    a. The sun

    b. Seagulls

    c. A beach ball

    d. All three of the above

    e. Only a and b

FP 8. OK, so seagulls were involved in summer, but were they painted on the balloon or just flocking under it?

    a. They were painted on it.

    b. They were flocking as if someone had dropped a French fry.

    c. They were both painted on and flocking under.

    d. They were perched on the rim going for a ride.

FP 9. The spring balloon was adorned with something pretty. What was it?

    a. A daffodil and butterflies

    b. A daisy and baby birds

    c. A rose and butterflies

    d. A bouquet of wildflowers

FP 10. What is happening under the springtime balloon?

    a. The rain is falling.

    b. Flowers are falling. I guess no one caught the bouquet.

    c. Butterflies are flying.

    d. Both b and c

    e. Both a and c

FP 11. All right, there were butterflies, but what color were they?

    a. Yellow with red design

b. Blue with pink design

c. Red with orange design

d. They were all different colors.

FP 12. The balloons each had a basket. On each basket rim, there was a design. Which one of the following was not on the rim of a basket?

a. Wave   b. Leaf

c. Butterfly   d. Ice

e. They were all there.

FP 13. There was something else hanging up with the balloons. What was it?

a. A giant mirrored ball; makes me want to boogie

b. A hang glider

c. Clouds

d. A globe of the Earth

FP 14. There was also something made of bright fabric ribbons that covered part of the ceiling. What was it? And what color were the ribbons?

a. The ribbons were red and white and formed a tent.

b. The ribbons were yellow and formed a sun.

c. The ribbons were blue and white and implied swirling wind.

d. The ribbons were red, orange, yellow, green, blue, indigo, and violet; they created a rainbow.

FP 15. What was visible on the globe?

a. Land

b. Water

c. Ice

d. All of the above

e. All you could really see were swirling clouds and some water.

16. If the things directly under the balloons were real and were affected by gravity, what would be the worst thing that could happen to you if you walked directly beneath them?

a. I could be wet.

b. I could be cold.

c. I could have dried leaves all over me.

d. I could have bird poop in my hair; eww!!!

End of Pop Quiz

FP **17. As you walked into this area, you saw a large flat globe overhead. What color was it?**

    a. Blue   b. Green

    c. Orange   d. Clear

FP **18. What continent was directly in the center of the globe?**

    a. Africa   b. Asia

    c. Europe   d. North America

Game Room

    You will find really cool interactive video games in this room. Enjoy playing. Then answer these questions when you leave the room and enter the hallway area.

FP **Bird Game (Questions 19 to 25)**

19. Which of these obstacles was not a bird bother?

    a. Water spouts   b. Bigger birds

    c. Falling trees   d. Boulders

20. Your bird flew past many landmarks on the race. Check off each thing the bird passed. You receive 1 point for each correct landmark.

    a. A river   b. A bridge

    c. A log cabin   d. A moose

    e. Mickey Mouse   f. A waterfall

    g. A cave   h. Cactus

    i. A stone arch

21. How were the birds controlled?

    a. You flapped your arms to gain height and lowered them to descend.

    b. You jumped to go up and crouched to go down.

    c. You leaned to the side to steer.

    d. You really can't control a bird, you know; it's a wild creature.

22. There was water below you. Were any boats on it?

    Yes / No

23. Was there ice on the water?

    a. Yes

    b. No

    c. Only for some birds, not for others

24. Which of these things was not visible at the top of the screen?
   a. A total of the number of objects hit
   b. A map showing your position and the position of other birds
   c. A timer
   d. Your current ranking
   e. They were all visible.

25. What did the bird perch on at the end of the race?
   a. A giant number
   b. A branch
   c. A rainbow
   d. Nothing, it just circled in the air. That bird loves to fly.

FP **Ball Game (Questions 26 to 35)**

26. Which of the following items could you play with in the tossing game?
   a. A soap bubble
   b. A beach ball
   c. A snowball
   d. An acorn
   e. You could play with them all.
   f. All but a

27. On one of the screens, there was something made of snow. What was it?
   a. A snow fort
   b. A regular old snowman
   c. Mickey
   d. A snow castle
   e. None of the above
   f. All of the above except d

28. In the beach scene, there was something made of sand. What was it?
   a. A sand dune
   b. A sand sculpture of Mickey
   c. A sand pile next to a bucket
   d. A sand castle

29. At the end of the game when the balls broke, what did the twig balls become?
   a. Birds
   b. Lizards
   c. Beavers
   d. Owls

30. When the beach balls popped, what animal appeared?
    a. A seagull
    b. A fish
    c. A crab
    d. A seahorse
    e. I think you are confused about what happens
       when a beach ball pops.

31. When the snowballs burst, what animal appeared?
    a. A rabbit   b. A fox
    c. A squirrel   d. A bird

32. What happened when the soap bubbles popped?
    a. A loud pop and then soap dripping all over the
       screen.
    b. Lots more bubbles appeared.
    c. Actual bubbles appeared in the room.
    d. What soap bubbles?

33. Was a cactus visible on any of the screens?
    Yes / No

34. Was Mickey Mouse visible on any of the screens?
    Yes / No

35. What could travel from one screen to the next?
    a. Snowballs   b. Beach balls
    c. Acorns   d. All of the above

FP Balloon Game (Questions 36 to 43)

36. What was the thief stealing from the castle?
    a. Gems
    b. Gold coins
    c. Pearls
    d. Who cares, he's a thief. Let's get him!

37. What was the thief using to collect his booty?
    a. A massive hand
    b. A magnet
    c. The world's biggest vacuum hose
    d. Trained birds

38. When your balloon traveled into the underworld, what dangers did you face?

    a. Blasting fire

    b. A giant worm

    c. Giant spiders bent on your destruction

    d. A river of hot lava. Don't want to swim there, just saying.

    e. All of the above except b

39. Was there any wind?

    a. Only when players waved their arms to create it.

    b. Well, the flags were waving, so I am going to go with yes.

    c. A tornado was sucking treasure away.

    d. No wind today.

40. What was mounted on the front of the villain's balloon boat?

    a. A huge bird skull

    b. A mermaid

    c. A pirate flag

    d. An extendable hand

41. Where exactly did the castle store its gems.

    a. In a treasure chest at the top of the tower

    b. In the royal balloon boat

    c. On the sides of the tower – and that is just asking for it if you ask me.

    d. In the sky. Those gems had floating qualities.

42. Who or what was heaving rocks in the underworld?

    a. A troll, and he should be stopped.

    b. Flying monsters

    c. Spiders

    d. Lava

43. What happens when you return the gems to the castle?

    a. You are rewarded with a chest full of gold.

    b. A rainbow appears.

    c. You are named the kingdom's greatest hero.

    d. Fireworks fill the air.

FP **Paint-throwing Game (Questions 44 to 45)**

44. There were many colored blobs on the screen. What happens if you pop them?
    a. Paint drips down the screen creating a rainbow.
    b. A picture starts to appear.
    c. You can use the splat to finger-paint a picture.
    d. They double.

45. Which color paint blob was missing?
    a. Green   b. Red
    c. Blue   d. Yellow
    e. None; they were
       all there.

Imagination!

Journey Into Imagination With Figment

1. Something special is going on at the Imagination Institute. What is happening?
    a. They are moving to a new location.
    b. They are having a 50th anniversary party.
    c. They are hosting an open house.
    d. It's different for everyone because it takes place in your imagination.

2. What is the symbol on Imagination Institute signs?
    a. A brain with wings
    b. A car with wings
    c. A dragon with no wings
    d. A light bulb with wings
    e. None of the above

3. There is a purple dragon who is up to something with paint. What is he doing?
    a. Adding his name to the ride's sign
    b. Painting a window on the Imagination Institute
    c. Painting himself with yellow spots
    d. I don't know, but a dragon with paint can't be good.

4. What is true of Cam-o-Rama 360?
    a. It earned for its creator the 89th annual Inventor of the Year award.
    b. It has lots of wires that make it globe-like.
    c. It has lights and camera all in one.
    d. All of these things are true.
    e. Hey, didn't Darth Vader use that thing to interrogate Princess Lea?

5. What is a Weebo?
    a. A kind of mischievous purple dragon best kept in the imagination
    b. A flying lab assistant
    c. Something that wobbles but doesn't fall down
    d. A recording device for your television

6. Treasure Hunt Time! It is time for a quick treasure hunt. Let's see how many of these items you can find, and how many may be a figment of my imagination.
    ❑ Human hair, not on a fellow guest
    ❑ A light-bulb lamp
    ❑ A notebook
    ❑ A blue tulip-shape
    ❑ A yellow square
    ❑ A vase with fake flowers
    ❑ A red-striped tie
    ❑ Wheels
    ❑ A purple phone
    ❑ A small screen
    ❑ The letter "C"
    ❑ Red and green lights
    ❑ Two horns

7. What is unusual about the Image Works Lab?
    a. It brings two-dimensional pictures to life.
    b. It takes things that are invisible and makes them visible – but only in purple.
    c. It deals in "what if's."
    d. No one works there.

8. What did Dr. Wayne Szalinski create that won him Inventor of the Year?
    a. Flubber
    b. Figment
    c. The Shrinking Gun
    d. The Porthole of Imagination

9. What invention made by an "Inventor of the Year" recipient seems to be getting on the floor?

    a. Figment

    b. Flubber

    c. The Shrinking Gun

    d. The Magnetic Mop Super Cleaner (as seen on TV)

10. Scientists are, well how shall we say it, "known" for keeping things in their pockets. Which of these items is not in the pocket of an "Inventor of the Year"?

    a. A mechanical pencil

    b. A ruler

    c. A thermometer

    d. A pocket protector

    e. They are all there.

11. There is a little something odd about Professor Phillip Brainard. OK, there is a lot that's odd. What did he get wrong?

    a. One of the gloves he is wearing is inside out.

    b. His glasses are broken.

    c. There is a rip in his pocket.

    d. His ensemble is sooooo last season's "geek." He should keep up with the times.

12. If I were looking to hang out in a really hot-pink room, and I am definitely not, but if I were, where would I look?

    a. The Flubber storage room

    b. The sensory labs

    c. In Figment's bedroom; dragons just love hot pink.

    d. Dimensions Hall

13. Why would I find it tricky to get into the pink room?

    a. Opening the door is inadvisable. It is filled to the brim with Flubber.

    b. The sensory lab rooms can be a bit hard on the senses.

    c. The hall leading to it is, well, smallish. Does anyone have an "eat me" cookie?

    d. Figment's room is safely tucked in his imagination and not easily accessed.

14. Figment is treating something like a trampoline. That naughty dragon! What is he bouncing off of?
    a. A light bulb   b. The walls
    c. Flubber   d. Everything

15. Treasure Hunt Time! You have arrived at a storage cage. See if you can find these scientific gadgets before the open house closes.
- ❑ A megaphone
- ❑ Four test tubes filled with liquid
- ❑ Cymbals
- ❑ 98
- ❑ A suitcase
- ❑ Four ecto globes
- ❑ A plastic fan
- ❑ Two apples
- ❑ A bird's abode
- ❑ A tiny face
- ❑ Three thermometers
- ❑ 100
- ❑ A color wheel
- ❑ Two mannequins
- ❑ A blue case

16. What got into the coffee and is now bouncing off the walls?
    a. Professor Brainard
    b. Figment the dragon
    c. Flubber
    d. My imagination

17. Which of these is Dr. Channing's title?
    a. Principal Scientist
    b. Head of Laboratories
    c. Chairman
    d. Manager of Everything Else
    e All of the above
    f. All but c

18. Which of the following is not the symbol of a lab you are about to visit?
    a. A pair of eyes   b. A nose
    c. An ear   d. A mouth
    e. They all are.   f. All but a, it is not a
                         complete set.

19. What is today's theme?
- a. How to capture the Flubber before it takes over the world
- b. How to capture your imagination
- c. How to capture your senses
- d. How to capture Figment; we don't want that dragon flying around loose.

Future World West Answers

The Seas with Nemo & Friends
The Seas with Nemo & Friends attraction

1) b. A small flock of self-centered seagulls
2) Yes
3) No
4) Yes
5) Yes
6) c. Octopus and turtle
7) Yes
8) No
9) a. 1
10) e. They were all there.
11) b. Pink
12) a. Yellow
13) d. Coral Caves
14) c. Seagulls
15) a. 5 a.m. to 11 p.m.
16) d. All of the above
17) c. A life jacket and a snorkel
18) c. Turtles
19) e. All of the above
20) b. Just swell
21) a. Darla's Beach Rentals
22) b. The flapjack octopus
23) Total Fishy Treasures found _____
24) d. A fish
25) Total Fishy Pictures identified _____
26) Total Underwater Treasures found _____
    Add 1 bonus point if you heard someone say, "Just keep swimming."

Turtle TalkWith Crush

1) c. The moon jelly
2) False
3) True
4) True
5) False
6) b. Hang upside-down in caves
7) a. They eat so much algae and sea grass that their body fat turns green.
8) d. The jellyfish
9) b. They are shedding excess salt from their eyes.
10) Total Ocean Treasures found _____

The Land
Circle of Life

1) b. He was on rocky ledge.
2) d. An environmental fable
3) a. North, South, and Central America
4) c. All three had welcoming smiles.
5) b. Pumbaa and Timon were being industrious.
6) a. They were making signs to direct us.
7) c. He was hammering a sign into the ground.
8) Yes
9) No
10) True
11) True
12) False
13) c. A paintbrush
14) a. He had put his name down as the star of the show.
15) b. A paintbrush
16) b. He painted over Timon's name on the sign and replaced it with his own.
17) d. Paint drippings on the grass

Living with the Land

1) c. Hans Christian Anderson
2) d. Be the one person who makes a difference.
3) b. George H.W. Bush
4) b. Than we have changed ourselves
5) a. Nature
6) c. Because you get punished if you make a mess
7) a. A patchwork quilt
8) b. Deceive us

9) a. For society and the environment to work
together

10) d. The world

11) c. Rewards nor punishments

12) a. 5

13) c. The Earth

14) Total number of members of your group who are
older than this ride _____

Soarin'

1) a. Four

2) b. The seasons

3) c. Seagulls and butterflies

4) d. All of the above

5) d. Both a and c

6) b. A snowflake

7) e. Only a and b

8) c. They were both painted on and flocking under.

9) a. A daffodil and butterflies

10) e. Both a and c

11) a. Yellow with red design

12) c. Butterfly

13) d. A globe of the Earth

14) b. The ribbons were yellow and formed a sun.

15) d. All of the above

16) a, b, c, and d are all correct; it is a matter of
perspective.

17) c. Orange

18) a. Africa

Bird Game

19) b. Bigger birds

20) a. River, b. Bridge, e. Mickey Mouse, f. Waterfall,
h. Cactus, i. Stone arch

21) c. You leaned to the side to steer.

22) No

23) c. Only for some birds, not for others.

24) a. A total of the number of objects hit

25) a. A giant number

Ball Game

26) f. All but a

27) c. Mickey

28) d. A sand castle

29) b. Lizards

30) c. A crab

31) *d. A bird*

32) *d. What soap bubbles?*

33) *Yes*

34) *Yes*

35) *d. All of the above*

Balloon Game

36) *a. Gems*

37) *c. The world's biggest vacuum hose*

38) *e. All of the above except b*

39) *b. Well, the flags were waving, so yes.*

40) *a. A huge bird skull*

41) *c. On the sides of the tower*

42) *a. A troll*

43) *d. Fireworks fill the air.*

Paint-throwing Game

44) *b. A picture starts to appear.*

45) *e. None; they were all there.*

Imagination!

Journey Into Imagination with Figment

1) *c. They are hosting an open house.*

2) *d. A light bulb with wings*

3) *a. Adding his name to the ride's sign*

4) *d. All of these things are true.*

5) *b. A flying lab assistant*

6) *Total Treasures found _____*

7) *c. It deals in "what if's."*

8) *c. The Shrinking Gun*

9) *b. Flubber*

10) *d. A pocket protector*

11) *a. One of the gloves he is wearing is inside out.*

12) *d. Dimensions Hall*

13) *c. The hall leading to it is smallish.*

14) *a. A light bulb*

15) *Total Scientific Treasures found _____*

16) *c. Flubber*

17) *e. All of the above*

18) *f. All but a*

19) *b. How to capture your imagination*

World Showcase

Mexico:
Gran Fiesta Tour Starring
the Three Caballeros

? **POP QUIZ!** As you enter this line, you'll pass under a painted sign telling you the name of the attraction. Have a good look at it.

1. What was hanging over the sign?
    a. Three sombreros
    b. Two guitars and one set of maracas
    c. A large, festive lantern
    d. A large bell

2. Who are the Three Caballeros?
    a. Donald Duck, Mickey Mouse, and Goofy
    b. Donald Duck and two of his bird amigos
    c. Donald Duck and two men playing guitars
    d. I don't know, but I am getting the feeling Donald Duck is involved somehow. Call it a hunch.

3. What instruments were the Three Caballeros playing?
    a. Two guitars and one set of maracas
    b. One guitar, one set of maracas, and one trumpet
    c. Three guitars
    d. No instruments; they were just waving.

End of Pop Quiz

4. Treasure Hunt Time! See how many of these Mexico pavilion treasures you can unearth before you float on down the river.
    ❑ A window shaped like a half circle
    ❑ A wrought-iron curlicue, up high

- ❏ Flowers
- ❏ Smoke
- ❏ A wrought-iron heart shape
- ❏ A potted tree
- ❏ A frown set in stone
- ❏ A circle in shiny gold
- ❏ A glowing red door
- ❏ Something that looks like it might blow its top

You will come to a poster for the Gran Fiesta Tour. Take a good look at it and then turn away. It is time to play Three Caballeros Memory.

5. All three Caballeros were wearing black bow ties.
- a. Yes
- b. No, two were wearing black bow ties and one was wearing none at all.
- c. No, the Three Caballeros were far more colorful than that. The ties were pink, green, and blue.
- d. These guys don't like bow ties; they did have snappy bolo ties though.

6. All three were wearing sombreros.
Yes / No

7. What were they standing on, besides their feet?
- a. A colorful blanket
- b. The desert
- c. A stage
- d. A balcony

8. How many fingers were they holding up?
- a. The first was holding up one finger, the second two fingers, and the third held up three.
- b. Their hands were busy playing instruments.
- c. Three each
- d. Birds don't have fingers. Now if you are talking feathers… I still don't remember.

9. One Caballero had a lasso tied to his belt.
Yes / No

10. One Caballero was wearing spurs.
Yes / No

11. There were musical notes in the background.
Yes / No

12. One of the guitars was pink.
Yes / No

13. What did only one of the three Caballeros have?
a. Pants
b. A jacket
c. A belt
d. All of the above; he was a lucky ducky
e. None of the above

14. Donald Duck was dressed in his normal blue sailor suit.
Yes / No

15. Treasure Hunt Time! If you are still waiting to sail off to Mexico, see how many of these treasures you can find before you climb aboard.
❑ A pink cactus
❑ A purple sun
❑ An orange pineapple
❑ Two yellow birds
❑ A smiling face
❑ Three yellow stars
❑ A white guitar
❑ Two blue feathers
❑ When the next concert will be

Norway: Maelstrom

FP **POP QUIZ!** It's time to test your powers of observation. Let's see what you noticed on your way into this line.

1. According to the sign as you entered, what is Maelstrom?
a. A Perilous Viking Voyage
b. The Ultimate Storm
c. A High Seas Norwegian Adventure
d. A grainy porridge best served with honey

2. The Maelstrom sign featured which of these things?
a. A Viking hat
b. A boat in a storm
c. A red flag with a cross
d. Two men in battle

3. OK, so there was a boat, but what did you notice about it? Put a check mark next to each of the following things that were in it.

> a. There were two sails.
>
> b. There was a man.
>
> c. The mast was cracked and hanging.
>
> d. There was lightning.
>
> e. There were red stripes on a flag.
>
> f. The Norwegian flag was ripped and hanging over the side.
>
> g. A man was overboard.
>
> h. There was a large wave.
>
> i. There was a man in the crow's nest.
>
> j. There were round shields on the side.
>
> k. There were gulls in the sky.

4. There was something above the main entry sign on the building. What was it?

> a. A window with lace curtains and a vase with flowers in it
>
> b. An arch with a large bell hanging in it
>
> c. A clock
>
> d. I'm going to play the odds here and say a Norwegian flag.

End of Pop Quiz

FP 5. Somewhere nearby, there are directions to the North and South Poles. Who is guiding your way to the poles?

> a. A Viking
>
> b. A troll
>
> c. A sailor with a map
>
> d. Hey, did I say I wanted to go to the Poles?

FP 6. What article of clothing did our guide forget to put on today?

> a. His shirt
>
> b. His pants
>
> c. His shoes
>
> d. Both a and c, but thankfully he remembered his pants.
>
> e. You know, I think that he could be a she... maybe... nah.

FP 7. **What is the Puffin's Roost?**
　　a. The name of a boat
　　b. The name of a lighthouse
　　c. A gift shop
　　d. That would be where a puffin goes to, well, catch
　　　a few winks

FP 8. **According to the sign, what kind of heritage does
Norway enjoy?**
　　a. A rich seafaring heritage
　　b. A vast heritage of discovery
　　c. A long heritage of life in harmony with nature
　　d. A proud heritage of people not afraid to make a
　　　statement with their hats

FP 9. **Treasure Hunt Time!** Once you arrive in the large
room with the murals, see how many of these treasures
you can find in the murals before you wash away.

Ocean mural
　　❑ A lighthouse
　　❑ A hard hat
　　❑ A boat in the ice
　　❑ Two canoes
　　❑ A clipboard
　　❑ An old hollow tree
　　❑ Lightning
　　❑ A man with a rope
　　❑ Two polar bears
　　❑ N-85
　　❑ A bracelet
　　❑ Two men on the ice
　　❑ Two seagulls
　　❑ A campfire
　　❑ Kids rock climbing
　　❑ A helicopter
　　❑ The Norwegian flag on a hat
　　❑ A herd of elk
　　❑ Two fishing nets
　　❑ A life vest
　　❑ A Viking vessel

Map mural
　　❑ A tongue
　　❑ Four crowns
　　❑ A person

- ❑ Four fleurs-de-lis
- ❑ A seahorse
- ❑ An intricate wagon
- ❑ A branch
- ❑ A polar bear
- ❑ A flying fish
- ❑ A sail with a yellow circle
- ❑ Three Viking-style boats
- ❑ A neighborhood
- ❑ Italy
- ❑ A ship in trouble
- ❑ A narwhal (a dolphin-like creature with a long horn)
- ❑ A red pennant
- ❑ Two axes
- ❑ A long vine
- ❑ Two trees
- ❑ A fork in the road
- ❑ North, south, east, and west

China: Reflections of China

Lucky Collection: There is a museum attached to the waiting area for this attraction. It hosts wonderful old objects on loan from China. While you wait for the next show, see how lucky you are. Search the museum and the waiting area for the items below, which are common in Chinese art and antiquities. You may not be able to find all of them because the museum exhibits change from time to time, but give yourself 1 point for each one you collect.

- ❑ A dragon
- ❑ A horse
- ❑ A lion
- ❑ A vase
- ❑ A weapon
- ❑ A flower
- ❑ A moon
- ❑ A tree
- ❑ A waterfall
- ❑ Fancy robes
- ❑ A battle

❏ Something from the Han dynasty
❏ Something from the Ming dynasty
❏ A phoenix
❏ A pearl
❏ A building hidden in the trees
❏ A bird
❏ Someone wearing armor

3 points bonus points for whichever treasure hunter finds the oldest thing _____

The American Adventure

Treasure Hunt Time! As you wait for the show, you can wander around the heritage museum in the front. While you explore see how many of these All-American treasures you can discover.

❏ Three profiles
❏ Yourself
❏ Red and green grapes
❏ A shovel
❏ A horn
❏ Something belonging to Will Rogers
❏ An eagle in flight
❏ A large metal hook
❏ A wet journey
❏ A pair of glasses in for a very long trip
❏ A patch for the Space Shuttle Columbia
❏ Spurs
❏ A bandana
❏ A letter from Benjamin Franklin
❏ A white picket fence
❏ A medal
❏ A wagon full of hay
❏ The Statue of Liberty
❏ A projector
❏ A Space Shuttle Discovery patch

France: Impressions de France

? POP QUIZ! How much did you notice as you entered this queue?

1. The Impressions de France sign was made from metal and has a sculpture worked into it. What was the sculpture of?
   a. The Eiffel Tower
   b. A girl's face
   c. Bread and cheese
   d. The French flag

2. There were doors with knockers on either side of the entrance. What did the knockers look like?
   a. A lion's head
   b. Mickey Mouse's head wearing a tam
   c. A fleur-de-lis
   d. Grapes

3. How many pillars were on the front of this building?
   a. 0   b. 2
   c. 4   d. 6

End of Pop Quiz

Inside Queue

4. Someone here is being very rude. Whose behavior is not up to snuff?
   a. A gargoyle is picking his nose; how foul.
   b. A gargoyle is eating with his mouth open; now that is not necessary.
   c. A gargoyle is spitting; ewe, gross!
   d. A gargoyle is doing all of these things.
   e. I am getting the idea that there is a gargoyle here somewhere.

5. Treasure Hunt Time! How many treasures with a hint of Paris can you find?
   ❑ A water lily
   ❑ A tree with no leaves
   ❑ Two hands with no body

- ❑ Someone sitting on a pier
- ❑ Yourself
- ❑ The number 8 with a hole in it
- ❑ Two bridges
- ❑ A dome-shaped rooftop
- ❑ A person pushing a cart
- ❑ An eagle gargoyle
- ❑ Two carved flowers
- ❑ Five swans
- ❑ A mast
- ❑ A horse
- ❑ Someone lying down
- ❑ A gold shell
- ❑ A fountain
- ❑ A sword
- ❑ A horn
- ❑ An architectural drawing
- ❑ A head that is definitely not where it belongs

Canada: O Canada!

Hunt More Treasure! This hunt is unique because you will be discovering treasures that you'd use to find, well, treasure. As you wait for your journey into Canada's beauty, you will find yourself entering what appears to be an old mining cave. It is filled with things you might see in a mine. Have a close look around, inside and out, to see how many of these buried treasures you can unearth before you depart for Canada.

- ❑ A gold sifter
- ❑ A wheelbarrow
- ❑ Two rusted chains
- ❑ An old metal bucket
- ❑ A roof that is peeling
- ❑ A turret reaching into the sky
- ❑ A lantern-like wall sconce
- ❑ Something with teeth but no mouth
- ❑ Three pickaxes
- ❑ A messy coil of rope on two pegs
- ❑ Four shovels
- ❑ Three pulleys with nothing attached them
- ❑ A barrel with yellow stripes
- ❑ A lantern hanging from a hook

❑ Two poles with rope coiled around them
❑ A device for measuring water level that seems to be providing other info today
❑ A red light
❑ A short ladder
❑ A gear in the rafters
❑ A big circle
❑ A very long saw blade

World Showcase Answers

Mexico: Gran Fiesta Tour Starring the Three Caballeros

1) d. A large bell
2) b. Donald Duck and two of his bird amigos
3) c. Three guitars
4) Total Treasures found _____
5) b. No, two were wearing black bow ties and one was wearing none at all.
6) Yes
7) a. A colorful blanket
8) c. Three each
9) No
10) Yes
11) Yes
12) No
13) d. All of the above
14) Yes
15) Total Treasures found _____

Norway: Maelstrom

1) c. A High Seas Norwegian Adventure
2) b. A boat in a storm
3) b. Man, d. Lightning, e. Red stripes on a flag, h. Large wave, j. Round shields
4) a. A window with lace curtains and a vase with flowers in it
5) b. A troll
6) d. Both a and c
7) c. A gift shop
8) a. A rich seafaring heritage
9) Total Treasures found _____

China: Reflections of China
Number of Lucky objects collected _____

The American Adventure
Number of All-American Treasures found _____

France: Impressions de France
1) b. A girl's face
2) a. A lion's head
3) c. 4
4) c. A gargoyle is spitting.
5) Total Treasures found _____

Canada: O Canada!
Number of Mining Treasures found _____

Epcot Scavenger Hunt

This hunt takes place in World Showcase. Good luck.

Mexico
❑ A stairway that you can't use
❑ A big cement ball
❑ A snake man
❑ A bird in a cage

Norway
❑ A roof that is sticking its tongue out at you
❑ A door frame that is biting itself
❑ A pretzel wearing a crown
❑ A living roof
❑ A horse walking on a sign
❑ Snowshoes

China
❑ A green man going for a ride on the rooftops
❑ Two snow white dragons
❑ A red phoenix with a blue tail
❑ A very big bell
❑ A red birdcage
❑ An elephant

Outpost
- ❑ An arrow pointing the way to the Bahamas

Germany
- ❑ A timely performance
- ❑ A standing bear
- ❑ Two hands – one with a star, one with a moon
- ❑ A dragon being slain
- ❑ An airplane
- ❑ A castle in glass

Canada
- ❑ A totem pole
- ❑ Something for a horse's hooves and something for a person's feet
- ❑ A bird with a face on its belly
- ❑ The making of maple syrup
- ❑ A red maple leaf

United Kingdom
- ❑ A flower wearing a crown
- ❑ A pig with an apple in its mouth
- ❑ A lion and a unicorn
- ❑ A king who is willing to spit

France
- ❑ A rooster holding plates
- ❑ A mold man
- ❑ A lady holding two paintbrushes

Morroco
- ❑ A star fountain
- ❑ A little metal bird resting on a pot
- ❑ An open book
- ❑ A hanging kettle

Japan
- ❑ A bird robe
- ❑ A door within a door
- ❑ A gold fish

The American Adventure
- ❑ A golden Eagle
- ❑ A hornet's nest

Italy
- ❑ A winged lion who is all about reading
- ❑ Hard grapes
- ❑ A fish door handle
- ❑ A trident
- ❑ A chandelier of many colors

Epcot
Scavenger Hunt Tally

Total Treasures found _____

Disney's Hollywood Studios

In this chapter, you'll find games for most of the park's ride queues as well as for shows that tend to have queues. They are organized by areas, in the order you will find them on your Guidemap, and then alphabetically within each area. Attractions that don't have queues are not included.

If you want to continue to play when you are walking around the park from one place to another, turn to the Disney's Hollywood Studios Scavenger Hunt at the end of this chapter. *Tip*: You may want to read over the list now and then stay on the lookout. The treasures on the scavenger hunt list are scattered throughout the park. You get 1 point for every treasure you find.

Note: When you see *FP* next to a question or section, it means you can find the answer (or gather Treasure or Collection items) from both the FASTPASS and standby lines. A **?** in the margin is your signal to look hard at something (often the attraction's sign) before you enter the queue.

Scoring: Unless specified otherwise, give yourself 1 point for each correct answer, 1 point for each Treasure you find, 1 point for each item you add to a Collection, and 1 point for any similar finds you make when you are hunting for something rather than answering questions. Don't forget to add 5 bonus points for each of your Collections with more than 10 items in it at the end of the day. Good luck!

Hollywood Boulevard

The Great Movie Ride

Treasure Hunt Time! See how many of these entertaining treasures you can find here in the courtyard before you are off to the movies.

- ❑ Kermit the frog
- ❑ A horse-drawn chariot
- ❑ A man with flames above his head
- ❑ The word "Love"
- ❑ A tiny gold man
- ❑ Ruby slippers
- ❑ Birds in flight
- ❑ A gold dragon on a red circle
- ❑ A big blue "O" in flames
- ❑ "Hollywood" in the hills
- ❑ An intricate wooden dragon
- ❑ A parasol being held
- ❑ The footprints of a famous mouse
- ❑ A dragon head with no body
- ❑ A heart
- ❑ A man holding a head (not his own)
- ❑ Mythical creatures with no fear of heights
- ❑ A face with VERY long, pointy teeth

Hollywood Boulevard Answers

The Great Movie Ride
Total Treasures found _____

Echo Lake

Indiana Jones™ Extreme Stunt Show!

Outside Queue

1. When you entered the queue, you passed under a sign featuring Indiana Jones himself. What was he holding in his hand?
   a. A snake
   b. An idol
   c. An emerald
   d. A whip

2. Were there any other people featured in this sign besides our fedora-wearing hero?
   Yes / No

3. Oh NO! It appears that there has been a crash. A plane carrying archaeological relics has crashed right here in the queue. As you make your way through the jungle, try your hand as an archaeologist. See how much treasure you can unearth while you wait in the "Queue of Doom." (a) Earn 1 point for each piece of plane wreckage you discover, (b) 1 point for each antiquity you dig up, and (c) 1 point for everything on the list below.
   ❑ Grass matting
   ❑ A book
   ❑ Trunks resting on crates
   ❑ A three-leaf clover
   ❑ A coil of rope with a hook on each end
   ❑ A crowbar
   ❑ A pickaxe
   ❑ A black case

Inside the Theater

4. Maya Treasure Hunt: Once you enter the theater
and take your seat, you will discover that you are in
a Mayan temple. How exciting! The temple is filled
with ancient treasure. Maybe you can discover some
before Indiana Jones arrives on the scene. After all, why
should he get all the fortune and glory? Can you find:

- ❑ Three skeletons with dangerous weapons
- ❑ A skull wearing hoop earrings
- ❑ An angry guy looking important and carrying
  a big stick
- ❑ A stockpile of weapons
- ❑ A mustache
- ❑ The tomb's treasure
- ❑ An eye with a vine about to grow through it.
  Gross!
- ❑ A headdress with blue paint still visible
- ❑ A carving of a pyramid
- ❑ A foot
- ❑ A skeleton not made out of stone
- ❑ A stone flower

Star Tours

Outside Queue

1. Jedi vs. Sith Contest: A long time ago in a queue
not so far away, there was a bit of a wait to enter the
spaceport. If you will be waiting outside for a time, this
game is for you. If not, move ahead to the next section.

In *Star Wars*, the good guys are the Jedi and the bad
guys are the Sith. To play, you must choose the Jedi or
the Sith (If multiple people are playing, split into two
teams.) Each description on the list below makes up
one round of the game.

During each round, both sides try to look for a
person wearing blue (Jedi) or red (Sith) who also fits
the description. The first team to spot a person fitting
the description while also wearing the team's color
wins the round, and play moves to the next entry on
the list. For example, in the first round both teams

look for "a person talking on a cell phone." If the Jedi side spots a person talking on a cell phone who is also wearing something blue before the Sith side spots a person talking on a cell phone who is wearing red, that round goes to the Jedi. Subjects wearing both colors are conflicted, and the first team to spot them may claim them. (Sorry Jedi, blue jeans don't count.)

Start your battle now and may the Force be with you.

A person talking on a cell phone
 ❑ Jedi (Blue)   ❑ Sith (Red)

A person with a lightsaber
 ❑ Jedi (Blue)   ❑ Sith (Red)

A person carrying a toy
 ❑ Jedi (Blue)   ❑ Sith (Red)

A person wearing Mickey Mouse ears
 ❑ Jedi (Blue)   ❑ Sith (Red)

A person wearing a baseball cap
 ❑ Jedi (Blue)   ❑ Sith (Red)

A person with a fanny pack
 ❑ Jedi (Blue)   ❑ Sith (Red)

A person wearing a windbreaker
 ❑ Jedi (Blue)   ❑ Sith (Red)

A person taking a picture
 ❑ Jedi (Blue)   ❑ Sith (Red)

A person wearing numbers
 ❑ Jedi (Blue)   ❑ Sith (Red)

A person with glasses on top of their head
 ❑ Jedi (Blue)   ❑ Sith (Red)

A person wearing a ribbon
 ❑ Jedi (Blue)   ❑ Sith (Red)

A person playing with an app
 ❑ Jedi (Blue)   ❑ Sith (Red)

A person wearing a hoodie
 ❑ Jedi (Blue)   ❑ Sith (Red)

A person in a button-up shirt
 ❑ Jedi (Blue)   ❑ Sith (Red)

A person with a team's name on their clothes
 ❑ Jedi (Blue)   ❑ Sith (Red)

A person wearing polka dots
 ❑ Jedi (Blue)   ❑ Sith (Red)

A person with a mustache
 ❑ Jedi (Blue)   ❑ Sith (Red)

People sharing a hug
 ❑ Jedi (Blue)   ❑ Sith (Red)

In the Spaceport

You are now entering the spaceport. In this area, you will have to listen and look for answers. You may not see what you need to answer every question in the time you are in the area. That is OK because it means you are getting closer to the ride!

Note: Questions coming from the screen or the robots will come in no particular order, so you may want to check ahead a bit. If you don't have time to answer these questions now, you can always come back to them when you're waiting in another queue and see what you can remember.

FP 2. Can you find an alien creature with a fish head?
> Yes / No

FP 3. What does the IC360 provide to Star Tours passengers?
> a. It takes you into the most extreme climates. Hmm… not sounding good so far.
> b. It takes you nose to nose with the galaxy's most dangerous creatures. Wait a minute … do I want that?
> c. It puts you squarely in the middle of the action when a battle for control of the galaxy is near at hand. Anyone know where the customer service desk is?
> d. It lets you see it all from the comfort of your own seat. Now that's sounding more like it.
> e. All of the above
> f. All but c

FP 4. What is the flight number of the nonstop starspeeder with service to Coruscant that is now boarding?
> a. 492   b. 705
> c. 6017   d. 1025

FP 5. What is the current security threat level?
> a. 5   b. Red
> c. 2   d. Orange

FP 6. What is R2-D2 fixing?
> a. The power couplings
> b. The hyperdrive motivator
> c. The thrusters

     d. Absolutely nothing – that lazy, overgrown scrap
       pile!

FP 7. What is every Starspeeder equipped with?
     a. A free checked-baggage area
     b. The most reliable pilot
     c. The most legroom
     d. The widest seats
     e. All of the above
     f. All but a

FP 8. On what planet can you visit the planet's core?
     a. Coruscant   b. Tatooine
     c. Naboo   d. Pluto

FP 9. What is the weather forecast for Cloud City?
     a. Snowy
     b. Sunny and bright
     c. Dust storms in the afternoon
     d. Cloudy, of course

FP 10. Who does C-3PO think is an ungrateful little twit?
     a. A passenger who did not bother to say thank
       you
     b. All scanning droids – and they are not very
       bright either
     c. R2-D2
     d. The head droid at the spaceport: "He thinks he
       does everything."

FP 11. What must all interplanetary travelers present?
     a. Visas
     b. Photo ID
     c. Current passport
     d. All of the above
     e. Only a and c

FP 12. What does a Tatooine vacation have?
     a. Everything under the suns
     b. Really rocking dust twisters
     c. Tattoos
     d. Some of the biggest slugs this side of Endor

**FP 13. Who should you try to catch a glimpse of when
visiting Naboo?**
     a. Jar Jar Binks   b. The queen
     c. The Emperor   d. Elvis

FP 14. **What planet does C-3PO think is most beautiful?**
    a. Endor   b. Tatooine
    c. Hoth   d. Naboo

FP 15. **Something tends to keep happening to R2-D2 while he works. What is it?**
    a. He gets hit with steam.
    b. He is forced to listen to C-3PO complain.
    c. He is spun around.
    d. He is zapped with electricity.
    e. All of the above
    f. Only a and b

FP 16. **Where can you party all night long?**
    a. In Tatooine at the Cantina
    b. On Coruscant in the famous club district
    c. On Endor in the forest party shack
    d. In a Starspeeder 2000. They are equipped with party room and custom disco balls.

FP 17. **What is required for all droid passengers?**
    a. Proof of ownership
    b. A restraining bolt
    c. A cargo payment receipt
    d. Nothing, droids are not allowed as passengers.

FP **Luggage Scan Area**

18. **Hey, that baggage droid looks like he could use a little of your help.** Here is a list of things commonly found in the scanned luggage of interplanetary travelers. Perhaps if you are good enough, you will find an awesome job here scanning luggage.
    ❑ A stuffed animal that the droid thinks is alive
    ❑ A stormtrooper helmet
    ❑ A Buzz Lightyear doll – to infinity and beyond
    ❑ A group of droid heads that like to say, "Roger"
    ❑ A Mickey Mouse hat
    ❑ A sorcerer's hat
    ❑ A genie's lamp
    ❑ A stowaway
    ❑ Boxer shorts with a heart pattern
    ❑ A droid lying on its back and having a look around
    ❑ A football
    ❑ Guns

- ❑ A lightsaber
- ❑ Extra hands
- ❑ A little ball shooting light
- ❑ WALL-E (a square robot with tank wheels and binocular eyes)
- ❑ A coil of rope
- ❑ A camera
- ❑ Glasses
- ❑ Flip-flops
- ❑ A head in a crystal ball
- ❑ Bagpipes
- ❑ A superhero costume
- ❑ Goofy's hat
- ❑ Tennis shoes
- ❑ A droid in pieces
- ❑ A monkey playing the drums
- ❑ A computer
- ❑ A bag belonging to Lando Calrissian
- ❑ Goggles
- ❑ A C-3PO head
- ❑ A baseball cap

FP Silhouette Area

19. It's time for a quick scavenger hunt. See how many of these silhouettes you can find before you space out.

- ❑ C-3PO
- ❑ A person carrying a purse
- ❑ A stormtrooper
- ❑ Something that gets shot down
- ❑ R2-D2
- ❑ Someone with a touchpad recording information
- ❑ R2-D2 getting pushed around
- ❑ Two people bowing in greeting
- ❑ A camera pestering a passenger
- ❑ A Jawa (short people in robes)
- ❑ People holding hands
- ❑ A person stretching from the top of the window all the way to the bottom
- ❑ R2-D2 doing a Mickey Mouse impression
- ❑ Someone dropping something
- ❑ Watto (a pudgy flying passenger)
- ❑ Someone carrying a stack of boxes
- ❑ A family of Ewoks (fuzzy teddy bear-like creatures)
- ❑ Someone putting up his hood

❑ Someone using a Jedi mind trick
❑ Jar Jar Binks (tall creature with buggy eyes and long floppy ears) getting a ride

FP Body Scan Area

Soon it will be time for your full body scan – required of all interplanetary passengers, no exceptions. Listen carefully to the body-scan droid while you are in his area. Then see how many of these questions you can answer.

20. What s the body-scan droid's favorite thing to say?
    a. "Nothing to see here."
    b. "Keep it moving."
    c. "Respect the droids."
    d. "Is that a Wookie or is it your boyfriend?"

21. What is the body-scan droid not programmed to deal with?
    a. Young humans   b. Rabid Gungans
    c. Begging   d. Your personal problems

22. What is a job in security?
    a. "A job in security"
    b. "My lot in life"
    c. "A great place to throw my weight around"
    d. "The most important thing any droid will ever do, so show some respect."

23. According to the body-scan droid, why are there no liquids allowed on board the flight?
    a. "Because I said so, that is all the reason you need, human."
    b. "The shuttle was built by droids who did not think to put in a bathroom."
    c. "Humans are known to be the clumsiest life form in the galaxy. Enough said."
    d. "Because it is rule number 458.2 in the Passenger's Conduct Handbook provided to you at booking."

24. The body-scan droid is very concerned with how the line is moving. According to him, when is it OK to stop moving?
    a. When frozen in carbonite
    b. When he says "STOP Humans!"

    c. When you have boarded your spacecraft and are belted into your seat

    d. When you bump into the person in front of you

25. How does the body-scan droid "like it"?

    a. He likes it when everything is moving smoothly.

    b. He likes it when all of the humans have boarded their flights and he can power down.

    c. He likes it with cream and sugar.

    d. He does not like it, what's to like?

26. The body-scan droid remarks about someone's strength. What does he say about it?

    a. "Do you need some help with your bag, mister? The kid next to you looks strong."

    b. "You look strong enough to deadlift Jabba the Hut."

    c. "You look strong enough to pull the ears off a Gondar."

    d. "Wow, that guy looks strong, must be part Wookie."

27. What advice does the body-scan droid give you for your tour?

    a. "Don't hire Gungans as tour guides or bodyguards."

    b. "Don't do anything I wouldn't do, and I wouldn't do anything."

    c. "Stay out of imperial sectors."

    d. "If you play games with the natives, let the Wookie win!"

28. Why could the body-scan droid use a little help?

    a. He is trying to practice Jedi mind tricks from his Jedi-By-Mail course. He needs a passenger with a very weak mind to practice on.

    b. He is about to power off and needs someone to continue the scanning process.

    c. He is running behind on his quota of passengers detained and would like volunteers.

    d. He accidently wiped his memory and can't remember who he is.

29. What note was left for the driver of a brown Landspeeder Model X-34?

    a. "This area is for the loading and unloading of droids only."

    b. "Parked in my space, you are. Have you towed, I will."

    c. "I find your lack of parking skill disturbing."

    d. "Chewie tells me you are looking for passage to the Alderaan system."

30. Some woman tried to waltz past security with something she was not allowed to have. What was it?

    a. Two cinnamon buns in her hair

    b. She had a small Ewok in her purse.

    c. She concealed a pod-racing betting form in her book.

    d. She had the plans for a death star stashed inside her droid.

31. How would the body-scan droid like you to act?

    a. More like a droid

    b. Like a more intelligent life form

    c. Like you are paying attention

    d. Less suspicious

32. What is the most fun thing he can think of?

    a. Scanning you

    b. A relaxing oil bath

    c. Assisting you with anything you might need

    d. He is not programmed to think of anything fun.

33. For some security droids, this is just a job. What is it to him?

    a. His primary program.

    b. An opportunity to be bored out of his mind

    c. Just a job

    d. "It's awful. Brain the size of a planet and I'm doing this."

34. What language is the body-scan droid shocked that you do not speak?

    a. Wookinease

    b. Ewakein

    c. Binary

    d. Bochi

35. What does he commend a gentleman for doing a good job of?
    a. Bumping into the person in front of him before stopping.
    b. Making his mind a complete blank
    c. Standing upright
    d. Nothing

36. Why are you not being thanked for your cooperation?
    a. "I am not programmed to be thankful. Don't want to be disingenuous here."
    b. "I am not a mealymouthed protocol droid."
    c. "It is my job to be as intimidating as possible. Are you feeling intimidated?"
    d. "Since your cooperation is mandatory, no thanks seem necessary."

37. There are no overhead compartments in the Starspeeder.
    True or False?

38. What does the body-scan droid say to those traveling with small children?
    a. "Good Luck."
    b. "There is absolutely no riding on a parent's lap or what have you."
    c. "Children with more than two arms must be properly restrained."
    d. "I am sorry, but restraining bolts are for droid use only."

39. What does he feel is suspicious human behavior?
    a. Laughing
    b. Sweating
    c. Blinking
    d. Breathing
    e. All of the above
    f. All but d

40. What new program is he trying out?
    a. Human-behavior simulator
    b. Speed scanning
    c. Small talk
    d. American Idol

41. What does the body-scan droid mistake someone's children for?

    a. Wookies   b. Jawas

    c. Master Yoda   d. Droids

42. How many different species of life forms can the scanner recognize?

    a. 6,000

    b. 10,000

    c. 14,000

    d. All known life forms

43. Is this the correct line for alien species?

    Yes / No

44. According to the body-scan droid, which is one of those funny words that just puts a smile on your face?

    a. Churro

    b. Supercalifragilisticexpialidocious

    c. Phlegm

    d. Diphthong

45. What restaurant does the scanning droid recommend?

    a. Cantina

    b. Dexter's Diner

    c. The restaurant at the end of the universe

    d. The Spaceport Skyroom

    e. He doesn't recommend human food; it smells just awful.

46. When the body-scan droid gets his wires wet, what happens?

    a. He gets the urge to put on his scuba gear and go for a swim.

    b. He shuts down, but it makes for a nice nap.

    c. He has to dry himself out with a hair dryer which is a bit humiliating.

    d. He ends up repeating himself every 20 minutes.

47. What does he say to someone who looks familiar?

    a. "You look familiar, but then all humans look the same to me."

    b. "Hey, are you my long lost brother? No? What about sister?"

c. "You look familiar; do you normally wear a large black helmet?"

d. "Haven't I scanned you somewhere before?"

48. What must all passengers have?
a. Tickets
b. Flight glasses
c. A pulse
d. "The ability to sit. This means you, sir."

49. How long do the security droid's relationships last?
a. 1 second
b. 5 seconds
c. 10 seconds
d. Forever, he never forgets a face.

The American Idol Experience

1. What is the name of the theater you are about to enter?
a. American Idol Theater
b. "When You Wish Theater"
c. Superstar Television Theater
d. Grauman's Chinese Theater
e. This is not a theater; it is a studio.

2. A caution sign is posted for you. What are you cautioned about?
a. The doors
b. The noise
c. The flashing lights
d. Possibly questionable singing voices

3. What is the name of the ship anchored a short distance from you?
a. The Queen Minnie
b. U.S.S. Min and Bill's
c. H.M.S. Dinosaur
d. S.S. Down The Hatch

4. What is it your turn for?
    a. To step up to the microphone
    b. To shine
    c. An American Idol Experience
    d. To go in please

5. You will see a video about how The American Idol Experience auditions went. What was the number of the featured audition room?
    a. 1
    b. 2
    c. 3
    d. It was not numbered.

6. Treasure Hunt Time! Let's see how many treasures you can find before it is time for your curtain call.
- ❑ A picture of an older couple. The lady is wearing a hat and the gentleman has a rather large nose.
- ❑ A lifesaving device with a sense of humor
- ❑ Spotlights
- ❑ A giant gold star
- ❑ A Chinese lion statue
- ❑ A giant gold moon
- ❑ Someone with eight legs
- ❑ A black-and-white checkered flag
- ❑ Two birds above a half sun
- ❑ A gloved hand with only three fingers
- ❑ A golden statue
- ❑ A grand piano
- ❑ Mickey dressed in a red robe
- ❑ A crab
- ❑ The song "When You Wish Upon a Star"
- ❑ A guitar
- ❑ Someone dressed as Elvis; blink and you will miss him.
- ❑ Six dragons
- ❑ A vertical experience
- ❑ A giant screen
- ❑ Mickey peeking out of the letter "O"

Echo Lake Answers

Indiana Jones Epic Stunt Spectacular!
  Outside Queue
    1) d. A whip
    2) No
    3) a. Number of pieces of plane wreckage found _____
       b. Number of antiquities found _____
       c. Total Treasures found _____
  Inside the Theater
    4) Total Mayan Treasures found _____

Star Tours
  Outside Queue
    1) Jedi vs. Sith Contest
       Total Jedi points _____ Total Sith points _____
  In the Spaceport
    2) Yes
    3) f. All but c
    4) c. 6017
    5) a. 5
    6) b. The hyperdrive motivator
    7) f. All but a
    8) c. Naboo
    9) d. Cloudy, of course
    10) c. R2-D2
    11) e. Only a and c
    12) a. Everything under the suns
    13) b. The queen
    14) d. Naboo
    15) f. Only a and b
    16) b. On Coruscant in the famous club district
    17) a. Proof of ownership
    18) Luggage Scan Area
        1-2 items found: Don't quit your day job.
        3-4 items found: Well, you probably won't be
        working here but not bad for a human.
        5-6 items found: I think there is a future here for
        you.
        7 or more items found: You're hired, please get
        fitted with a restraining bolt and get to work!
    19) Number of Silhouettes spotted _____

Body Scan Area

20) b. "Keep it moving."
21) d. Your personal problems
22) a. "A job in security"
23) b. "The shuttle was built by droids who did not think to put in a bathroom."
24) d. When you bump into the person in front of you
25) a. He likes it when everything is moving smoothly.
26) c. "You look strong enough to pull the ears off a Gondar."
27) b. "Don't do anything I wouldn't do, and I wouldn't do anything."
28) d. He accidently wiped his memory and can't remember who he is.
29) b. "Parked in my space, you are. Have you towed, I will."
30) a. Two cinnamon buns in her hair
31) d. Less suspicious
32) a. Scanning you
33) c. Just a job
34) c. Binary
35) b. Making his mind a complete blank
36) d. "Since your cooperation is mandatory, no thanks seem necessary."
37) True
38) a. "Good Luck."
39) e. All of the above
40) c. Small talk
41) b. Jawas
42) c. 14,000
43) No
44) a. Churro
45) b. Dexter's Diner
46) d. He ends up repeating himself every 20 minutes.
47) d. "Haven't I scanned you somewhere before?"
48) b. Flight glasses
49) b. 5 seconds

The American Idol Experience

1) c. Superstar Television Theater
2) a. The doors
3) d. S.S. Down The Hatch
4) c. An American Idol Experience
5) b. 2
6) Total Treasures found _____

Streets of America

Lights, Motors, Action!® Extreme Stunt Show

? **POP QUIZ!** As you walk up to the entrance, you'll see a very big sign for this show. Take a good look at it and then join the queue and test your memory with Questions 1 to 5.

1. There was something unusual about one of the letters on the sign. What was unusual?
  a. The "O" was a tire.
  b. The "M" in "motors" was bright red and flashing.
  c. The "O" was an odometer.
  d. The "A" was tipped on its side with tire marks.

2. How many cars were there?
  a. 1
  b. 3
  c. 4
  d. 10; it was a regular traffic jam.

3. What colors were the cars?
  a. Red and black
  b. Red and white
  c. Black and silver
  d. Black, silver, and red

4. Most of the cars were parked beneath the sign. Name one other parking place.
  a. On top of another car
  b. On top of the word "Show"
  c. Upside-down and underneath the word "Extreme"
  d. All the cars were parked beneath the sign.

5. What is the speed limit on the road leading up to the show?

    a. 5 mph

    b. 10 mph

    c. 15 mph

    d. 25 mph

End of Pop Quiz

6. Treasure Hunt Time! See how many of these treasures you can find before they roll away:

- ❏ A license plate from somewhere besides the U.S.A.
- ❏ A traffic light without the yellow light
- ❏ A bus-stop sign
- ❏ A clock
- ❏ A parking lot that is not for cars
- ❏ Something that is full of hot air and is not a family member
- ❏ A water tower
- ❏ Two smokestacks: one tall, one short
- ❏ A fire escape
- ❏ A bell
- ❏ A TV antenna
- ❏ A red door
- ❏ A white door
- ❏ A car bursting through flames
- ❏ A spray can lying on its side
- ❏ A green tag
- ❏ A pair of pants not on a person
- ❏ A movie director's clapboard with a black star on it
- ❏ A propeller
- ❏ Doors that open to nowhere
- ❏ Mickey Mouse ready to go for a fly

7. There is a picture of a speedometer. What is it reading?

    a. 5 mph

    b. 100 mph

    c. 150 mph

    d. Oh my gosh! It's all the way in the red! Slow down!!!

8. There are three cars performing a trick that I hope my car never does. What are they doing?
 a. Riding on two wheels in synchronization
 b. One car is jumping the other two.
 c. Flipping
 d. Flying off the roof

9. There is a picture of a motorcycle rider. What is the rider doing?
 a. A wheelie
 b. Jumping
 c. Driving onto the back of a truck
 d. Spinning out

10. What is significant about the number 55?
 a. It is the number on the plane.
 b. It is the speed on the speedometer in the pictures.
 c. It is a door for Cast Members only.
 d. It comes before 56?
 e. Both c and d

11. There are three soda vending machines. What appears to have happened to them?
 a. They were squished by a jumping motorcycle that landed on them.
 b. They have been smashed in two.
 c. They are covered with tire marks; some people just can't stay on the road.
 d. I don't know, but a cold drink sure sounds good.

Inside The Stadium
 While you wait for the action, see if you can rack up some more points.

12. Something by the name "Deep Search" has had its original name crossed out. What was that name?
 a. Calypso
 b. Beatle
 c. Jacqueline
 d. Search and Rescue #4

13. Treasure Hunt Time! Can you find these treasures before Lights, Motors, Action! begins?
 ❑ A pig in trouble
 ❑ A collection of baguettes

- A car with a flat
- A jet ski
- Tiny purple grapes
- A Hawaiian shirt
- A lady with a cracked head
- An old-fashioned bicycle
- A child's bicycle
- A word leaning to the left
- Sunflowers
- A life saver
- Lace curtains
- A wheel of cheese missing a slice
- Laundry
- A ball in a net
- A hotel
- Three surfboards
- A girl with boards
- Half a motorcycle
- A teeny tiny chair
- A yellow-striped cloth
- A barbeque grill
- A blue door with no windows
- A motor scooter

MuppetVision 3D

Outside Queue

The following questions are for the extended outside line. If you go right in, skip to Question 25.

1. In the Bride of Froggen-Schwein, what part does Miss Piggy lend her talents to?
- a. The Monster
- b. Mrs. The Monster
- c. Eyesore the Cretin
- d. Both b and c
- e. None of the above

2. What has been called "another exercise in dampness" by Muppet Labs?
- a. "20,000 Frogs Under the Sea"
- b. "Das Bear"

    c. "Pigseidon Adventure"
    d. Anytime you introduce a pig to water

3. In the movie "It Called from Outer Space," how do you power the phone booth?
    a. You plug it in, how else?
    b. It is wind powered. Hey, is there wind in space?
    c. Bike pedals, of course
    d. You must attach it to a rat on a wheel and hope he feels like a bit of a run.

4. You are in a special experiment being run by the famous Muppet scientist Dr. Honeydew. What is the experiment?
    a. 4-D audience, hope your health insurance covers that.
    b. The world's first experimental line
    c. The living building experiment. Parts of the building will be coming to life, such as the pipes, and we will see how you handle that.
    d. I don't remember signing a waiver.

5. You are being congratulated! What did you do?
    a. Left here
    b. Wound up there
    c. Successfully achieved no forward progress but avoided any backward pull
    d. Nothing, but I will gladly accept any congratulations offered.

6. According to the E-Z Location Finder, what is up a ways?
    a. Here
    b. There
    c. The sky
    d. Somewhere

7. If you were to end up here, what would the E-Z Location Finder have you do?
    a. Come here
    b. Go back a ways
    c. You missed it. Here was way back there.
    d. Now you are just messing with me, right? I am here. You're the one who is there.

8. If you just stay on course, where are you likely to end up?

a. Somewhere   b. Here

c. There   d. The show, I hope

9. According to the posted sign, what have the Muppet Lab and the E-Z Location Finder accomplished?

a. They got you from here to there.

b. They took you somewhere.

c. They confused you about whether you are actually here or not.

d. You say something was accomplished?

10. Something has come to an end, what is it?

a. The experiment

b. The "here and there" signage

c. My interest in being a participant in this crazy experiment that seems to be going nowhere

d. The line

e. Sadly all of the above but d

11. In the U-Do-It Rumor Rebound Experiment, what rumor are you encouraged to share?

a. Kermit the frog is really a toad.

b. If you look really closely while you are Soarin', you can see the Muppets wave to you from a golf cart.

c. Kermit will soon be Grand Marshal of the Rose Parade! Wait, that already happened.

d. I saw Elvis waiting in line at MuppetVision 3D.

12. If you complete the U-Do-It Phantom Fingertip Experiment, what must you do?

a. Make an extra pinky finger appear on both hands.

b. Make a fingertip appear to float in midair.

c. Make a finger disappear.

d. Make a fingertip turn blue.

13. What is the goal of the "Guide to MuppetVision's 3D Glasses"?

a. To help users distinguish between these glasses and sunglasses

b. To make it to *The New York Times* Best Seller lists

    c. To make it clear, once and for all, which eye the
      red lens goes on

    d. To keep MuppetVision 3D glasses on your face
      and off the floor

14. Treasure Hunt Time! Have a look at the "Getting
to Know Your MuppetVision Glasses" poster. See how
many of these 2D treasures you can find.
- ❑ A plane
- ❑ A light bulb that can see
- ❑ A balloon man
- ❑ A "To Do" list
- ❑ An arrow's path
- ❑ A splat
- ❑ A rocket
- ❑ A nose
- ❑ An idea
- ❑ Cheating at tic tac toe
- ❑ Pinocchio
- ❑ An ear shelf
- ❑ An asteroid
- ❑ Two eyes
- ❑ The location of Muppet Labs

**15. According to "How to Operate Your 3D Glasses,"
what makes an interesting fashion statement?**
    a. Tying a ribbon into a bow around the center of
      your glasses
    b. Wearing your glasses on the back of your head
      instead of the front
    c. Wearing glasses on both of your ears
    d. Bell-bottoms have always been an interesting
      fashion statement.

**16. There is a printed list of five reasons why you
should return your 3D glasses, with many more
reasons written in. Which of the following reasons is
neither printed nor written in?**
    a. We have robotic space attack hamsters – enough
      said.
    b. Forced to use the automated 3D glass retriever
    c. Hit by an anvil
    d. Buried in the ground upside-down with your
      feet sticking out
    e. All of the above were reasons.

17. Why shouldn't you look up?
   a. If you don't see the anvil, it can't land on your head.
   b. There is an enormous scoop of ice cream and it is about to drip on you.
   c. You might see the top-secret FX-Gen-R8R.
   d. Made you look!

18. In the poster for "BEAK · E," what is the robot holding in his hand?
   a. A cheese
   b. A sponge
   c. A teddy bear
   d. A sandwich; robots get hungry too.
   e. All of the above
   f. All but a

19. In the poster that brings you "The Best of Both Worlds," who is Miss Piggy dressed as?
   a. Piggy Longstocking
   b. Hamlet
   c. An Oincksternaut
   d. Hammah Montana

20. In "Follow the Feet," which of the following creatures is dancing?
   a. A frog   b. A pig
   c. A rat   d. A bear
   e. They all are.   f. All but d

21. In "Dive Hard 2", which of the following things was the diver using for his dive?
   a. A thermos
   b. An alarm clock
   c. A flotation ring
   d. Flippers
   e. All of the above
   f. None of the above, but he did have a rubber ducky.

22. In "High School Mayhem," what are the Muppets doing?
   a. Destroying a perfectly good locker
   b. Playing instruments
   c. Having a food fight
   d. Passing notes in class

23. Kermit the pirate has some seafaring knowledge to share. What is it?

    a. If you can't swim with the big frogs, stay in the puddle.

    b. Flies are harder to come by in mid sea.

    c. Yo Ho! Yo Ho! An amphibian's life for me.

    d. On the high seas, it is easy to turn green.

24. On the poster for Cleopigtra, there are some unusual hieroglyphs. What animal is featured in these?

    a. Pig

    b. Frog

    c. Bear

    d. Rat

Inside Queue

25. If you wanted to get into the security station, what would you do?

    a. Yell "Free Donuts."

    b. Look under the mat.

    c. Try to break in.

    d. Ring the bell for service.

26. Oh No! Miss Piggy is featured on a wanted poster. Who is she wanted by?

    a. Absolutely everyone

    b. A frog who enjoys moonlit swims and dinner with flies

    c. Her agent; his payment is overdue.

    d. The make-up department. It takes time to make a sow look like a silk purse, you know.

27. Who committed the crime of impersonating a comic?

    a. Miss Piggy

    b. Fozzie Bear

    c. Gonzo

    d. The whole lot of them

28. What sort of animal is the officer on duty?

    a. Frog

    b. Bear

    c. Pig

    d. Rat

29. What about "Box A"? What is located there?
 a. Department of Gift Wrapping and Silly Gift
  Giving
 b. Institute of Heckling & Browbeating
 c. Whatever is not located in "Box B"
 d. The Academy of Amphibian Science

30. Someone has been cleaning and they left their dustpan out. What is featured on the dustpan?
 a. A monster Muppet named Animal
 b. A picture of a broom with a sneezing face
 c. Dust bunnies
 d. A rainbow

31. Find a part of the building that is not what it looks like. What is it?
 a. It is a ceiling, or at least it should be.
 b. It is a wall, or maybe not.
 c. It is a door, or could that be an artificial reality?
 d. It is a window, or at least I think it is. I guess I
  will never know.

32. Muppet 3D Labs has some rather unexpected departments you will pass on your way in. Which of the following is not a department of Muppet 3D Labs?
 a. The Department of Making Things More
  Expensive Than We Can Afford
 b. The Stress Testing Department
 c. The Division of Fashion Technology
 d. The Institute of Advanced Chronology

33. Where might I find something that is really, really Tippy-Top Secret?
 a. The Department of Mind Your Own Business
 b. Miss Piggy's dressing room
 c. Through that trapdoor at the very tippy top of
  the ceiling that's marked "Top Secret."
 d. Stage 3D

34. Whose autograph is ripped?
 a. Kermit the Frog
 b. Animal
 c. Ralph
 d. The Great Gonzo

35. Treasure Hunt Time! It is time for a great big treasure hunt! You have now entered the prop storage area. It is packed full of Muppet treasures. See how many you can discover before curtain time.

- ❏ A bird cage containing a fish
- ❏ A wooden propeller
- ❏ A green bike
- ❏ A yellow feather boa
- ❏ Banana puree
- ❏ A teetering stack of barrels
- ❏ A green football helmet
- ❏ A catch of the day that has already been cleaned
- ❏ Mold and spores
- ❏ Butterflies: one yellow, one pink, one white, and one orange
- ❏ A parade of pack camels
- ❏ A boxing glove that is harder than brick
- ❏ Kermit, out for battle
- ❏ A place where no one can find their shoes
- ❏ Something that should be kept refrigerated
- ❏ A periodic table of the elements
- ❏ A cannon
- ❏ A flying tooth
- ❏ Something that requires some assembly
- ❏ An insult
- ❏ A pair of lava lamps
- ❏ Saturn
- ❏ A mallet
- ❏ A really big pencil
- ❏ 2D Fruities
- ❏ A movie reel
- ❏ A soldier with a pretty bow
- ❏ A celestial swine
- ❏ A light that also serves as a nose
- ❏ A guitar
- ❏ A violin
- ❏ An octopus
- ❏ A snorkeler
- ❏ A sleepy gauge

Studios Backlot Tour

1. As you walked in, you passed three large red signs that looked like directors' clapboards. What did they say?

    a. Quiet on the set. This is a take.

    b. Lights. Camera. Action.

    c. Back. Lot. Tour.

    d. Hollywood. Back Lot Tour. Take One.

    e. Is this a trick question? Signs don't talk.

2. There was a big red vehicle parked outside the tour building. What kind of vehicle was it?

    a. A camera crane

    b. A fire engine

    c. A tour bus

    d. It could turn into all three of these things and a mighty fighting robot, too.

    e. None of the above; there was no vehicle.

3. A sign for this ride was painted on the garage door you passed under as you walked in to take the tour. There was something painted on the sign besides the attraction's name. What was it?

    a. A movie camera

    b. A tour bus

    c. A spotlight

    d. A director's chair

    e. All of the above

    f. All of the above except d

4. What is significant about "39A"?

    a. It's the number of the bus parked out front.

    b. It is the set number of the closed set you are now entering.

    c. It is the street address of the Backlot Tour building.

    d. It's the number of the parking area your car is in.

5. Across from the entrance to the ride, there is a sign for a catering company. What is it called?

    a. Director's Choice Refreshments

    b. First Act Catering

c. Roach Coach Catering

d. High Octane Refreshments

6. Out front you passed what rather large food or drink item?

a. An ice cream cone

b. A hamburger

c. A bottle of Coca-Cola

d. This is Hollywood Studios, baby; they're all huge here.

7. You will come to a row of framed posters for current Disney movies. Take a good look at them, and give yourself 1 point for:

a. Everything you find in the posters that you could also find in your home _____, and

b. Anything you spot in the posters that you can also see on someone else waiting in line _____

8. Extra points!!! If you can locate all of the letters of the alphabet in the posters, you get 5 bonus points. Cross off letters as you spot them.

A B C D E F G H I J K L M
N O P Q R S T U V W X Y Z

9. Treasure Hunt Time! See how many of these movie treasures you can find around you before the director yells "Action!"

❑ A bird

❑ A dragon

❑ A parrot

❑ A ship's anchor

❑ A battleship

❑ Destruction on wheels

❑ Sails that have seen better days

❑ A pile of cannonballs

❑ An angel

❑ A ship's wheel

❑ A ship's wheel in use

❑ A merman

❑ A white flag with a red "X"

❑ Two model planes

❑ A collection of 12 Polaroid photos

❑ An explosion

❑ A very wet man with a big camera

❑ A life preserver the right size for a mouse

❏ A red flag with a yellow cross
❏ "36"
❏ Two cannons that could shoot stars
❏ A ship's deck that is missing its ship

10. What is SER. NO. N3544887?
    a. A boat designation
    b. A nuclear device
    c. The part number on the cannon's right side
    d. I think it is the scan number for my favorite
       breakfast cereal.

Streets of America Answers

Lights, Motors, Action! Extreme Stunt Show
    1) c. The "O" was an odometer.
    2) c. 4
    3) a. Red and black
    4) b. On top of the word "Show"
    5) d. 25 mph
    6) Total Treasures found _____
    7) d. It's all the way in the red!
    8) a. Riding on two wheels in synchronization
    9) b. Jumping
    10) e. Both c and d
    11) c. They are covered with tire marks.
  Inside the Stadium
    12) d. Jacqueline
    13) Total Treasures found ____

MuppetVision 3D
  Outside Queue
    1) b. Mrs. The Monster
    2) c. The movie the "Pigseidon Adventure"
    3) c. Bike pedals
    4) b. The world's first experimental line
    5) a. Left here
    6) b. There
    7) b. Go back a ways
    8) c. There
    9) a. They got you from here to there.
    10) e. All of the above but d
    11) d. I saw Elvis waiting in line at MuppetVision 3D.

12) b. Make a fingertip appear to float in midair.

13) d. To keep MuppetVision 3D glasses on your face and off the floor

14) Total 2D Treasures found _____

15) c. Wearing glasses on both of your ears

16) a. We have robotic space attack hamsters.

17) c. You might see the top-secret FX-Gen-R8R.

18) b. A sponge

19) d. Hammah Montana

20) f. All but d

21) e. All of the above

22) b. Playing instruments

23) d. On the high seas, it is easy to turn green.

24) d. Rat

Inside Queue

25) b. Look under the mat.

26) a. Absolutely everyone

27) b. Fozzie Bear

28) c. Pig

29) b. Institute of Heckling & Browbeating

30) a. A monster Muppet named Animal

31) c. It is a door.

32) a. The Department of Making Things More Expensive Than We Can Afford

33) d. Stage 3D

34) b. Animal

35) Total Prop Treasures found _____

Studios Backlot Tour

1) b. Lights. Camera. Action.

2) c. A tour bus

3) e. All of the above

4) a. It is the number of the bus parked out front.

5) d. High Octane Refreshments

6) c. A bottle of Coca-Cola

7) a. Number of poster items that you'd also find at home _____
b. Number of poster items that you saw on other people in line _____

8) Add 5 bonus points if you found all 26 letters of the alphabet _____

9) Total Movie Treasures found _____

10) b. A nuclear device

Pixar Place

Toy Story Midway Mania!®

Outside the Building

1. The Midway Mania sign is constructed out of which of the following toys? Check all that are correct.
   a. Scrabble letters
   b. Alphabet-letter blocks
   c. Puzzle pieces
   d. Chess pieces
   e. Super-bouncy balls
   f. Tinkertoys
   g. Dominos
   h. Plastic toy tanks
   i. Building blocks
   j. Pencil
   k. Doll
   l. Yoyo
   m. Baseball mitt

2. Why are the numbers 3, 1, 2, 4, 1, 4 important?
   a. They are the numbers visible on the dominos.
   b. They are the numbers on the playing cards.
   c. They are the numbers on the Scrabble pieces of the Midway Mania sign.
   d. Well, let's see 1, 2, 3, and 4 are obvious but I'm not sure about the extra 1 and 4.

3. Wait a minute, the toy soldiers seem to be sending you a message. What do they want you to know?
   a. You've Got a Friend in Me.
   b. Toy Meeting Tonight, Andy's Room.
   c. Meet the Toys.
   d. Let's Play.
   e. Both b and c
   f. Both a and d
   g. Both a and c

4. There is a monkey going for a ride. What is he taking out for a test drive?
    a. A rocket ship
    b. A toy car
    c. A tank
    d. A boat

5. There is a plunger being put to a purpose. What is it being used for?
    a. It is unplugging a barrel of monkeys.
    b. It is holding up a menu.
    c. As a weapon by the Green Army Men.
    d. It is the measuring sign to make sure riders are tall enough to ride.

6. The Green Army Men are moving a Mr. Spell game. What are they using as a tool to move it?
    a. Sheer Army-Man power and a Slinky
    b. A Tinkertoy cart
    c. Monkey movement
    d. A jump-rope

7. Treasure Hunt Time! See how many of these childhood treasures you can find before they all end up in the toy box.
    ❑ A card with the corner bent
    ❑ A yellow balloon with a happy face
    ❑ A spouting whale
    ❑ An Army Man using binoculars
    ❑ A green crayon
    ❑ A sheriff's badge
    ❑ A planet with a green ring
    ❑ A bridge of monkeys
    ❑ A pink crayon
    ❑ A dinosaur
    ❑ An alien's eyes
    ❑ A red checker piece and two black ones
    ❑ The king of clubs
    ❑ A kite's string
    ❑ A die
    ❑ The five of hearts
    ❑ A musical note
    ❑ Someone monkeying around with the letter "L"
    ❑ A Green Army Man very concerned about me
    ❑ A black star on pink
    ❑ A baseball and bat

Inside the Building

8. As you walk inside, you will find a childhood safety device. What is it?
    a. A night light
    b. A booster seat
    c. A lock for baby-proofing a cabinet
    d. A sippy cup

9. What is the queen of hearts holding in her hands?
    a. A necklace   b. Hearts, of course
    c. Flowers   d. She has hands?

10. What would cost you $4.95 here or $50.00 in Canada?
    a. A Woody the Cowboy doll
    b. Candy Land
    c. Tinkertoys
    d. Buzz Lightyear Attack on Zorg

11. Who or what is featured on the viewer disks?
    a. Peter Pan   b. Tomorrowland
    c. Cinderella   d. Lady and the Tramp
    e. Both a and b   f. All but b

12. What are being used as columns to hold up the ceiling?
    a. Tinkertoys   b. Checkers
    c. Blocks   d. Both b and c
    e. All of the above

13. What is Blue Sky?
    a. A space on the Candy Land board
    b. A little wooden airplane
    c. The name of the western town created around
       Andy's room
    d. The title of the crayon artwork on the wall

14. Andy's Room Treasure Hunt! Andy's room is a bit messy. See if you can help him figure out where he put his toys before they become lost. When you arrive at Mr. Potato Head, be sure to listen. He is one funny potato. This treasure hunt lasts until you leave the room.
    ❑ A place to start
    ❑ A periwinkle crayon
    ❑ A white guitar
    ❑ A cupcake

- ❏ A yellow pawn
- ❏ A checkered racing flag
- ❏ A bell
- ❏ Tinker Bell glowing yellow
- ❏ A block with the letter "L"
- ❏ An octopus
- ❏ Spinning Rocket Jets
- ❏ A chance to move two yellow spaces
- ❏ Someone wearing a flotation ring held up by suspenders
- ❏ A puzzle piece
- ❏ A die with the five up
- ❏ A man with a beard
- ❏ A Crazy Eights card
- ❏ A saw
- ❏ A green pawn
- ❏ A girl picking apples
- ❏ A ladder
- ❏ A yellow-green crayon
- ❏ A sideways cowboy
- ❏ A gold hook
- ❏ The ten of spades
- ❏ Yellow glasses
- ❏ A map
- ❏ A wanted poster
- ❏ A dragon
- ❏ A desk lamp
- ❏ A polka-dot bow tie
- ❏ The state of Washington
- ❏ A cow with a bell
- ❏ A puzzle piece with yellow, orange, red, and green on it
- ❏ The bank
- ❏ A horseshoe
- ❏ Two tents made of cards
- ❏ A bar code
- ❏ A horse
- ❏ A postage stamp

❓ Mr. Potato Head Memory Game

I hope you were paying attention to Mr. Potato Head, he hates to be ignored. See how many of these questions you can answer. Just remember there are no wrong answers, just right answers and the ones that aren't.

15. Why can't Mr. Potato Head hear you?
   a. Because he never stops talking
   b. He is all eyes, not all ears.
   c. See how well you'd hear with plastic ears.
   d. He pulled his ear out.

16. What is it time to do while Andy is away?
   a. It is time to play.
   b. It is time to find moving buddies. I claim Mrs. Potato Head.
   c. It is time for a meeting of the toys.
   d. It is time to prepare for Andy's birthday party. Has anyone seen the Army Men?

17. When Mr. Potato Head says, "Well, at least you're honest," to what is he referring?
   a. He is talking about the fact that you do like French fries.
   b. He is talking about the fact that you don't want to raise your hand anymore.
   c. He is referring to the fact that you do not think he is particularly skinny.
   d. He is talking about the fact that you do not think that Mr. Potato Head is the star of *Toy Story*.

18. What does Mr. Potato Head do to make people happy?
   a. He pulls off his ear.
   b. He sings a song.
   c. He stops singing a song.
   d. He offers to introduce everybody to Buzz and Woody next time they are around.

19. How does Mr. Potato Head tell you that the games will be in 3D?
   a. He puts on 3D glasses.
   b. He tells you that the games will be in 3D and he hopes you will be, too.
   c. He asks you to give him a "D" three times and then asks what you've got.
   d. He sings a little song about the 3D games on the midway.

20. Mr. Potato Head tells you that there is nothing to be afraid of and that you should trust him. Why?
   a. Potatoes never lie.
   b. If he is lying, you can take off his mouth.
   c. He is a hot potato.
   d. If there was something to be afraid of, he would have spotted it. He has a lot of eyes.

21. Mr. Potato Head offers you a hint. What is it?
   a. The secret to doing well in the game is to be sure to pull the trigger.
   b. This is the part where you clap.
   c. Be sure to put your glasses on.
   d. Keep your eye on the ball. He is really good at that, having all those eyes.

22. What kind of music scares balloon animals?
   a. Bebop, it's way too close to "be popped."
   b. Hard rock
   c. Pop songs
   d. All music makes them feel a bit deflated.

23. Why shouldn't Mrs. Potato Head get plastic surgery?
   a. She has three noses already.
   b. What if the surgeon was in the mood for French fries?
   c. Potatoes are supposed to be round.
   d. Potatoes shouldn't have surgery, they are too thin-skinned.

24. What whined a little when Rex stepped on it?
   a. Himself. He stepped on his own feet.
   b. A squeaky ball
   c. Woody
   d. A grape

25. What is Toy Story Midway Mania! more fun than?
   a. A day with all of his pieces in the right spot
   b. A barrel of monkeys
   c. His first day playing with Andy
   d. A day without drool (When is that baby going to stop teething anyway?)

26. What is Mr. Potato Head hoping someone will say?
    a. That he is their favorite toy
    b. That spuds make the best friends
    c. That they promise never to eat another potato for as long as they shall live
    d. That he should be elected head toy; after all, he is all head

27. What does Mr. Potato Head like to call people in the audience?
    a. Sweet potato   b. Rotten potato
    c. Hockey puck   d. Fans

28. What does Mr. Potato Head wish the Little Green Men would stop saying?
    a. "We come in peace."
    b. "Ooh, Strangers."
    c. "The Claw! It decides who will go and who will stay."
    d. "We are eternally grateful."

29. What makes Mr. Potato Head a commentator?
    a. He has a microphone and you are listening.
    b. He is a potato and he makes comments.
    c. Have you ever encountered an uncommentator?
    d. To be a commentator you have to have a pretty big head, and he is all head.

30. What kind of hat was Mr. Potato Head wearing?
    a. A cowboy hat
    b. A bowler hat (a rounded old-fashioned hat)
    c. A straw hat
    d. No hat at all. Is it customary for potatoes to wear hats?

31. Was Mr. Potato Head wearing shoes?
    a. Yes, tennis shoes
    b. Yes, black and shiny
    c. Yes, gray men's dress shoes
    d. Do potatoes have feet?

32. How many fingers did Mr. Potato Head have in all, not counting his thumbs?
    a. 6
    b. 8

    c. 10

    d. 12 – He had an extra hand on the floor.

33. Did Mr. Potato Head have sideburns?

    Yes / No

34. Did Mr. Potato Head have a mustache?

    Yes / No

35. There were buttons somewhere on Mr. Potato Head's clothes. Where were they?

    a. On his cuffs

    b. Around the rim of his hat

    c. On his spats (the white covers on his shoes)

    d. On his shirt front. Wait a minute, that potato had no shirt!

36. There was a power button on his display. What did it say?

    a. "Start"

    b. "Push Here"

    c. "Try Me"

    d. Sometimes you can really push my buttons; get it, my buttons?

37. What was in Mr. Potato Head's hand the whole time?

    a. A cane

    b. An extra part

    c. A microphone

    d. Nothing

38. Mr. Potato Head had some spare parts just lying around on the stage. What parts did he have to spare? Check all that are correct.

    a. Ear

    b. Eyes

    c. Nose

    d. Hand

39. What color were Mr. Potato Head's sleeves?

    a. Red-and-white striped

    b. Green-and-white striped

    c. White

    d. I already told you, that potato wasn't wearing a shirt.

40. What was Mr. Potato Head's title as it was printed on his stage?
  a. Andy's Favorite
  b. The only talking potato you are ever likely to see
  c. World's Best Toy
  d. Boardwalk Barker
End of Mr. Potato Head Memory

Final Room
  Are you ready for some new challenges?

FP **41. Treasure Hunt Time!** If you have a few more moments before your ride, Andy's mom would appreciate your help in finding a few last things that Andy has misplaced.
  ❑ Toy Story Midway Play Set proof-of-purchase bar code
  ❑ A dog
  ❑ A sharp pencil
  ❑ A yellow arrow
  ❑ A ball being fired
  ❑ A night light
  ❑ Woody the Cowboy and Jessie the Cowgirl
  ❑ A wagon wheel
  ❑ A group of ants
  ❑ Five alphabet blocks
  ❑ Twister (the game)
  ❑ Mouse Trap
  ❑ Babes in Toyland
  ❑ A domino
  ❑ Operation

Pixar Place Answers

Toy Story Midway Mania!
Outside the Building
  1) a. Scrabble letters, b. Alphabet blocks, d. Chess pieces, f. Tinkertoys, g. Dominos, i. Building blocks, j. Pencil, l. Yoyo
  2) c. They are the numbers on the Scrabble pieces of the Midway Mania sign.
  3) g. Both a and c
  4) a. A rocket ship

5) b. It is holding up a menu.
6) d. A jump-rope
7) Total Childhood Treasures found _____

Inside the Building

8) a. A night light
9) c. Flowers
10) d. Buzz Lightyear Attack on Zorg
11) e. Both a and b
12) e. All of the above
13) b. A little wooden airplane
14) Total Andy's Room Treasures found _____

Mr. Potato Head Memory (Answers 15 to 40)

15) d. He pulled his ear out.
16) a. It is time to play.
17) b. He is talking about the fact that you don't want to raise your hand anymore.
18) a. He pulls off his ear.
19) c. He asks you to give him a "D" three times and then asks what you've got.
20) c. He is a hot potato.
21) b. This is the part where you clap.
22) c. Pop songs
23) a. She has three noses already.
24) d. A grape
25) b. A barrel of monkeys
26) a. That he is their favorite toy
27) c. Hockey puck
28) d. "We are eternally grateful."
29) b. He is a potato and he makes comments.
30) c. A straw hat
31) b. Yes, black and shiny
32) a. 6
33) No
34) Yes
35) a. On his cuffs
36) c. "Try Me"
37) c. A microphone
38) b. Eyes, c. Nose
39) a. Red-and-white striped
40) d. Boardwalk Barker

Inside the Building

41) Total Andy Treasures found _____

Animation Courtyard

Disney Junior— Live on Stage!

1. Mickey Mouse has sprinkled lots of colors around for you to enjoy. See how many of these colors you can find on the buildings around you and on the other people waiting in line.

- ❑ Red
- ❑ Yellow
- ❑ Orange
- ❑ Pink
- ❑ Silver
- ❑ White
- ❑ Blue
- ❑ Green
- ❑ Purple
- ❑ Gold
- ❑ Black

2. Look at the kids waiting in line with you. Can you spot any who are jumping? 1 point for each jumper.

3. Take another look at them. Are any of them dancing? 1 point for each dancing guest you see.

4. Are any of the kids around you are singing? 1 point for each singer you find.

5. Bonus Points just for Kids Under 6:
- (a) Earn 3 points for bouncing like a ball.
- (b) Earn 5 extra points if you sing a song.
- (c) Earn 5 more points for your very best dance. If another kid dances with you, you get 2 additional points!

6. Mickey Mouse can be seen in several places around you. Get 1 point for each Mickey you find.

Voyage of The Little Mermaid

As you got in line, you passed under a large sign for the show. Ariel and several other characters from *The Little Mermaid* were there greeting you.

1. Which of these characters was not on the welcoming committee?
   a. Flounder the fish swam away.
   b. Sebastian the crab was too crabby to attend.
   c. King Triton was too busy with his royal duties to wish you hello.
   d. They were all there. The inhabitants of the sea are a very welcoming bunch.

Welcome to fish school. Let's test out your brain coral. Look at the framed art from *The Little Mermaid*. Give yourself as long as you like to gaze at the multiple pictures in each frame. Then turn away and check your memory before moving on to the next frame.

Frame 1

2. Sebastian the crab has a close-up in one of the pictures. What is he doing in that picture?
   a. Looking very frightened of an angry King Triton
   b. Chasing a runaway mermaid
   c. Singing into his version of a microphone
   d. Riding in a chariot
   e. Sebastian was not in any of these pictures.

3. There were six pictures in this frame. How many of them contained Ariel herself?
   a. Three
   b. Four
   c. Five
   d. All six of course; she is the star of the show.

4. In one picture, lots of fish have gathered in a ring around a rock. They are all looking at the rock. What do they see?
    a. Sebastian the crab
    b. Ariel
    c. King Triton
    d. Just a bare rock. You never know what will entertain fish.

5. In one of the pictures, Ariel is wearing a pink dress.
    True or False?

Frame 2

6. In one of the pictures, Ariel is messing with her hair. What is she using to fix her hair?
    a. A fork
    b. Her hands
    c. A brush
    d. A crab, she was hoping to get it cut.

7. How does Ariel show her father affection?
    a. She kisses him.
    b. She hugs him.
    c. She puts a sea flower in his hair.
    d. She does what she is told. Just kidding, she would never do that.

8. Ariel is being told off by someone. Who is giving her a piece of their mind?
    a. King Triton
    b. Sebastian the crab
    c. Her sisters
    d. Ursula the sea witch
    e. No fights here. It's always better down where it's wetter, take it from me.

9. There was a picture of Ariel in her wedding gown.
    True or False?

Frame 3

10. Scuttle the seagull is offering his expert opinion on human treasures for Ariel's benefit. What human artifacts are the topics of his wisdom?
    a. A book
    b. A fork
    c. A pipe
    d. Both b and c
    e. All three; seagulls have a lot to say.
    f. No one should ever listen to a seagull.

11. Sebastian the crab is hanging out with three new buddies. Who are they?
    a. Sea anemones
    b. Sea snails
    c. Blow fish
    d. Flamingos

12. Ariel is showing something new and exciting to Scuttle. What is she showing him?
    a. Her new clam shells
    b. Her new friend
    c. A music box with dancers
    d. Her new human legs

13. Ariel is reading a book to Scuttle.
    True or False?

Frame 4

14. What does Ursula the sea witch wear around her neck?
    a. Seaweed
    b. A shell
    c. A bottle with something muddy-looking inside it on a chain.
    d. Nothing, beautifying herself is not her priority.

15. In one picture, Ursula is accompanied by a pet. What kind of pet does she keep?
    a. An eel
    b. A snake
    c. A shark
    d. A cute little seahorse; hey, she is a complex character.

16. Ariel is looking very hard at something. What is she examining?

    a. A cauldron   b. Sebastian the crab

    c. A contract   d. Ariel never looks hard at anything.

17. In one of the pictures, Ariel has on a dress and also has a tail.

    True or False?

Frame 5

18. Someone is doing a little dance. Who feels like dancing?

    a. Ariel and Prince Eric

    b. Ariel and Flounder the fish

    c. The chef is light on his feet.

    d. Sebastian the crab is a crab of many talents.

19. There were three open clamshells. What was inside?

    a. Mermaids

    b. Human treasure

    c. "Instrument-playing" fish

    d. Pearls, of course

20. The human world appears to be having a shipboard celebration. How are they celebrating?

    a. With dancing   b. With fireworks

    c. With a feast   d. All of the above

21. Ariel appears to have made friends with a group of rather unusual looking seahorses. What is out of the ordinary about these seahorses?

    a. They have horses' heads on seahorse bodies.

    b. They have big heads with lots of pink hair.

    c. They are wearing tiny reins.

    d. Together they are playing a big harmonica for her.

Frame 6

22. Together Ariel and Prince Eric seem to be very busy in this set of pictures. Which of the following activities is not on their list of romantic to-dos?

    a. Dancing on a garden terrace

    b. Canoeing on a private lagoon

c. Getting married

d. They did all that. They are an active couple.

e. They didn't do any of that stuff, those couch potatoes.

23. What animals were featured in these pictures?
  a. A crab   b. A dog
  c. A crane   d. A fish
  e. Both a and b   f. All but d

24. How many different outfits was Princess Ariel wearing in these pictures?
  a. 1
  b. 2
  c. 3
  d. 4, at least, or maybe 5. She is a princess after all.

25. Princess Ariel and Prince Eric ride off into the sunset in a horse-drawn carriage.
  True or False?

You have finished the framed art quizzes. If you are still outside, it is time to play "There's Something Fishy Around Here." If you are going inside now, skip to the Treasure Hunt.

26. "There's Something Fishy Around Here"
Look around. You will see a number of large happy-looking fish nearby. You will also find many happy-looking guests. Pick the fish closest to you and have a good look. Then find a guest who is dressed in clothing that is reminiscent of the designs or color (or both) of your chosen fish. See who can find the fishiest "twins" in the audience. Remember not to point; neither fish nor people like to be pointed at. Get 1 point for each twin you find.

Inside Queue

27. Treasure Hunt Time! Look around you. There are many human treasures Princess Ariel would love to get her flippers on. See how many you can discover before they are all washed away.
  ❑ A windmill
  ❑ A bottle in the shape of a fish
  ❑ A pair of rubber boots

- ❑ Something belonging to Geppetto
- ❑ A red lantern
- ❑ A gasoline can
- ❑ Something useful when hunting mermaids
- ❑ A peg leg belonging to a famous seagoer
- ❑ Something Sebastian the crab should keep well away from
- ❑ Something important to "The Old Man and the Sea"
- ❑ The first electric ship light
- ❑ A shark
- ❑ A hook hand
- ❑ Two lengths of rope
- ❑ An antique "paint by number"
- ❑ A sea star
- ❑ Two gold chalices
- ❑ A pair of green glass bottles
- ❑ A trident
- ❑ Brain coral
- ❑ A "before" shot
- ❑ A convenience for peg legs
- ❑ Hemingway's recreation gear
- ❑ A walrus
- ❑ Something used by Tom Thumb
- ❑ A rusty hook
- ❑ A squid beater
- ❑ A ship's wheel
- ❑ A diving suit
- ❑ A basket
- ❑ A mer-monkey

Animation Courtyard Answers

Disney Junior—Live on Stage!
1. *Number of colors found* _____
2. *Number of jumpers found* _____
3. *Number of dancers found* _____
4. *Number of singers found* _____
5. *Number of bonus points earned* _____
6. *Number of Mickeys found* _____

Voyage of The Little Mermaid
    1) d. They were all there.
Frame 1
    2) c. Singing into his version of a microphone
    3) b. 4
    4) a. Sebastian the crab
    5) True
Frame 2
    6) b. Her hands
    7) c. She puts a sea flower in his hair.
    8) a. King Triton
    9) False
Frame 3
    10) d. Both b and c
    11) b. Sea snails
    12) d. Her new human legs
    13) False
Frame 4
    14) b. A shell
    15) a. An eel
    16) c. A contract
    17) True
Frame 5
    18) c. The chef is light on his feet.
    19) a. Mermaids
    20) b. With fireworks
    21) b. They have big heads with lots of pink hair.
Frame 6
    22) d. They did all that.
    23) f. All but d
    24) c. 3
    25) False
"There's Something Fishy Around Here"
    26) Number of fishy "twins" found_____
Inside Queue
    27) Total Human Treasures found _____

Sunset Boulevard

Beauty and the Beast —Live on Stage!

If you are waiting outside, you can use your time to rack up some more points.

1. What is the closest street corner?
    a. Hollywood and Vine
    b. Mickey Ct. and Donald Dr.
    c. Sunset Strip and Hollywood Blvd.
    d. Highland Ave. and Sunset Blvd.

2. Can you find a boat that sails in all directions but never leaves its spot?
    a. Yes
    b. No, there is no water here, so a boat couldn't sail anywhere.

3. Treasure Hunt Time! See how many of these beautiful treasures you can find before you get beastly bored.
    ❑ A sweet smell under glass
    ❑ A feather duster
    ❑ Spent wishes
    ❑ A flame
    ❑ A chance to scream
    ❑ A glove with a star on it
    ❑ A windmill
    ❑ Sky high mouse ears
    ❑ A chip
    ❑ A trolley
    ❑ A marquee
    ❑ A mustache that is more than a facial ornament
    ❑ A big tooth
    ❑ A circle that isn't round

4. Can you find some evidence of hands that are where people's feet should go?
  a. Yes, people around here seem to walk on their hands, strange really.
  b. No, all the hands seem to be where they belong.

5. There are a lot of numbers around here. Check below your feet and see if you can spot these numbers:
  0 1 2 3 4 5 6 7 8 9

6. Treasure Hunt Time! There is a sidewalk area full of handprints. If there are not too many people standing on it, hunt the sidewalk for these treasures.
  ❑ A flower
  ❑ A pair of glasses
  ❑ A heart
  ❑ Someone who seems to have three hands of varying sizes
  ❑ A question
  ❑ A very fancy "Y"
  ❑ Two sets of prints in the same square
  ❑ A very light set of handprints
  ❑ A corner that broke
  ❑ Footprints
  ❑ An upside-down hand
  ❑ A directional designation

Fantasmic!

The bad news is that the wait for Fantasmic! is normally quite lengthy. The good news is that the show is worth the wait. I suggest that in addition to enjoying the activities here in the book, you spend the time enjoying a picnic dinner.

? **POP QUIZ!** There is a large billboard for Fantasmic! Have a quick look at it and then see how many of these questions you can answer.

1. Mickey was doing battle with a dragon. Very daring of him. The Dragon was green with a purple belly.
  True or False?

2. The dragon had her tongue hanging out of her mouth. Very sloppy.
    True or False?

3. Mickey was wearing a hat. It had stars and a moon on it.
    True or False?

4. The dragon was wearing a hat with fire on it. Dragons can be fashionable.
    True or False?

5. Mickey's ensemble included a belt.
    True or False?

6. The ground was crumbling beneath the dragon's feet.
    True or False?

7. There were stars in the sky.
    True or False?

8. There was a full moon.
    True or False?

9. The dragon had five claws on each foot.
    True or False?

10. The dragon's nostrils were glowing. I do not want to be there when she blows her nose.
    True or False?

11. Mickey was using a magic wand.
    True or False?

12. Mickey had a sword in his belt.
    True or False?

13. Mickey's robe was too long for him. It was trailing behind him. Now that's bound to be a hazard if he needs to run, which seems likely.
    True or False?

14. Mickey had a bow on his outfit.
    True or False?

15. Lightning appears to be coming out of Mickey's fingers.
    True or False?

16. There was smoke in the picture.
    True or False?

17. The dragon had spikes on her tail.
    True or False?

18. The dragon had horns.
    True or False?

19. The dragon's wings had sharp spikes of their own. I am not going to mess with her.
    True or False?

20. Mickey had pointy-toed shoes.
    True or False?

End of Pop Quiz

21. Treasure Hunt Time! See how many of these treasures you can find before the dragon gets a bit peckish and eats them all up.
    ❑ Searchlights
    ❑ Wood
    ❑ A very skinny window
    ❑ A traffic light
    ❑ A moon
    ❑ An Asian rooftop
    ❑ Two chimneys
    ❑ Something defying the laws of gravity
    ❑ A stone arch
    ❑ Four white wooden X's
    ❑ The perfect accessory for someone whose head is
       a bit too big

22. "Toons vs. Dragons" Game
    In Fantasmic!, Mickey, a "toon," does battle with a powerful dragon. While you wait to see their battle, it's time to play "Toons vs. Dragons." To play you must choose to be a "Toon" like Mickey or a "Dragon." (Hey, dragons are not all bad!). If multiple people want to play, split into teams. Your goal is to build up your forces by spotting the toons or dragons hiding among you.
    The game is divided into rounds. In each round, each side looks for a person wearing its colors (orange

for the Toons, green for the Dragons) who also fits the description in the list below, beginning with "A person wearing Mickey Mouse ears." The first team to spot a person fitting the description who is also wearing that team's color wins the round. Then play moves to the next entry on the list.

For example, in the first round, if the Toon side first finds a person with Mickey Mouse ears who is wearing something orange, that round goes to the Toons. If the subject is wearing both colors, they are confused, and the first player or team to spot them may claim them.

The side with the largest force at the end of the battle wins.

- A person wearing Mickey Mouse ears
  - ❑ Toons (orange)   ❑ Dragons (green)
- A person wearing a hat
  - ❑ Toons (orange)   ❑ Dragons (green)
- A person with a purse
  - ❑ Toons (orange)   ❑ Dragons (green)
- A person eating a turkey leg
  - ❑ Toons (orange)   ❑ Dragons (green)
- A person with a backpack
  - ❑ Toons (orange)   ❑ Dragons (green)
- A person carrying a bag from a gift shop
  - ❑ Toons (orange)   ❑ Dragons (green)
- A person carrying a stuffed animal
  - ❑ Toons (orange)   ❑ Dragons (green)
- A person wearing a Disney character
  - ❑ Toons (orange)   ❑ Dragons (green)
- A person with a single ponytail
  - ❑ Toons (orange)   ❑ Dragons (green)
- A person with two ponytails
  - ❑ Toons (orange)   ❑ Dragons (green)
- A person with braids
  - ❑ Toons (orange)   ❑ Dragons (green)
- A person eating a hot dog
  - ❑ Toons (orange)   ❑ Dragons (green)
- A person carrying a child
  - ❑ Toons (orange)   ❑ Dragons (green)
- A person drinking something
  - ❑ Toons (orange)   ❑ Dragons (green)
- A person in a dress or a skirt
  - ❑ Toons (orange)   ❑ Dragons (green)
- A person with a jacket
  - ❑ Toons (orange)   ❑ Dragons (green)

- A person wearing stripes
  - ❑ Toons (orange)   ❑ Dragons (green)
- A person with a beard
  - ❑ Toons (orange)   ❑ Dragons (green)
- People holding hands
  - ❑ Toons (orange)   ❑ Dragons (green)
- A person eating ice cream
  - ❑ Toons (orange)   ❑ Dragons (green)
- A baby
  - ❑ Toons (orange)   ❑ Dragons (green)

Inside the Theater

23. Collection Time! It is time to build a Character Collection. Below is a list of Disney characters who are pictured in this theater. Try to find them all.

❑ Beast   ❑ Mickey
❑ Jafar   ❑ Pocahontas
❑ Maleficent   ❑ Sebastian
❑ Scar   ❑ Ursula
❑ Witch   ❑ Hades

? POP QUIZ! OK, now that you have found them, let's see what you remember? Circle the correct character.

24. What character's hands are in the air like he or she doesn't care?
  a. Hades
  b. Ursula
  c. Mickey
  d. Sebastian. Hey, wait a minute; crabs don't have hands. Well, claws then.

25. What character could be said to be "kind of fruity" today?
  a. The Witch   b. Pocahontas
  c. Scar   d. Beast

26. Who had on a lot of blue eye shadow?
  a. The Witch
  b. Ursula
  c. Jafar
  d. Maleficent

27. Whose collar stuck up past their ears – a real fashion no no?
    a. Jafar
    b. Maleficent
    c. Hades
    d. Scar. Wait, that's a mane not a collar.

28. Who was wearing a feather?
    a. Jafar
    b. Beast
    c. Pocahontas
    d. Mickey

29. How many characters were wearing clothing on their heads?
    a. 0 (Hats are so yesterday.)
    b. 2
    c. 3
    d. 4

30. Who had blue hair?
    a. Hades
    b. Ursula
    c. Maleficent
    d. Beast

31. Who was wearing jewelry?
    a. Pocahontas
    b. Ursula
    c. Maleficent
    d. All of the above
    e. Only a and b

32. Who was wearing a necklace with a charm?
    a. The Witch
    b. Maleficent
    c. Ursula
    d. Pocahontas

End of Pop Quiz

33. Collection Time! If you are still waiting, and it is not too dark yet, this would be a great time to work on your Collections.

Rock 'n' Roller Coaster® Starring Aerosmith

? **POP QUIZ!** Before you get into line, have a quick look outside at the large guitar and rather unusual car. After you give yourself one minute with each of these beauties, head in to the queue. Your first game will test your memory to see if it's rockin' or has just rolled away.

FP **1. You saw a very large guitar just before you entered this line. It had three knobs. What were those knobs?**
   a. Fast. Faster Brakes. Where are the brakes?
   b. Volume. Tone. Tone.
   c. Forward. Backward. Upside-down. (You did know you will be upside-down, didn't you?)
   d. Loud. Earsplitting. Aerosmith.

FP **2. Was the guitar the only giant instrument in this display?**
   a. Yes.
   b. No, there was also a giant drum set.
   c. No, there was also a giant keyboard.
   d. No, there was also a giant tambourine.
   e. You know, you would think I would have noticed a giant guitar but …

FP **3. What was unusual about the guitar's pick?**
   a. It said "Hanes" on it.
   b. It said "Aerosmith – a moving experience"
   c. It was a hologram.
   d. There was no guitar pick. With a guitar that big you might really want one, just saying.

FP **4. Did the guitar have the normal six strings?**
   Yes / No

FP **5. Not including black and white, the guitar's paint job was red and one other color. What was the other color?**
   a. Sky blue   b. Orange
   c. Gold   d. Red was the only color. You're trying to trick me.

FP 6. Was there a broken string on this guitar?

    Yes / No

FP 7. Were there numbers on the guitar?

    Yes / No

FP 8. There was something on this guitar's neck that is not found on your average guitar. What was it?

    a. A musical note

    b. A car

    c. A picture of Mickey Mouse

    d. This guitar is neckless … soooooo not average.

FP 9. Now it is time to turn your memory upside-down. That's right, we are going to talk about the car. What color was it?

    a. Sky blue   b. Star silver

    c. Midnight black   d. Candy apple red

FP 10. What decorations were on the car's body?

    a. Racing stripes, naturally

    b. Lightning bolts

    c. Wings with a star in the center

    d. None

FP 11. What did the car's back license plate say?

    a. Road Runner

    b. Aerosmith

    c. Rock 'n' Roller Coaster

    d. Nothing, it was blank.

FP 12. What did the license plate on the front say?

    a. Rock 'n' Roller Coaster

    b. Road Runner

    c. Aerosmith

    d. Nothing, isn't that illegal? Or are the rules different when your car can drive upside-down?

FP 13. How many taillights were present?

    a. 2   b. 4

    c. 6   d. 8

FP 14. The car's make was on it. What was it?

    a. Cadillac   b. Rock 'n' Roller Coaster

    c. Mustang   d. DeLorean, perfect for an upside-down car, don't you think?

FP 15. **What was inside the car for making music?**
    a. A radio   b. An iPod
    c. A CD player   d. A guitar

FP 16. **How many headlights did the car have?**
    a. 1   b. 2
    c. 3   d. 4

FP 17. **Was there was a picture painted on the hood of the car?**
    Yes / No

FP 18. **Was the car a four-door?**
    Yes / No

FP 19. **Did the car have a back seat?**
    Yes / No

FP 20. **Did the car have whitewall tires?**
    Yes / No

FP 21. **What was the car parked on?**
    a. A wall
    b. The underside of a sign
    c. Part of the guitar
    d. A parking lot, I hope

FP 22. **What was the name of the company that made the giant guitar?**
    a. Ibanez
    b. Taylor
    c. Stretch
    d. Fender

FP 23. **What was the road made of?**
    a. Normal asphalt, just very high
    b. Guitar strings; that guitar was all strung out.
    c. Sheet music
    d. There was no road; the car was upside-down in the air. Didn't you see?

FP 24. **Was the car approaching or leaving the Rock 'n' Roller Coaster?**
    a. Approaching
    b. Leaving
    c. I think it was just hanging around.

End of Pop Quiz

25. You are now entering the record company's building. The door going in is decorated in what way?
    a. It has a guitar on it.
    b. It has a wavy keyboard on it.
    c. It has musical notes on it.
    d. All of the above
    e. Only a and c

26. What does the symbol for this recording company look like?
    a. Like a circle with a pie piece tipping out of it
    b. Like a CD with wings
    c. Like a red guitar of course
    d. Like a collection of three overlapping circles
        with notes spinning off of them

27. What is the name of the record company?
    a. Sound Waves Music
    b. One Mouse Records
    c. Blue "Car Tunes"
    d. G-Force Records

Poster Room

28. "If I Were a Rock Star"
    You have entered a room filled with posters of musical performers. It's time to play "If I Were a Rock Star."

    To play everyone in your group must look around at the posters and decide which one looks most like they would if they could be a rock star. Shhhh! Keep this information to yourself; you never know when the paparazzi may be around.

    Then one at a time, starting with the youngest, each member of the group asks the others "Which rock star am I?" The others each tell who they think you are and why. (It could be because of looks, or because they think that's the kind of costume you would wear, or it could even be because of the instrument you play or might play.)

    The person who asked, "Which rock star am I?" earns 1 point each time someone picks the star they secretly chose to represent themselves. Each person in the group takes a turn. (Yes, Mom and Dad can be rockers, too.)

29. If you are still in the poster room, then it is time to play "Alphabet Rock Soup." Try to find each letter of the alphabet on one of the posters. Cross off the letters you locate.

A B C D E F G H I J K L M
N O P Q R S T U V W X Y Z

30. By the way, do you notice anything special about the pillars in the poster room?
    a. They are made from a guitar part.
    b. They are constructed from gold records stacked one on top of another.
    c. They are made entirely of mosaic triangles.
    d. They have musical notation on them.

31. What is on the ceiling?
    a. An upside-down car. Hey, I thought that thing was parked outside.
    b. Something dangling with an intricate mobile made from CDs
    c. A gold record
    d. Popcorn. How out of date is that?

Recording Studio Equipment Room

32. What is 7 3 3 3?
    a. The model number for the disk cutter
    b. The setting on the mix console
    c. The street number of the G-Force studio
    d. The lucky numbers of the Aerosmith band members. I wonder which band member didn't choose three?

33. What led some artists to claim that G-Force engineers were "not playing with a full deck"?
    a. Their tendency to wear mouse ears during recording sessions
    b. They often forgot to turn on the microphones during recording sessions.
    c. The strange fact that they insisted on playing cards after recording sessions but refused to use the queen of hearts.
    d. They often ran out of tape in the middle of a session.

34. What sometimes caused a "Tube Bad" to occur?
- a. The cancellation of a scheduled broadcast of an artist over the Tube
- b. The explosion of tube number 6 during recording
- c. The artists arrived before the vacuum tubes had an hour to warm up.
- d. I don't know, but I think this joke may be Tube bad.

35. Treasure Hunt Time! See how many of these musical treasures you can find before it is time to jam.
- ❑ Something used for cutting
- ❑ A knot in some wood
- ❑ The legendary "G-Force One"
- ❑ Sub B
- ❑ Two tape reels
- ❑ Headphones
- ❑ A red switch
- ❑ A blue button
- ❑ A ring of light
- ❑ The symbol for "General Electric"
- ❑ Proof that "Les" was more
- ❑ Six microphones
- ❑ A green marble

FP T-Shirt Room

36. Check out the shirt for a dance concert presented in the San Francisco style. It features a flying bird. Who is to be admitted free to this dance concert?
- a. Ladies
- b. Children under 3
- c. Seagulls
- d. Everyone, it's a free concert.
- e. Nothing is free.

37. What are the Go-Gos doing on their T-shirt?
- a. Painting their nails
- b. Having a facial treatment
- c. I don't know exactly, but I think it's time to get dressed.
- d. All of the above

38. Who has maximum R and B?
   a. That's right, "Who" does have maximum R and B.
   b. The Steve Miller Band
   c. Rod Stewart
   d. No one yet, I'm still waiting.

39. MC5 shirt features a very unusual animal. What is this animal able to do?
   a. Fly
   b. Breath fire
   c. Shoot lightning from its flanks
   d. All of the above
   e. All but b; a lion breathing fire, now that's just silly

40. What is Rod Stewart doing?
   a. Playing a guitar in the bathtub
   b. Looking wistfully from a car window
   c. Napping
   d. Riding a motorcycle

41. A member of MC5 seems to be very fond of something. What is it?
   a. A girl
   b. A car
   c. A French horn
   d. His teddy bear
   e. All of the above
   f. All but d; he gave up his bear.

42. In the poster for the Velvet Underground, what body part is not attached to a person?
   a. An eye with a brow and everything
   b. A hand
   c. A mouth
   d. Both a and b
   e. None of the above

43. Who is doing a squatting dance move on their T-shirt?
   a. Janet Jackson
   b. Michael Jackson
   c. The Jackson 5
   d. I am getting the feeling it is a Jackson.

44. Which of these animals is not making an appearance at the Invisible Circus?
    a. A bird
    b. A tiger
    c. A wolf
    d. A dragon
    e. They are all there.
    f. Now how would I know if they are invisible?

45. Treasure Hunt Time! It's time for a micro hunt that is limited to a single T-shirt. Have a look at the Ziggy Marley Melody Makers Shirt. Try to find each of these 100% cotton treasures before your time here shrinks to nothing.
    ❑ A yellow striped mask
    ❑ An "i" that is an eye for two reasons
    ❑ A sun
    ❑ A lion with a scepter
    ❑ A hooved animal
    ❑ A crown
    ❑ A hand holding something that glows
    ❑ XL

46. What is pictured on the Big Brother & the Holding Co. T-shirt?
    a. A gargoyle
    b. A tower
    c. A guy with a top hat
    d. All of the above
    e. All but c

47. What famous treasure has donned a pair of sunglasses?
    a. The Mona Lisa
    b. President Lincoln on Mount Rushmore
    c. The sphinx
    d. Mickey Mouse. It's his rock star look.

48. How much would you expect to pay in admission if you were to attend the Cosmic Car Show?
    a. $1.00
    b. $10.00
    c. $13.50
    d. Free, baby, free!

FP Alleyway

49. Treasure Hunt Time! You've almost reached your concert coaster. See how many of these alley treasures you can find before you step into your limo.
- ❏ A club
- ❏ An arrow
- ❏ An orange cone
- ❏ A door covered in posters
- ❏ A key pad
- ❏ A chain-link fence
- ❏ A round mirror
- ❏ A stuffed dog
- ❏ A traffic advisory
- ❏ A blue guitar
- ❏ A peace symbol
- ❏ A copy of *Billboard* magazine
- ❏ Something that is free
- ❏ A ladder
- ❏ A bike
- ❏ A picture of a pet wearing a Santa hat
- ❏ Hours of operation
- ❏ Key # 12

The Twilight Zone Tower of Terror™

FP **1. What is the name of the hotel you are about to check into?**
- a. The Tower of Terror
- b. The Hollywood Tower Hotel
- c. The Hollywood Tower of Terror Hotel
- d. The Hotel at the End of the Universe

2. What year was the hotel established?
- a. 1899
- b. 1908
- c. 1917
- d. 1923

3. There is a rather ominous warning sign posted on the gates. What does it tell would-be hotel guests?

    a. Danger high voltage! The sign gives off sparks.

    b. Private property, no admittance!

    c. No vacancy!

    d. Keep out! (The rest of the sign's message has vanished, but I get the feeling I am unwanted.)

    e. Beware of dogs!

4. The wait-time sign for this ride is unique. What's unusual about it?

    a. It is shaped like a sundial.

    b. It appears to have been hit by lightning.

    c. Both a and b are true. There were two different signs, though only one still tells time.

    d. There is no need for a sign here; we are entering the Twilight Zone.

5. The sign contains some Roman numerals. Which of these numbers is not designated on the sign?

    a. 3

    b. 5

    c. 8

    d. They arc all there.

    e. The Romans were confused. I don't see any numbers, but there sure are a lot of initials.

6. The Hollywood Tower Hotel has several signs listing some impressive amenities. Check off all of the benefits a guest could expect to enjoy during her stay.

a. Bowling Green	b. Rose Garden
c. Gentleman's Club	d. Library
e. Pool	f. Tennis Courts
g. Beauty Salon	h. "Band Pavillion"
i. Movie Theater	j. Grand Terrace
k. Dog Park	l. Natatorium
m. Arboretum	n. Gymnasium
o. Stables	p. Foyer

7. What is Olea Europaea?

    a. An olive plant

    b. A spa treatment provided in the salon to the rich and famous

    c. The hotel restaurant's dinner special

    d. If Olea Europaea is not an opera singer, then I am stumped.

8. This garden is very fancy. Look for a statue of a lady. She is holding something. What is it?
- a. A small dog. She'd better hide him, I'm not sure this hotel accepts pets.
- b. A pitcher of overflowing water
- c. A lute
- d. Wheat

9. Treasure Hunt Time! Try to find these garden treasures quickly before you check in.
- ❑ A bird of paradise
- ❑ The initials HTH. There are many. You get 1 point for each set you find.
- ❑ Four long chains meeting at a single point
- ❑ A date
- ❑ A heart that blocks light (this one is hard)
- ❑ A metal leaf
- ❑ A very large crack
- ❑ A spiral column
- ❑ A stone bowl of fruit

Inside the Lobby

FP **POP QUIZ!** You have entered the hotel lobby. As there are a lot of guests waiting to check in, you may as well have a look around. On your left when you come inside, you will notice a table that appears to have been used by hotel guests a very long time ago. On your right, is the concierge desk. Have a quick look at these, then turn away and start your quiz.

10. What was the guest table being used for?
- a. The table was being used for a wine tasting.
- b. Playing a friendly game of mahjong
- c. A tarot card reading. The death card was up, now that can't be a good sign.
- d. All of those things were happening.

11. There was a vase of dead flowers on the table.
True or False?

12. A cart stood ready to deliver tea.
True or False?

13. There was a menu available.
True or False?

14. There was a plate of small sandwiches and tea cookies.
    True or False?

15. There was a newspaper on the cart.
    True or False?

16. Someone left her sweater over the back of a chair.
    True or False?

17. It appears that someone was seeking help from the concierge. Which of these things can we guess based on the evidence left behind? Check all that apply.
    a. The guest's initials were R.T.
    b. The guest was in a hurry.
    c. The guest used a cane.
    d. The guest was a man.
    e. The concierge wore glasses.
    f. All these things are true.
    g. All are true except b.

End of Pop Quiz

18. There is a sizable empty vase standing on the floor near a fire alarm. What is pictured on it?
    a. Dogs
    b. A mountain
    c. Someone playing an instrument
    d. People riding horses
    e. All of the above
    f. All but c

FP 19. It appears to have been some time since Maid Service and Maintenance have attended to the lobby. What indicators suggest that management needs to hire new help?
    a. Cobwebs
    b. Dead plants
    c. Dust
    d. Cracked and crumbled walls
    e. All of the above
    f. All but d

20. Treasure Hunt Time! Look around the lobby and see how many of these dusty treasures you can find before they disappear into the Twilight Zone.

- ❏ An Asian planter
- ❏ The number 308
- ❏ Two tassels
- ❏ A wine bottle
- ❏ A bell
- ❏ A dusty bird of the night
- ❏ Three pieces of stemware
- ❏ An animal with a ring in its mouth
- ❏ A battle
- ❏ A long tongue being put to good use
- ❏ An orchestra
- ❏ A tapestry
- ❏ Something out of order
- ❏ Six pieces of luggage

21. One of the previous guests was keeping up with the news. What room was he staying in?
- a. Room 409
- b. Room 809
- c. Room 1313; he really should have seen it coming
- d. Whatever room he was in, I'm pretty sure it's vacant now.

22. You have come to a directory. Where would you go if you wanted to visit the Sunset Room?
- a. Lower Level
- b. The Top of the Tower
- c. Penthouse
- d. Lobby Level

FP **23. Time to head to the library. If you go to the left you will see a lovely display of gifts that you might buy in the hotel gift shop. What do they offer?**
- a. Three ornate glass bottles, three handbags, a necklace, and a compact.
- b. Three handbags, a bracelet, a letter opener, and a statue
- c. A statue, a necklace, three glass bottles, and a key chain
- d. A stuffed Mickey Mouse and a Hollywood Tower bathrobe.

FP 24. If you turn to the right, there is a bust on a table. Look at the bust while counting to ten then turn around. How observant were you? Mark everything that is true about the bust.

    a. He has a beard.

    b. He has a mustache.

    c. He wears a jeweled crown.

    d. His lower face is covered with fabric.

    e. He holds a sword.

    f. You cannot see a hand.

    g. He wears armor.

    h. He wears a medallion.

FP ❓ LIBRARY POP QUIZ!

When you enter the library, direct your attention to the TV screen. You will be shown a brief story of "The Twilight Zone." When it is over, you will undoubtedly be shown to your room to relax. After you depart the library, see how much you remember from the TV clip.

25. What did you need to unlock the door?

    a. The key to fantasy

    b. The key to imagination

    c. The key to fear

    d. The key to your room

26. What was beyond the door?

    a. An imaginary dimension

    b. The fourth dimension

    c. The lost dimension

    d. Another dimension

27. What were the three things you are told about the dimension beyond the door?

    a. It is a dimension of sight, smell, and mind.

    b. It is a dimension of sound, sight, and thought.

    c. It is a dimension of sound, sight, and mind.

    d. It is a dimension of senses, feeling, and thought.

28. Something made of glass was broken. What was it?

    a. A mirror. There's seven years bad luck right there!

    b. A wine glass. I hope it wasn't red wine. It can be murder to get out of the carpet.

    c. A window. Do they have homeowner's insurance in this dimension?

    d. Oh, no an elevator! Do you think that's a
       foreshadowing?

29. Which of these things was not seen in the introduction on the TV screen?

    a. $E=mc^2$
    b. A phone
    c. An eyeball
    d. A clock
    e. They were all seen.

30. What year was it?

    a. 1910
    b. 1926
    c. 1939
    d. 1953

31. Who liked to come to the Hollywood Tower Hotel?

    a. The show business elite
    b. The very rich
    c. Families traveling on a budget
    d. Unknowns hoping to be discovered

32. Who got onto the elevator? Circle all who got aboard.

    a. An older gentleman with a cane
    b. A fabulously dressed couple
    c. A set of twins
    d. A bellhop
    e. A little girl
    f. A little boy
    g. An older woman who might be the nanny
    h. A pet dog

33. Was the child carrying a toy?

    Yes / No

34. What disaster occurred at the Hollywood Tower Hotel on that fateful night?

    a. An earthquake hit
    b. A volcano surfaced just under the elevator shaft.
    c. Lightning struck
    d. All of the above. It was a very bad time to be
       staying at that hotel.

35. When the disaster struck what happened?
    a. The building was covered in lightning.
    b. The guests lit up like a Christmas tree.
    c. The elevator plummeted.
    d. Part of the hotel's facade disappeared.
    e. All of the above

36. What is still in operation waiting for you?
    a. A guest elevator
    b. A service elevator
    c. An escalator
    d. The stairs; I think I could use some exercise.

37. Where does the elevator travel?
    a. To the basement
    b. To the 13th floor
    c. To your room, of course
    d. Directly to the Twilight Zone

End of Library Pop Quiz

FP **Boiler Room**

38. Treasure Hunt Time! Look around the boiler room for these strange, discarded, and just plain dirty items.
    ❑ Wheels
    ❑ At least 15 gauges
    ❑ Coal
    ❑ The way to the laundry
    ❑ Fire
    ❑ Cold water; good to have if there is fire
    ❑ A wrench in a bucket
    ❑ A small, red, corroded door
    ❑ A hammer
    ❑ A cone-shaped fire bucket
    ❑ A wooden ladder
    ❑ An express elevator to the lower lobby
    ❑ A wooden crate
    ❑ A rope
    ❑ A rusted chain on the floor
    ❑ An old radio
    ❑ Work gloves
    ❑ "What happened at 6:30 a.m. on 7/20/39?"
    ❑ An oilcan
    ❑ A toolbox

❏ A sweater
❏ A life philosophy
❏ Two horses
❏ A book

Sunset Boulevard Answers

Beauty and the Beast—Live On Stage!

1) d. Highland Ave. and Sunset Blvd.
2) Yes, a weather vane
3) Total Treasures found _____
4) Yes
5) 2 points for finding all ten numbers, 0 to 9 _____
6) Total Sidewalk Treasures found _____

Fantasmic!

1) False
2) True
3) True
4) False
5) True
6) False
7) True
8) False
9) False
10) True
11) False
12) False
13) True
14) True
15) True
16) True
17) False
18) True
19) True
20) True
21) Total Treasures found _____
22) Highest score:
    Toons ___ Dragons ___
    5 points for the winning team

Inside the Theater

23) Number of characters collected ___

24) c. Mickey
25) a. The Witch
26) b. Ursula
27) b. Maleficent
28) a. Jafar
29) d. 4
30) a. Hades
31) e. Only a and b
32) c. Ursula
33) Number of items collected _____

Rock 'n' Roller Coaster Starring Aerosmith

1) b. Volume. Tone. Tone.
2) c. No, there was also a giant keyboard.
3) a. It said "Hanes" on it.
4) Yes
5) d. Red was the only color.
6) No
7) Yes
8) b. A car
9) a. Sky blue
10) d. None
11) c. Rock 'n' Roller Coaster
12) d. Nothing
13) d. 8
14) b. Rock 'n' Roller Coaster
15) a. A radio
16) d. 4
17) No
18) No
19) No
20) Yes
21) c. Part of the guitar
22) d. Fender
23) b. Guitar strings
24) b. Leaving
25) e. Only a and c
26) a. Like a circle with a pie piece tipping out of it
27) d. G-Force Records

Poster Room

28) Each member of the group earns 1 point each time someone picks the star they chose for themselves.

Person 1 _____   Person 2 _____
Person 3 _____   Person 4 _____

29) Number of letters found_____
30) a. They are made from a guitar part.
31) c. A gold record

Recording Studio Equipment Room

32) b. The setting on the mix console
33) d. They often ran out of tape in the middle of a session.
34) c. The artists arrived before the vacuum tubes had an hour to warm up.
35) Total Musical Treasures found _____

T-Shirt Room

36) c. Seagulls
37) d. All of the above
38) a. That's right, "Who."
39) e. All but b
40) b. Looking wistfully from a car window
41) c. A French horn
42) d. Both a and b
43) a. Janet Jackson
44) c. A wolf
45) Total T-shirt Treasures found _____
46) d. All of the above
47) c. The sphinx
48) a. $1.00

Alleyway

49) Total Alley Treasures found _____

The Twilight Zone Tower of Terror

1) b. The Hollywood Tower Hotel
2) c. 1917
3) d. Keep out!
4) c. Both a and b are true.
5) d. They are all there.
6) a. Bowling Green, b. Rose Garden, e. Pool, f. Tennis Courts, h. "Band Pavillion," j. Grand Terrace, l. Natatorium, m. Arboretum, o. Stables
7) a. An olive plant
8) d. Wheat
9) Total Garden Treasures found _____

Inside the Lobby

10) b. Playing a friendly game of mahjong
11) False
12) True
13) True
14) False

15) *True*

16) *False*

17) *g. All are true except b.*

18) *f. All but c*

19) *e. All of the above*

20) *Total Dusty Treasures found* _____

21) *b. Room 809*

22) *a. Lower Level*

23) *a. Three ornate glass bottles, three handbags, a necklace, and a compact.*

24) *a. He has a beard. b. He has a mustache. e. He holds a sword. g. He wears armor.*

Library Pop Quiz (Answers 25 to 37)

25) *b. The key to imagination*

26) *d. Another dimension*

27) *c. It is a dimension of sound, sight, and mind.*

28) *c. A window*

29) *b. A phone*

30) *c. 1939*

31) *a. The show business elite*

32) *b. A fabulously dressed couple, d. A bellhop, e. A little girl, g. An older woman who might be the nanny*

33) *Yes*

34) *c. Lightning struck*

35) *e. All of the above*

36) *b. A service elevator*

37) *d. Directly to the Twilight Zone*

Boiler Room

38) *Total Treasures found* _____

Disney's Hollywood Studios Scavenger Hunt

- ❏ Mickey with a director's clapboard
- ❏ A pink television
- ❏ An Emmy award
- ❏ The top of Bill Cosby
- ❏ A bird on a pineapple
- ❏ The number of miles to Paris
- ❏ A skunk
- ❏ A gas pump
- ❏ A giant camera
- ❏ Mickey Mouse telling time
- ❏ Hugo "Bark's" job
- ❏ The intersection of Hollywood and Vine
- ❏ A can of succotash
- ❏ A fedora hat
- ❏ Artifact number 53
- ❏ The Toon Patrol
- ❏ A traffic light
- ❏ A yellow submarine
- ❏ A blank horse
- ❏ A pig with chocolate
- ❏ A melted snowman
- ❏ A fire hose
- ❏ A lion who is a little blue
- ❏ The answer to "What does the Mona Lisa love?"
- ❏ A laundry line
- ❏ Dalmatian number 1
- ❏ The public library
- ❏ A subway to nowhere
- ❏ Pixar's little hopping lamp
- ❏ A sunken battleship
- ❏ A flying tiger
- ❏ An unusual scarecrow
- ❏ A place where dinos have walked

Hollywood Studios Scavenger Hunt Tally

Total Treasures found _____

Disney's Animal Kingdom

In this chapter, you'll find games for most of the park's ride queues as well as for shows that tend to have queues. They are organized by lands, in the order you will find them on your Guidemap, and then alphabetically within each land. Attractions that don't have queues are not included.

If you want to continue to play when you are walking around the park from one place to another, turn to the Disney's Animal Kingdom Scavenger Hunt at the end of this chapter. *Tip*: You may want to read over the list now and then stay on the lookout. The treasures on the scavenger hunt list are scattered throughout the park. You get 1 point for every treasure you find.

Note: When you see *FP* next to a question or section, it means you can find the answer (or gather Treasure or Collection items) from both the FASTPASS and standby lines. A **?** in the margin is your signal to look hard at something (often the attraction's sign) before you enter the queue.

Scoring: Unless specified otherwise, give yourself 1 point for each correct answer, 1 point for each Treasure you find, 1 point for each item you add to a Collection, and 1 point for any similar finds you make when you are hunting for something rather than answering questions. Don't forget to add 5 bonus points for each of your Collections with more than 10 items in it at the end of the day. Good luck!

Discovery Island

It's Tough to be a Bug! /
Tree of Life

In the center of a very mysterious island stands the most magical tree ever seen. It is called the Tree of Life. Every inch of this giant tree is covered by bark that forms its own story of life. Well-camouflaged in the bark are over 325 individual animals. These animals make up one enormous "Collection" for you to find – if you have a really sharp eye. Are you ready to go hunting?

Below is an incomplete list of animals spotted on the Tree of Life. It is in alphabetical order. As you hunt, you receive 1 point per animal found; 10 points for discovering the well-hidden rearing elephant. If you spot an animal that is not on the list, you get 5 points for that creature.

Note: You can help the list grow by taking a really excellent picture of the animal you've discovered and submitting it to LotsToDoInLine.com. If we include your find, your name will be added to the Acknowledgements section of the web page and the next edition of this book.

Tip: By far the best place to spot animals is in line for "It's Tough to be a Bug." All the animals you can find in this area are marked with a 🕷.

- ❑ 🕷 Aardvark
- ❑ 🕷 Alligator
- ❑ Ant
- ❑ Anteaters (including a B-pangolin, which looks like an armadillo with scales)
- ❑ Ape, baboon (or circle Baboon)
- ❑ Ape, bonobo, which looks a lot like a chimp (or circle Bonobo)
- ❑ 🕷 Ape, chimpanzee (or circle Chimpanzee)
- ❑ Ape, gorilla (or circle Gorilla)
- ❑ Ape, orangutan (or circle Orangutan)

- ❑ ⊛ Armadillo
- ❑ Baboons (apes, two)
- ❑ Bats (five)
- ❑ Bear(s), general
- ❑ Bear, grizzly catching salmon
- ❑ ⊛ Bear, sun bear
- ❑ Beaver
- ❑ Beetles, battling one another (two)
- ❑ Beetles, horned (both European and Australian *rhinoceros* species)
- ❑ ⊛ Beetles, with spots (two)
- ❑ Bird, cassowary
- ❑ Bird, barn swallow
- ❑ Bird, cockatoo
- ❑ Bird, crane
- ❑ Bird, crow
- ❑ Bird, dove-like
- ❑ Bird, ducks (two on the wing)
- ❑ Bird, eagle or hawk with spread wings
- ❑ Bird, great horned owl (or circle Owl, great horned)
- ❑ Bird, heron
- ❑ Bird, kookaburra
- ❑ ⊛ Bird, sparrow
- ❑ Birds, sparrow-like
- ❑ Bonobo (an ape)
- ❑ Buffalo
- ❑ ⊛ Bug, next to aardvark
- ❑ ⊛ Bugs with pincers
- ❑ Butterfly
- ❑ ⊛ Camel
- ❑ Camel head
- ❑ ⊛ Chameleon
- ❑ Cheetah
- ❑ ⊛ Chimpanzee (an ape)
- ❑ Cobra
- ❑ Crab
- ❑ Crawfish
- ❑ Crocodile
- ❑ Deer, female
- ❑ Dinosaur, Ankylosaurus (a short, armored dino)
- ❑ Dinosaur, Ichthyosaurus
- ❑ ⊛ Dinosaur, Pterodactyl (a flying dino)
- ❑ Dinosaur, Tyrannosaurus rex (or circle Tyrannosaurus rex)

- ❑ Dogs
- ❑ Dolphin
- ❑ Eagle or hawk with spread wings
- ❑ Eel, slender giant moray
- ❑ 🕷 Elephants, African
- ❑ 🕷 Elephants, Indian
- ❑ Elephant, rearing
- ❑ 🕷 Fish
- ❑ Fish head, very large
- ❑ Fish tail
- ❑ 🕷 Fish, anglerfish
- ❑ Fish, largemouth bass
- ❑ Fish, salmon (three)
- ❑ Flamingo
- ❑ Foxes
- ❑ Frog
- ❑ Giraffe head
- ❑ 🕷 Giraffes (including two with necks crossed)
- ❑ 🕷 Gorilla (an ape)
- ❑ Hedgehog
- ❑ Hippopotamus
- ❑ Hornet
- ❑ 🕷 Horses (one bucking)
- ❑ Iguana
- ❑ Japanese spider crab (a large arachnid with long, skinny jointed legs)
- ❑ Jellyfish (more than one)
- ❑ Kangaroo
- ❑ Koala bear
- ❑ Komodo dragon
- ❑ 🕷 Lemur
- ❑ Lion
- ❑ 🕷 Lizard
- ❑ Lobster
- ❑ Manatee mom and baby
- ❑ Meerkat
- ❑ Millipede
- ❑ Monkey, cotton-top tamarin
- ❑ 🕷 Monkey, howler
- ❑ 🕷 Monkeys, general
- ❑ Moose
- ❑ Octopus
- ❑ Okapi
- ❑ Opossum
- ❑ Orangutan (an ape)

- ❑ Oryx butting heads
- ❑ Ostrich
- ❑ Owl, great horned
- ❑ Peacock
- ❑ Pelican
- ❑ Penguin
- ❑ Platypus
- ❑ Porcupine
- ❑ Praying mantis
- ❑ Rabbit
- ❑ Ram
- ❑ Rat
- ❑ Ray
- ❑ Reindeer (three)
- ❑ Rhinoceros (one with his head down)
- ❑ Roadrunner
- ❑ Scorpion
- ❑ Sea lion
- ❑ Seal, elephant
- ❑ Seahorses (two)
- ❑ Shark
- ❑ Snail
- ❑ Snake
- ❑ Spider with very long back legs
- ❑ Squid
- ❑ Squirrel, flying
- ❑ Squirrels, ground (two)
- ❑ Starfish
- ❑ Tapir, Mountain
- ❑ Tiger
- ❑ Tortoises (one atop a hedgehog)
- ❑ Turtles (both river and sea)
- ❑ Tyrannosaurus rex (a dinosaur)
- ❑ Viper
- ❑ Wallaby
- ❑ Walrus
- ❑ Wart hogs
- ❑ Water buffalo (two)
- ❑ Whale, beluga
- ❑ Whale, humpback
- ❑ Wildebeest herd
- ❑ Wolf
- ❑ Wombat

Discovery Island Answers

Number of animals found on the Tree of Life

———

Camp Minnie-Mickey

Festival of the Lion King

1. Let's Go Hunting! It is good that you got to the festival a little early because the animals are on parade! Look around you at your fellow guests. They can be real animals. Fortunately, I have a list of the animals expected in the parade and maybe you will find even more. Earn 1 point for each "animal" you find.

- ❑ Koala, (a child being carried by a parent)
- ❑ Rabbit (a person who is jumping up and down)
- ❑ Fish (a person who is drinking)
- ❑ Bush baby (a person wearing sunglasses)
- ❑ Turtle (a person wearing a hoodie)
- ❑ Duck (a person with a visor)
- ❑ Chameleons (two or more people who are dressed alike)
- ❑ Horse (a person with a ponytail)
- ❑ Poison dart frog (a person wearing neon)
- ❑ Caterpillar (a person eating)
- ❑ Giraffe (a person taller than your dad)
- ❑ Whale (a person talking on a cellphone)
- ❑ Kangaroo (a person wearing a pouch)
- ❑ Magpie (a person wearing sparkly clothes)
- ❑ Peacock (a person with painted toenails)
- ❑ Tasmanian devil (a person spinning)
- ❑ Skunk (a person wearing stripes)
- ❑ Stork (a person wearing heels)
- ❑ Polar bear (a person wearing fur)

❑ Kitten (a person wearing boots)
❑ Snake (a person wearing multiple shirts)
❑ Bird (a person with a balloon)
❑ Zebra (a person wearing black and white)
❑ Dalmatian (a person wearing spots)
❑ Lion (a person with big curly hair)

2. Collection Time! This queue is a bit different from most. You will be waiting outside for a while and not moving around until it is time to go in. While you wait to see the king of the beasts, work on some Collections. Here are a few suggestions:

❑ Different stuffed animals
❑ Disney T-shirts
❑ Mickey Mouse ears

Camp Minnie-Mickey Answers

Festival of the Lion King
 1. *Number of "animals" found* _____
 2. *Number of items collected* _____

Africa

Kilimanjaro Safaris

? **POP QUIZ!** Have a quick look at the Kilimajaro Safaris poster, then join the queue.

1. Which of the following animals were featured on the poster?

 a. Lion and zebra
 b. Rhinoceros and water birds
 c. Elephants and giraffe
 d. People – yes, we are part of the animal kingdom as well.
 e. All of the above
 f. Only a and c

2. Were there any animals in the trees?
Yes / No

3. Was there any water?
Yes / No

4. What vehicle was present in the picture?
- a. A jeep
- b. A bus
- c. A train
- d. Animals don't drive.

End of Pop Quiz

5. If you have not yet done so, look up at the animal signs and then look back down. What animal's Swahili name is Twiga?
- a. Elephant
- b. Lion
- c. Giraffe
- d. That is the word for people who don't stay on marked trails.

6. What animal's Swahili name is Tembo?
- a. Elephant
- b. Giraffe
- c. Lion
- d. Monkey

7. What animal's Swahili name is Simba?
- a. Giraffe
- b. Monkey
- c. Elephant
- d. Lion. Now where are Timon and Pumbaa?

8. What will your "care of the animals you meet" ensure?
- a. Their survival
- b. Their safety
- c. Your safety
- d. The circle of life
- e. All of the above
- f. Both a and b

9. There are more animals overhead. Have a quick look and then look down. How many horns was that rhino sporting?
- a. 1
- b. 2
- c. 3
- d. There was a rhino?

10. Which of these animals has a name starting with "P"?
- a. Zebra
- b. Rhino
- c. Both of them
- d. This is a trick question right? Zebra starts with 'z' and rhino starts with 'r.'

11. What service is provided to the safari staff by the crowned cranes?
  a. They act as guards much as dogs would. You don't want to mess with a crowned crane.
  b. They wake the staff every morning by crowing like roosters.
  c. They keep down the insect population.
  d. Now even cranes must have jobs?

12. There are some beautiful crowned cranes for you to enjoy. While you are "royal watching," give yourself 1 point for each crane you spot. In addition, give yourself 1 point for each different kind of bird you find. _____

13. Someone is a temperature reader. What animal knows how hot it really is?
  a. Elephant
  b. Crane
  c. Giraffe
  d. I don't think I really want to know that; I'm melting faster than my ice cream cone.

14. It is time to head into the safari booking office. There is no staff at the front desk. What do they want you to do?
  a. Proceed
  b. Wait
  c. Leave money on the counter
  d. Visit the gift shop

15. Treasure Hunt Time! See how many of these office treasures you can find before the booking agent returns.
  ❑ A phone
  ❑ A giraffe
  ❑ Four pairs of binoculars
  ❑ A coffee mug
  ❑ Two baskets
  ❑ A gourd
  ❑ A zebra head
  ❑ Money
  ❑ A stapler
  ❑ A safari hat

16. There is a group of three similar things high on the walls. What are they?
    a. Blankets
    b. Tribal shields
    c. Animal skulls
    d. Purses, or pouches

17. There are two animal heads presiding over this office from on high. One appears to be an African antelope. What is the other?
    a. An elephant   b. A water buffalo
    c. A hippo   d. A squirrel, very cute

18. Find a map of the Harambe Wildlife Reserve. Then find the skull and crossbones on it. What do they warn of?
    a. Unsafe gas in the air
    b. Territorial elephant family, danger of trampling
    c. Bad water
    d. I don't know, but I think I will avoid the area.

19. If you were to visit the Seasonal Swamp, and I think you definitely should, what animal would you likely encounter?
    a. Hippopotamus   b. Giraffe
    c. Elephant   d. Thanks, I don't care for
                       swamps much.

20. Look around for a wooden lion. What is unusual about him?
    a. He has two heads.
    b. He only has half a mane – how sad.
    c. He has six legs – now that is weird.
    d. His tail is as straight as an arrow.

21. Outside the office you will find a pile of three things. What are they?
    a. Trunks   b. Canoes
    c. Tires   d. Books filled with records of
                       past safaris

22. What lone animal is seen on the sign outside the door for Kilimanjaro Safaris?
    a. Giraffe   b. Rhinoceros
    c. Lion   d. It's Mickey Mouse wearing
                       a safari hat.

23. You are entering a long covered-walkway area. If you look around you will find another mode of transportation waiting here. What is it?
    a. Motorcycle
    b. Canoe
    c. Elephant-riding saddle
    d. Hot air balloon

There is a video playing. It will give you facts about some of the animals you may encounter on safari. Let's see if you can find the answers to the following questions in the video.

24. In a family group of lions, who does most of the hunting?
    a. The young males
    b. The females
    c. The dominant male
    d. They steal their food from other animals.

25. What is a group of elephants known as?
    a. A herd   b. A pride
    c. A family   d. A pack

26. If elephants had a president, who would it be?
    a. The elephant with the largest tusks
    b. A young strong male
    c. Elephants rotate control daily.
    d. An older female – finally, a female president

27. What rhino has a flexible pointy upper lip?
    a. White rhino   b. Black rhino
    c. Both

28. Which is true about zebra stripes?
    a. They are unique to individual zebras, like fingerprints to humans.
    b. The stripe pattern has been the same since the earliest recorded zebras.
    c. Zebra siblings share the same pattern.

29. What animal has the distinction of being the fastest animal on earth?
    a. Gazelle   b. Lion
    c. Cheetah

30. What are a warthog's upper tusks used for?
    a. Digging
    b. Inflicting damage on a predator
    c. Looking big and bad

31. When a Thomson's gazelle makes abrupt upward leaps what is it called?
    a. Fluking   b. Pronking
    c. Bouncing

32. When a hippo opens his mouth in a wide yawn, what does it mean?
    a. He is asserting dominance; it is a threat display.
    b. He is hungry.
    c. He is sleepy. Hippos have to sleep too, you know.

33. How does the Marabou stork get most of her meals?
    a. She steals eggs from nests.
    b. She attacks smaller prey from the sky.
    c. She is a scavenger.

34. How do male giraffes battle for dominance?
    a. They rear up on their hind legs and try to push the other giraffe with their front legs.
    b. They wrap their necks around each other in an arm-wrestling-like fashion.
    c. They play rock, paper, scissors.

35. How does the male lion spend most of his day?
    a. Hunting
    b. Sleeping
    c. However he wants; are you going to argue with a lion?

FP **36. According to posted signs, who always has the right of way?**
    a. Wild animals   b. Reserve rangers
    c. Tour vehicles   d. Whoever gets there first

FP **37. According to the postings, why should you never feed the animals?**
    a. They may take more than the handout you offer; they may take a hand.
    b. They should not be exposed to human germs.
    c. They shouldn't get that close to the tour vehicles.

    d. They eat natural diets and should not become
       dependent on handouts.

FP 38. The safari sign reminds guests that it's improper to:
    a. Discard any litter
    b. Disturb or feed birds and animals
    c. Leave designated roads or trails
    d. All of the above
    e. All of those, plus you left one out! You're not
       supposed to cut or destroy any vegetation.

FP 39. What should you keep ready at all times?
    a. Your passport   b. Your camera
    c. Your ticket   d. Your patience; animals
                        don't work on schedule.

FP 40. Treasure Hunt Time! Soon you will be on safari.
Before you set off, see how many of these treasures you
can spot.
- ❑ A lantern with a red bottom
- ❑ A giraffe getting her "close-up"
- ❑ A monkey
- ❑ A tribal owl
- ❑ A red triangle with no other triangles around it
- ❑ A tablecloth
- ❑ A pair of sunglasses
- ❑ Antlers
- ❑ A shield in red, black, and white
- ❑ A hippopotamus
- ❑ An elephant with his ears up
- ❑ The Endangered Animal Rehabilitation Center
- ❑ Two tires not attached to a vehicle
- ❑ A gas can
- ❑ A circular face
- ❑ A plane landing

Africa Answers

Kilimanjaro Safaris
1) e. All of the above
2) No
3) Yes
4) b. A bus
5) c. Giraffe
6) a. Elephant

7) d. Lion

8) a. Their survival

9) b. 2

10) a. Zebra

11) c. They keep down the insect population.

12) Number of crowned cranes found _____
    Number of different kinds of birds found _____

13) c. Giraffe

14) a. Proceed

15) Total Office Treasures found _____

16) d. Purses, or pouches

17) b. A water buffalo

18) c. Bad water

19) a. Hippopotamus

20) d. His tail is as straight as an arrow.

21) b. Canoes

22) b. Rhinoceros

23) d. Hot air balloon

24) b. The females

25) a. A herd

26) d. An older female

27) b. Black rhino

28) a. They are unique to individual zebras.

29) c. Cheetah

30) a. Digging

31) b. Pronking

32) a. He is asserting dominance.

33) c. She is a scavenger.

34) b. They wrap their necks around each other in an
    arm-wrestling-like fashion.

35) b. Sleeping

36) a. Wild animals

37) d. They eat natural diets and should not become
    dependent on handouts.

38) e. All of those, plus you're not supposed to cut or
    destroy any vegetation.

39) b. Your camera

40) Total Treasures found _____

Rafiki's Planet Watch

Wildlife Express Train: to

1. When it comes to safaris, what do the people at Kilimanjaro Safaris do?
    a. Go all out
    b. Go native
    c. Go wild
    d. Go, go, go; really, they don't stop until you get there.

2. What animals are featured in the Kilimanjaro Safaris' poster hanging here in Harambe station?
    a. Zebras
    b. Giraffes
    c. Birds
    d. Lions
    e. All of the above
    f. All of the above except d

3. According to the poster, how does it appear that visitors to Kilimanjaro Safaris get around while viewing the animals?
    a. On elephants
    b. In some rather filthy Jeeps
    c. On foot
    d. On an old rickety bus

4. Search closely for a notice from the Harambe Town Counsel. It tells us that continuous railroad service to Bwanga Station has been cancelled. Why is this?
    a. Because of massive flooding in the area
    b. Because a pride of wild lions has moved in
    c. Because erosion has damaged the tracks
    d. Bwanga just isn't that interesting; no one was buying train tickets.
    e. The notice included all of the above, so you can take your pick.

5. What will you find around the message board where the Harambe Town Council notice is posted?
    a. Two closed booking windows
    b. A flyer offering private tours to Bwanga at your own risk
    c. Prices for train tickets to Bwanga
    d. A second Town Council notice declaring the area safe for service

6. What does Usivute Sigara mean?
    a. Do not leave bags unattended.
    b. Smoking is prohibited.
    c. Do not feed the lions.
    d. I don't know but I hope I am not doing it.

7. What does "Mwizi Ya Pembe Kujihadhari!" mean?
    a. Restrooms Out of Service!
    b. Live Electric Wires!
    c. No Unattended Baggage!
    d. Ivory Poachers Beware!

8. How many times should a would-be poacher think before killing for ivory?
    a. More then once   b. 10
    c. 100   d. 1,000

9. What animals are featured on the "Ivory Poachers Beware" poster?
    a. An elephant and a hippopotamus
    b. An elephant and a hornbill
    c. An elephant and a rhinoceros
    d. It is just an elephant, but he looks mad. I think they should leave his tusks right where they are.

10. Treasure Hunt Time! See if you can find all of these indoor treasures before you step outside.
    ❑ A pair of hiking shoes
    ❑ An overturned basket
    ❑ A bungee cord
    ❑ A brown backpack
    ❑ A rope handle
    ❑ A hotel sticker
    ❑ A ladder
    ❑ Loose frayed wires
    ❑ A man fishing

11. What actions are corrupt according to the Harambe Town Council?
  - a. Insulting the condition of the train station
  - b. Soliciting passengers to buy ivory or other animal products
  - c. Taking an unauthorized break
  - d. Tendering or accepting tips

12. If you search closely, and I do mean closely, you will find a waterbuck with something to say about Cap'n Bob's Super Safaris. What's his comment?
  - a. I love Cap'n Bob and so will you.
  - b. Give me one good reason why.
  - c. I'd rather be running.
  - d. If you want to see me, see Cap'n Bob first!
  - e. Nothing, waterbucks can't talk.

13. What does Cap'n Bob guarantee?
  - a. Animals
  - b. Your safety
  - c. Fun
  - d. Memories for a lifetime
  - e. All of the above
  - f. Nothing, to no one

14. What does Jorodi make?
  - a. Animal carvings
  - b. Masks and beads
  - c. Safari gear
  - d. The best sandwich in Harambe

15. Who should you report poaching to?
  - a. Your bus driver
  - b. A policeman
  - c. The nearest ranger station
  - d. No one, but you should glare at poachers really menacingly.

16. If you have 51 cents just burning a hole in your pocket, what could you get?
  - a. A souvenir safari pamphlet
  - b. A full meal at Cap'n Bob's
  - c. A ride on the train to Bwanga – if the train is operating
  - d. A pressed penny with a picture of Tarzan
  - e. All of the above plus a complimentary beverage
  - f. Probably nothing but bubblegum; it costs 51 cents.

17. If you see the sign "Mizigo tu," what does it mean?
    a. Luggage only   b. No spitting
    c. This way out   d. Come again

18. What would you need to access the station keys?
    a. Authorization from the stationmaster
    b. The key to the case they're in; it's locked.
    c. To be the conductor
    d. A translator to read the signs for you

19. What are children forbidden to do?
    a. Become disorderly
    b. Ride on top of the train
    c. Climb on the parapets
    d. Sing

20. If you look around, you can find pictures of each of the following modes of transportation, except one. Which one is missing?
    a. A truck/jeep   b. A cruise ship
    c. A plane   d. A hot air balloon
    e. They are all there.

21. Which of these are northbound stops?
    a. Nairobi   b. Kisangani
    c. Kampala   d. Nakuru
    e. These are all
       northbound stops.

22. What does having a platform ticket not entitle you to?
    a. Board the train
    b. Bring luggage
    c. Board at the time indicated on your ticket
    d. A return trip

23. Treasure Hunt Time! Try to find as many of these railway treasures as you can before your train pulls into the station.
    ❑ A sleeping bag
    ❑ A basket inside a basket
    ❑ Men's shoes
    ❑ A gas can
    ❑ Loose wires
    ❑ A red lantern
    ❑ A guitar case

- ❏ A hat
- ❏ A peephole
- ❏ A green backpack
- ❏ Two tiny elephant silhouettes facing each other
- ❏ Three dollies; I don't mean the baby doll sort
- ❏ A travel agency with a giraffe on its card
- ❏ A map
- ❏ A grass/straw roof
- ❏ An alarm
- ❏ Mickey, Minnie, and friends
- ❏ A key chain
- ❏ A teeny tiny gear picture
- ❏ A spoked wheel
- ❏ The stationmaster's door
- ❏ A stool
- ❏ A coil of rope
- ❏ A bed roll
- ❏ A woven suitcase

Wildlife Express Train: from

Collection Time! If you find yourself waiting for the train back to Harambe, this would be a good time to work on a Collection or two. Here are some possibilities:

- ❏ People with stuffed animals; give yourself 1 additional bonus point for each different kind of plush animal you spot.
- ❏ People texting
- ❏ People with shoes that don't tie

Rafiki's Planet Watch Answers

Wildlife Express Train: to
1) *c. Go wild*
2) *f. All of the above except d*
3) *d. On an old rickety bus*
4) *c. Because erosion has damaged the tracks*
5) *a. Two closed booking windows*
6) *b. Smoking is prohibited.*

7) d. Ivory Poachers Beware!

8) b. 10

9) c. An elephant and a rhinoceros

10) Total Treasures found _____

11) d. Tendering or accepting tips

12) b. Give me one good reason why.

13) a. Animals

14) b. Masks and beads

15) c. The nearest ranger station

16) d. A pressed penny with a picture of Tarzan

17) a. Luggage only

18) b. The key to the case they're in

19) c. Climb on the parapets

20) e. They are all there.

21) e. These are all northbound stops.

22) a. Board the train

23) Total Railway Treasures found _____

Wildlife Express Train: from

Number of items collected _____

Asia

Expedition Everest:
Standby Line

Note: See page 284 for FASTPASS line games.

Expedition Everest Queueseum

On the way to your train to the "Roof of the World," you will pass through a very beautiful "queueseum," my name for a very long, very detailed line with Disney magic to spare. In most cases if the line passes through a queueseum, you would be missing a lot of the fun if you could skip it. It's designed to keep you entertained during what will probably be a long wait for a great ride. 5 bonus points if you can guess the words I combined to form "queueseum."

1. What is the name of the tour company you are using to explore Everest?
    a. Everest Treks   b. Himalayan Escapes
    c. The Yacking Yeti   d. Sherpa's Incorporated

2. What animal is the mascot for the tour company?
    a. A mouse in trekking gear: "Remember, it was all started by a mouse!"
    b. A yeti: "We Keep You Steady And Avoid The Yeti."
    c. A flying yak: "Here And Back With The Flying Yak"
    d. A dragon: "Lucky-Garden Golden Dragon Treks"

3. Which of the following items cannot be found on the expedition company's patio?
    a. Digital clock   b. Plate
    c. Bells   d. Hiking boots
    e. All these things are there.

4. What should you check at the desk?
  a. Your payment, of course
  b. Your stamped permits
  c. Your gear
  d. Your waiver

5. The person who should be helping you has left you a message. What do they want you to know?
  a. "Mt. Everest is big. It's mind-bogglingly big. Are you sure you want to go?"
  b. "Yeti sightings in and around Everest have increased; proceed at your own risk."
  c. "Out to Lunch"
  d. "Be Right Back"

6. Where is the office calculator?
  a. On the floor
  b. On the safe
  c. In a fancy wooden box
  d. In the trash

7. Someone wants to remember something for the summit. What is it?
  a. Champagne and film
  b. Oxygen and warmest undergarments
  c. Ropes and camera
  d. Mickey Mouse plushy for cool photo op

8. Treasure Hunt Time! See how many of these high-mountain treasures you can spot before it is time to prepare for your journey.
  ❑ A white teapot
  ❑ A projector
  ❑ A knit hat
  ❑ Shoes with no laces
  ❑ An empty soda bottle
  ❑ A headlamp
  ❑ Packing tape
  ❑ Scale
  ❑ A crocodile head
  ❑ A calendar
  ❑ Green boots
  ❑ A helmet
  ❑ OKI
  ❑ The height of Mt. Everest
  ❑ Framed money

❑ A dragon sticking out his tongue
❑ A plum
❑ A tiger

9. Outside the door, you will see a covered patio off to the side. It has lots of useful stuff hanging from its covering. Which of these things is not hanging on that patio?
    a. Garlic
    b. A lantern
    c. A basket
    d. Peppers
    e. All these things are there.

10. There is a mountaineering association that appears to have everything you will need for your expedition. What is the name of the association?
    a. Top Of The World Mountaineering Association
    b. The Clever Camel Mountaineering Association
    c. Chomolungma Mountaineering Association
    d. Anandapur Mountaineering Association

11. Which of these things can you see on display at the mountaineering association?
    a. Backpacks
    b. Harnesses
    c. Ropes
    d. All of the above
    e. All but a

12. Part of the building appears to be looking at you. What part?
    a. The windows
    b. The trim
    c. The columns in the rafters
    d. Buildings don't look at people. I think you need some shade.

13. Treasure Hunt Time! This area contains treasures. See how many you can find before they roll down the mountain.
    ❑ A blue barrel
    ❑ A stocking
    ❑ A bent tool
    ❑ Door handles with rings
    ❑ A bowl with a square cut out of the side

❑ A prayer flag with a lion
❑ A pulley
❑ A fancy light
❑ An urn

14. What does local custom say of the yeti?
    a. He is responsible for the snow.
    b. He is a curse to all who climb the great mountain.
    c. He is a guardian of the sacred mountain.
    d. He's just this guy; you know?

15. There is a statue garden with a number of yeti statues. They have received an offering. What did they get?
    a. Fruit
    b. Money
    c. Chalices
    d. All of the above
    e. Only a and b

16. The yeti are holding something. What is it?
    a. Mountains   b. Fruit
    c. People   d. Snow cones

17. The yeti are adorned. With what?
    a. Flowers
    b. Red paint
    c. Jade
    d. Nothing, they are just plain yeti.

18. Treasure Hunt Time! In the statue garden, there are many treasures belonging to the yeti. See how many you can find.
    ❑ Someone who lost his head
    ❑ A bell with another bell coming out of it
    ❑ Seven upside-down buckets
    ❑ A lime
    ❑ A rock with a hole in it
    ❑ A man with both his hands held in front of him
    ❑ Mt. Everest
    ❑ An orange
    ❑ A stone statue with some broken trim
    ❑ Two metal dragons with full mouths
    ❑ A prayer flag featuring a horse

19. You are coming to a fancy building all carved of wood. Something is in the rafters holding up the roof. Who or what is it?
   a. Dragons
   b. Yaks
   c. Looks like yeti again; I guess they can be very useful.
   d. A group of workers who don't look like they enjoy their jobs much.

20. You will find a set of doors tied shut. What is on them?
   a. Yeti riding yaks
   b. Yeti lifting the mountains
   c. Yeti beating their chests
   d. No yeti, just a sign that says "Temple Staff Only, Keep Out"

21. There is a guy made of stone who is wearing an animal or animal part. Which of these is he sporting?
   a. A snake
   b. Yak horns
   c. A yeti pelt
   d. A foxtail

22. This fancy wooden building has many decorations. See if you can complete three Special Collections while you go around the building.

   Get 1 point for each unique bell that you find on this building. _____

   Get 1 point for each unique yeti image. It can't be the same as any other yeti images that you have counted. _____

   Get 1 point for each different fruit or vegetable you spot _____

23. You are coming to a high-mountain shop. What's for sale that's displayed outside the shop?
   a. Lanterns
   b. "I climbed Mt. Everest" T-shirts
   c. Shovels
   d. Folding furniture
   e. All except b
   f. Only a and d

24. What must expedition members do to reach the museum?

    a. Climb, the museum is at the summit. I bet they don't get too much traffic.

    b. Leave a fruit or money offering in the statue garden.

    c. Complete the ride, the museum is at the other end.

    d. Go through the shop.

25. What must visitors not do?

    a. Leave anything behind on the mountain

    b. Pose for a picture while sitting on a yeti statue

    c. Pick the tea

    d. Point, it's rude after all.

26. Tashi's Trek and Tongba Shop has something displayed over its entrance. What is it?

    a. A yeti, naturally

    b. A picture of Tashi and family

    c. A ram's head, so cute

    d. Some dried garlic

27. This shop sells many things, but let's suppose you are musical. Can you find an instrument to play when you reach the summit? Bells don't count.

    Yes / No

28. Treasure Hunt Time! See how many of the goods on this shopping list you can find in the store before it is time to check out.

    ❑ A T-shirt that is watching you

    ❑ A newspaper

    ❑ A place for a nap

    ❑ An old radio

    ❑ A cooking pot and ladle combination

    ❑ A phone

    ❑ A shovel

    ❑ A gold statue

    ❑ Gloves in orange, brown, and white

    ❑ A tiger

    ❑ A chain of carabiners

    ❑ A hat

    ❑ A pitchfork

    ❑ "The Yeti Expedition" patch

    ❑ A lady with ten arms

❑ A great success of a local scientist
❑ A parrot
❑ A ladder
❑ A selection of boots
❑ Canned food
❑ Binoculars
❑ A lemon
❑ A red lantern

29. You have arrived at the Yeti Museum. There is a picture featuring the yeti. What is the yeti bigger than in the picture?
   a. The people
   b. The mountains
   c. Some of the clouds
   d. All of the above
   e. All but a

30. There is a newspaper article about a local scientist. What did he do to get in the paper?
   a. He has the largest selection of petrified yeti scat (poop) known to exist anywhere.
   b. He climbed Mt. Everest.
   c. He took a group of local children on a yeti hunt at base camp. They even had s'mores.
   d. He proved the yeti is real.

31. You will come to a display case featuring things used by local people. Which of these things is not found in that case?
   a. A sewing kit   b. Linen
   c. Salt   d. Small metal flowers
   e. They are all there.

32. There is a comb in this case; what is its purpose?
   a. To comb the carpet
   b. To comb a child's hair
   c. To comb a cow
   d. All of the above; I do not want to use that comb.

33. Treasure Hunt Time! We are in a museum full of treasures, so it is definitely time to hunt them. See how many of these treasures you can unearth before the museum closes for the day.
   ❑ A lantern
   ❑ A tea company sign

❑ Someone making butter from yak milk
❑ A bell with a yeti on top
❑ A wooden yeti mask with small bits of rags creating fur
❑ A costume used in a yeti dance
❑ Binoculars
❑ A map with push pins
❑ *Life* magazine
❑ A ripped tent
❑ A dented teapot
❑ A totem featuring a yeti about to make a snack of a yak
❑ People and yaks crossing water in art
❑ A wooden box with eyes for you
❑ Wooden double doors

34. You will discover a picture display of lowland jungle animals. One of them is an important representative of Nepal. Which one?
a. King cobra, he is the yeti's friend and assistant
b. Danfe pheasant, the national bird; quite an honor
c. Peacock pansy butterfly, considered a national treasure
d. Chital, the national animal

35. There is a display of masks. Which mask has golden eyebrows?
a. Yeti
b. Leopard
c. Deer
d. Nilgai
e. You say these animals have eyebrows?

36. Do any of the masks have closed eyes?
Yes / No

37. Do any of the masks have beaks?
Yes / No

38. A wolf has left something behind that is now on display. What is it?
a. A footprint
b. Petrified poop; yuck!
c. Bones from its meal of yak
d. Little Red Riding Hood's basket

39. Which of the following traps is on display?
- a. Honey trap, sounds sticky
- b. Pit trap
- c. Camera trap. Smile, you're on Candid Animal Camera!
- d. All of the above
- e. All but a

40. What animal is thought by scientists to match closely the description of a yeti?
- a. Spotted leopard
- b. Black bear
- c. Tiger
- d. The old mountain man who never shaves

41. How many toes does a Himalayan yeti have?
- a. 2. Just enough for a kicky pair of thongs.
- b. 4
- c. 5
- d. 6

42. Something was recovered from the Forbidden Mountain Range. What was it?
- a. Primitive pictorial yeti writing that, when translated, appears to mean, "Keep Off My Mountain."
- b. A very big yeti footprint; I mean I don't know what size shoe that yeti wears, but I don't think they carry it at Payless.
- c. Yeti scat; I don't think I would want to recover that.
- d. All of the above
- e. All but a; yeti don't write.

43. When visiting the sacred mountain, who risks the wrath of the yeti?
- a. People without respect for the natural environment
- b. People without respect for the creatures of the mountain
- c. People who declare that the yeti is fiction
- d. People who smell like yak.
- e. Both a and b
- f. Both b and d

44. What special thing does the "base camp" cook do?
   a. He makes even yeti meat taste delicious. It is
      normally gamey.
   b. He cooks anything at altitude even if the fire
      keeps going out.
   c. He feeds large groups of people.
   d. He combines local foods with expedition
      supplies to create varied meals for months.

**45. How much weight do the expedition porters
normally carry?**
   a. 50 pounds
   b. 75 pounds
   c. 100 pounds
   d. 125 pounds or more

Expedition Everest: FASTPASS Line

FASTPASS lines are designed to move quickly;
therefore, so is this game. It is all in treasure hunt form
with hunts for each area you will go through. Find as
many treasures as you can as you move closer to your
trip to the top of the world.

1. Inside the First Room
   See if you can find these Himalayan treasures before
you go outside:
   ❑ A bottle
   ❑ A bike
   ❑ Something being weighed
   ❑ Binoculars
   ❑ A teapot
   ❑ The summit of Mt. Everest
   ❑ A draining spoon
   ❑ A wok
   ❑ A fruit
   ❑ Boots
   ❑ The time
   ❑ A sleeping mat
   ❑ A butter churn
   ❑ A bell
   ❑ Jewelry
   ❑ Five masks

❑ Firewood
❑ A stamp
❑ A lantern

2. Outside the First Building
❑ A large black ball
❑ Garlic
❑ A yak
❑ Someone who has gone red in the face
❑ A tomato
❑ Mountains made of stone
❑ A metal urn
❑ Upside-down buckets
❑ A ladder
❑ A teapot with a long spout
❑ A wooden bucket
❑ A star fruit
❑ Red/green rope
❑ A yellow case
❑ A place to grind
❑ An onion

3. Anandapur Mountaineering Association's Supply Area
❑ Smiling beams
❑ Mittens: orange and red with blue thumb
❑ First-aid kit
❑ Two tiger statues
❑ A rainbow hat
❑ A monkey on a stool
❑ Fruit
❑ A headlamp
❑ Two yellow canisters
❑ A phone
❑ A broom
❑ A calendar
❑ A green muffler
❑ A carabineer chain
❑ A pink water bottle
❑ Rainbow gloves
❑ A red baseball cap
❑ A book called "The Himalayan Experience"

4. Highlights from the Yeti Museum Area
❑ A head with curly horns
❑ Three bracelets

- ❑ A large wooden yeti
- ❑ A ritual knife
- ❑ A gold face
- ❑ A drawing of a yeti on a hilly green field
- ❑ A ceremonial robe
- ❑ A way to weigh your fortunes
- ❑ An elephant
- ❑ A rice sifter
- ❑ A way to keep your hands warm (not mittens)
- ❑ A yellow push pin
- ❑ A compass
- ❑ A pocket knife
- ❑ Two ice screws
- ❑ A big tooth, a very big tooth; Did I mention that it's BIG?
- ❑ Footprints in the snow
- ❑ A less then useful shovel
- ❑ A scat collection (Ewe!!!!!)
- ❑ A warning followed by a letter of disagreement

Flights of Wonder

If you arrive at the Flights of Wonder show early, you will have a chance to meet and learn about an owl. Be sure to pay attention: you never know when there will be a pop owl quiz. No, seriously, there is going to be a pop owl quiz.

1. Two birds are sharing the show times for Flights of Wonder with you. What kind of birds are they?
- a. Peacocks
- b. Owls
- c. Roosters
- d. Hummingbirds

2. Treasure Hunt Time! Try to locate all of these treasures before they flutter away.
- ❑ Two baskets
- ❑ Two blue elephants
- ❑ A bedroll made of reeds
- ❑ A pail
- ❑ A brick adornment that looks like it might just fall
- ❑ A rug with a zigzag pattern

❑ A hawk perched up high
❑ A yellow butterfly
❑ A coil of rope hanging from two bent nails
❑ Folded blankets
❑ A frayed rope
❑ Scraps of fabric in red, yellow, and white tied to a rope
❑ An intricate umbrella that stands no chance of holding off the rain
❑ A large rusty jug
❑ Three embroidered birds
❑ A tassel
❑ A bell with points on the end
❑ A tiger that is in front of a tree
❑ A bell that looks like an upside-down flower
❑ Three lanterns
❑ A large striped piece of ribbon
❑ A fish
❑ A collection of beads
❑ A large urn
❑ Pink silk flowers

Inside the Theater:

? **POP OWL QUIZ!** If you got here in time, you were treated to a talk about owls. Let's see what owl facts you remember. (If you did not get to meet an owl, let's see "whoo" is best at guessing.)

3. How many vertebrae do owls have in their necks?
    a. Twice as many as people
    b. Twice as many as giraffes
    c. Only one, that is why their necks are so short.
    d. The same number as any mammal
    e. Both a and b

4. What is unusual about owl eyes?
    a. They have no eyelids.
    b. They can't move in their sockets.
    c. They are blind in the daytime.
    d. They produce tears in the daylight to protect them from the light.

5. An owl can turn its head all the way around.
    True or False?

6. In relation to the size of their heads, owls and humans have the same size eyes. The owl's eyes look larger because they are very bulgy.

True or False?

7. How is it possible for giraffes to have only half the number of neck vertebrae as owls?

    a. Giraffes have much bigger vertebrae.

    b. Giraffes don't need as many vertebrae because they have such large muscles in their necks.

    c. It is not possible; have you seen a giraffe's neck?

Wow, you are as smart as a wise old owl. (Yes, I went there.) Your owl quiz ends here.

8. How many different places on stage can you find for a bird to rest his weary wings? Earn 1 point for each perch you spot. _____

9. Treasure Hunt Time! Look around the theater for these treasures before the performers fly in.

    ❑ A tilted lamp on a post

    ❑ A stump

    ❑ A movable curtain

    ❑ A coiled rope with a frayed rope tassel

    ❑ A scrap of white cloth

    ❑ A stack of square rocks

    ❑ A covered window with a hole at the bottom

    ❑ Two scraps of blue cloth

    ❑ A bricked-in window

    ❑ At least 20 small blue squares

    ❑ At least 3 red scraps of fabric

    ❑ Fringe

    ❑ A metal roof

Kali River Rapids

FP Outside Hike

1. Kali River Special Collections

For the outside portion of the queue, you will play the role of archaeologist. (You can bring your own fedora, but bullwhips are frowned upon.) A major museum has hired you to search out rare tribal artifacts in the jungle. Carefully inspect the edges of the path you are following. Look at the walls, too. If you are good at your job, you will find both whole statues and broken bits of ancient treasure. You'll also spot monkeys on an island on your left.

Each time you make a discovery, you get 1 point. Before you proceed inside, check the answer key to see if the museum curator is happy with your efforts. Also, remember to check the river whenever you get the chance. Watching people get wet can be fun!

Things that count toward your score:

    Whole Statues _____

    Broken pieces of artifacts _____

    Monkeys _____

    Wet People _____

Front Porch

2. On the front porch of the "queueseum" you are about to enter there are lots of bells. What is hanging out of the bells?

    a. Pretty red cloth with gold trim

    b. Handles shaped like teeny tiny monkeys hanging upside down from the bells

    c. Leaves

    d. All of the above

    e. Both a and c

Kali River Queueseum

If it is adventure you are after, a trip down Kali River should be just the thing. Before you challenge the river rapids, you will pass through a very beautiful "queueseum," my name for a long queue filled with lots of things to find. You will discover it when you step inside.

As you enjoy the queueseum, please bear in mind that the questions you'll be able to answer will depend on where the line flows the day of your visit, because the route will depend on the length of the line. There are a total of six rooms you may visit on your way to the rapids: the Statue Room, the Fountain Room, the Duck Room, Mr. Panika's Shop, the Paddle Room, and the River Art Room. Questions are grouped by room, and you may have to flip ahead or go back in your book to find the questions for the room you are entering.

Statue Room

3. As you enter this room, you will see a large screen. Which of these animals are pictured on the screen?
    a. Turtle and lion
    b. Bird and cobra
    c. Horse and rhino
    d. Elephant and lizard
    e. All of the above
    f. All but d

4. There is a very large statue in the center of the room. What kind of creature holds center stage?
    a. A snake
    b. An elephant with many hands
    c. A cat; who doesn't like cats? Sure dog people don't, but who else?
    d. A crane

5. A meal seems to have been offered to the room's central statue. What snack is she going to enjoy?
    a. Fruit
    b. Meow Mix
    c. Peanuts
    d. Seeds

6. Treasure Hunt Time! See how many of these well-hidden treasures you can find before you leave the statue room.
    ❑ A lap with no body
    ❑ Two red umbrellas
    ❑ A yellow umbrella

- ❏ A purple umbrella
- ❏ An orange umbrella
- ❏ A blue umbrella
- ❏ A toothy grin
- ❏ A trunk with red legs
- ❏ Four gold elephant heads holding four bells
- ❏ A flower lei
- ❏ A bunch of bananas
- ❏ A collection of spears
- ❏ A flat, colorfully painted dragon with good rhythm
- ❏ A xylophone
- ❏ Someone sticking his tongue out
- ❏ Two dragons sporting hats
- ❏ A gong
- ❏ A mask with skulls along its top like a crown
- ❏ An offering plate with only one kind of fruit
- ❏ A star fruit
- ❏ Four hummingbirds topping bottles
- ❏ Sleeves so long they would touch the ground
- ❏ Masks with veil-like fabric draped on them
- ❏ Three intricate platters

7. Cool, it looks like there is food service nearby. Where do locals get a little snack?

    a. In sack lunches sold in the gift shop

    b. At a small restaurant called Temple Treats and Eats

    c. From a bicycle food cart

    d. There is a food truck just outside the window.

8. A mannequin is wearing a black top and red pants. Which of these things is true about him?

    a. He might need braces.

    b. He has a unibrow (eyebrows that join in the middle to make one long brow).

    c. He has a flower in his hair; now that is unexpected.

    d. He seems fond of dreadlocks.

    e. He has all of these and more.

    f. He has all but b.

Fountain Room

9. Someone is not minding his manners. Who is spitting?
- a. An intricately painted elephant; to be fair, I think she is taking a bath.
- b. A golden cobra
- c. A bronze dragon
- d. That man over there; how rude!

10. What is sitting on the fountain steps?
- a. A heavy metal urn
- b. An offering of corn
- c. A small statue of a monkey
- d. Me – I'm tired.

11. Along the wall, there are niches with statues in them. Which statue has been given some jewelry?
- a. The dragon
- b. The monkey
- c. A woman
- d. A beast with sharp fanglike teeth; let's call him the lion.

12. One of the niches contains a statue that is squatting down. Why?
- a. He is lifting something on his head.
- b. He is placing an offering.
- c. He is crowning a child.
- d. He is doing his leg exercises.

13. Which of the statues seems to have been given an offering?
- a. The man; he's gotten incense.
- b. The fanged lion-like creature; with those teeth I would offer him something, too.
- c. The dragon; apparently he likes fruit.
- d. All these statues seem to have received gifts today.

14. What is that around the lion's neck?
- a. A collar with spikes; like he needs them!
- b. A bell, of course, to warn the birds
- c. A necklace made of shells
- d. His neck is bare.

15. Which of the statues is wearing a crown?

    a. The lion; he's the king.

    b. A human

    c. The dragon

    d. The cobra

    e. None of them has a crown.

16. There is a stack of three things that are alike. What is stacked?

    a. Boxes   b. Offerings of fruit

    c. Statues   d. Large cauldrons

? POP QUIZ! There is a display with a bicycle inside this room. Take a quick look at it and then turn your back.

17. Which of these items were in the bicycle display?

    a. A metal barrel containing two watermelons

    b. A green umbrella

    c. A crate of fruit

    d. A large metal jug

    e. A bike horn

    f. A spare tire

    g. Several brooms in a basket

    h. Several mats in a basket

    i. A bike lock and change

    j. A handlebar-basket full of bottles

    k. A pointy hat

    l. A blue bike

    m. A crate full of durian fruit (spiky green fruit)

    n. A purple plastic basket

    o. Money

End of Pop Quiz

18. It is time to play "Find That Platter or Bowl." There is a vast display of platters and bowls hanging from the walls and ceiling. See if you can find these exact items from among the stock:

    ❑ A platter featuring a parade of elephants

    ❑ A pot with a face on it where the handle attaches to the bowl

    ❑ A teakettle

    ❑ A copper pitcher

    ❑ A platter featuring a man and a beast

    ❑ A pot with a pouring spout

    ❑ A platter with two birds: one upside-down, one right-side up

19. Hey look! There is an advertisement for a local hotel. Which of these luxuries is not listed in the ad?
 a. Bathroom with running water on both floors
 b. Rooms with windows available
 c. Toilet paper, just a little extra
 d. Locks available on most doors
 e. All these amenities are listed.

Duck Room

In this room, there are many beautifully illustrated stories. See how many answers you can find on the ceiling.

20. Who teaches the human king to care about all living things?
 a. The king of the deer
 b. The swan with the golden feather
 c. The brave lion
 d. The human queen, and she means business

21. In the story of "The Swan with the Golden Feather," what color is the feather held up by the boy?
 a. Gold, naturally
 b. White; now that's odd.
 c. Black with gold stripes
 d. There is no boy holding a feather.

22. Who gets a lift on a crocodile?
 a. A mouse (not Mickey)
 b. The king of the lions
 c. A brave human child
 d. A monkey

23. Why is the jackal teased by the iguana?
 a. Because lion is bigger than he is
 b. Because he makes a silly sound when he talks
 c. Because only the foolish pretend to be kings
 d. Because his mother wears army boots

24. What must the tortoise do to catch a ride?
 a. Paint his shell
 b. Give a gift
 c. Close his mouth
 d. Hold out his thumb, that is, if he has one

25. In which story are people sleeping in a bed?
   a. "The Swan with the Golden Feather." Feathers are comfy for sleeping.
   b. "Banyan Deer"
   c. "Fearless Lion and the Brave Elephant"
   d. "Monkey and the Crocodile"

26. In which story can you find a person with wings?
   a. "Banyan Deer"
   b. "Tortoise and the Geese"
   c. "The Swan with the Golden Feather"
   d. "Dumbo"

27. Who does battle with the multi-headed serpent?
   a. Tiger
   b. Elephant
   c. Lion
   d. All of the above
   e. Only b and c; tiger is a scaredy-cat.

28. What animal is sticking his tongue out?
   a. Deer
   b. Lion
   c. Goose
   d. Iguana
   e. No animals would behave so rudely.
   f. Both a and d

29. What animal is sporting a checkered skirt?
   a. Elephant
   b. Swan
   c. Iguana
   d. Monkey

Mr. Panika's Shop
   This shop sells many exciting knickknacks you could use in your home as dust magnets… I mean decorations.

30. At the shop entrance, what does Mr. Panika offer for free?
   a. Looking
   b. Touching
   c. Advice
   d. Nothing my friend; this is a shop.

31. What large winged creatures are over the store's entrance?
> a. Flying tigers
> b. Falcons
> c. Dragons
> d. Hummingbirds of unusual size

32. As you enter, look to the left and find the cabinet with the black-wheeled horse on the second shelf. How many teapots does it contain?
> a. 2
> b. 3
> c. 4
> d. None, and I could have done with a spot of tea.

33. Does it contain a rabbit?
> Yes / No

34. The office area for this shop is vacant. Where is the shopkeeper?
> a. Having a rest upstairs; quiet, please!
> b. Watching you; no sticky fingers, please!
> c. Out to lunch, will return in an hour
> d. At the temple, please wait.

35. The shopkeeper has a crowded desk. Which of the following items is not on the shopkeeper's desk?
> a. A bookend
> b. A picture of a lady
> c. A coupon for ½ off on lunch at the Curry Hut
> d. A phone
> e. They were all there.

36. Treasure Hunt Time! See how many of these treasures you can find in the shopkeeper's office before he returns.
> ❏ A spotted goose
> ❏ The Eiffel Tower
> ❏ A broom
> ❏ Information about Nepal
> ❏ A banana
> ❏ Two horse heads
> ❏ A fuse box
> ❏ A large metal urn
> ❏ A giraffe
> ❏ A business card

- ❏ A yin yang symbol
- ❏ A Hollywood sign
- ❏ Two elephant heads
- ❏ A lizard

37. There is a door with a sign on it way up high. What does the sign say?
- a. "Storage/To Be Shipped"
- b. "Staff Only"
- c. "Private Please No Entry"
- d. "Your message here"

38. Treasure Hunt Time! See how many of these high-flying souvenirs you can find before the store closes for the day.
- ❏ A flying frog
- ❏ A wicker bird
- ❏ A bunny's head
- ❏ A wagon wheel
- ❏ A flying horse
- ❏ A frog with a big mouth
- ❏ A parade of metal birds
- ❏ A flying turtle
- ❏ Shoes
- ❏ A butterfly
- ❏ A sari (Indian dress)
- ❏ A very big snake
- ❏ Twin birds
- ❏ A birdhouse that looks hungry
- ❏ A dragon
- ❏ A sea turtle
- ❏ A man with his hat in his lap
- ❏ A marionette
- ❏ Two men at work
- ❏ A desk

39. What will get you better prices in this store?
- a. Haggling
- b. Being a member of the shop owner's family
- c. Paying with a credit card
- d. Paying in U.S. dollars
- e. Nothing, the price is the price.

40. There is a short glass cabinet. Have a look inside and then look away. Which of these treasures were displayed in the short cabinet? Mark all that you saw. No peeking!

    a. A small wooden crocodile
    b. A brass elephant
    c. A horse head
    d. An ornate mirror
    e. A wooden dagger
    f. A key resting in the cabinet lock
    g. A wooden box
    h. A white bowl with a ram's head

41. Find the cabinet with the elephant on wheels in repose on the top shelf, far right. This cabinet seems to have mice and I don't mean Mickey and Minnie. What are the mice sitting on?

    a. A lion's head
    b. Wheels; they are pull toys.
    c. An urn or vase
    d. The mousetrap, thankfully

42. There is a display cabinet with a large brass cow on the second shelf having a bit of a lie-down. Something is looking over that peaceful cow. What is it?

    a. An ape
    b. A horse
    c. A goat
    d. It's just the head of the goat, and he is smiling at me.

43. Does this cabinet contain a frog?
    Yes / No

44. Up high you will find a wonderful display of artificial animal heads for your consideration. Is there a parrot head?
    Yes / No

45. One of those heads is sticking its tongue out at us, and it is gold! Who has the Midas tongue?

    a. Horse
    b. Dragon
    c. Cow
    d. Cat
    e. A gold tongue indeed!

46. What forms of payment are accepted in this shop?
- a. Cash only
- b. Travelers checks
- c. Three milking goats is good for most things
- d. MasterCard and Visa
- e. All of the above
- f. All but c

47. There is a blue knickknack cabinet that contains a turtle on the bottom right shelf. What creature in this cabinet has way more heads than are strictly necessary?
- a. Crow
- b. Dragon
- c. Cow
- d. Horse

48. The blue cabinet also displays golden cobras on a left-hand shelf. What else is for sale on that side of the cabinet?
- a. A bird on a perch
- b. An elephant with a head coming out of both sides of its body
- c. A stone cow
- d. A pitcher
- e. All of the above and more; just ask about our coupons.
- f. All but d are there; but perhaps I could interest you in this camel figurine?

Paddle Room

49. What has been caused by recent illegal logging activities?
- a. An increase in forest fires
- b. Habitat destruction along the river
- c. The closure of Sector 8
- d. Many cute spotted owls are without a tree.

50. According to the map of the Kingdom of Anandapur, where would you go if you wanted to catch a plane?
- a. Ciater in the Bugis Sea
- b. The Tamilaya District
- c. Madja in Luk Mountain Range
- d. Drukdzong in the Drukhimal District
- e. You could catch your flight in all of the above.
- f. All but c

51. What can you look forward to after you board?
   a. A safe, exciting, and wet trip
   b. A spine-tingling, heart-pounding journey along a beautiful river
   c. A view of the local wildlife as you race along the rapids
   d. A three-hour tour

52. Who is biting deep into the jungle?
   a. Villagers
   b. Poachers
   c. Logging companies
   d. Tigers; have you seen the mouths on those things?

53. What will help the jungles' chances of surviving?
   a. Replanting
   b. Locking up poachers
   c. Tarzan
   d. People caring about them

54. Treasure Hunt Time! See how many of these treasures you can find before they float away.
   ❑ A paddle that looks like a guitar
   ❑ A backpack being held until the end of the summer
   ❑ A life preserver
   ❑ A black-collared starling
   ❑ A white-throated kingfisher
   ❑ A water bottle
   ❑ The top of the world
   ❑ Four gas lamps
   ❑ A green trunk
   ❑ An oar painted blue, yellow, and white
   ❑ A black-and-white oar
   ❑ A rusty metal hook
   ❑ A drawing of a girl's face
   ❑ A crocodile
   ❑ A cup holder
   ❑ A big metal wheel

In the Office

55. There is a blackboard for boat-tracking. What boat should have returned yesterday?
    a. Manaslu Slammer
    b. Java Jumper
    c. Bali Bumper-Car
    d. Missing boat you say?

56. There is a desk/cabinet area with a note telling us that the office personnel have "gone to temple." Take a good look at this area and then turn your back. Circle all of the things that were in the area.
    a. Binoculars
    b. Three cameras
    c. Typewriter
    d. First-aid kit
    e. A clipboard
    f. Film
    g. A can containing a selection of pens
    h. A bee smoker
    i. A small basket
    j. A weathered old box
    k. A container of sales receipts

River Art Room

57. On your left as you enter the room there is a cabinet with mesh doors. Inside it, you can see postcards on a bulletin board. Which of these things is pictured on a postcard?
    a. Cactus
    b. Surfing
    c. Oranges
    d. All of the above
    e. Only a and b

58. There are colorful artifacts of people sitting on top of the bulletin board. How many have beards?
    a. 1
    b. 2
    c. 3
    d. They are all clean-shaven.

59. There are some beautiful paintings of the river ride. What happens when the raft passes through So Sari?

  a. Oh no, you hit rocky white-water; that looks dangerous!

  b. You float into a market selling beautiful, colorful saris for very reasonable prices.

  c. The raft flips over and the people go for a swim. Hmm…that doesn't seem right.

  d. Huge waves fill the boat and the people are forced to bail it out.

60. These paintings seem to be very telling. What happens at Bali Bumper-Car?

  a. The river narrows and the boats speed through at breakneck speeds.

  b. The rafts collide with one another as the rough water pushes them together.

  c. The raft takes to the air as it flies over the waterfall. It doesn't look like this part goes well.

  d. Are you sure you want to go with this rafting company?

61. Which painting shows a raft meeting with a whirlpool?

  a. Durgas Delight   b. Trisuli Twister

  c. Sherpa Surfer   d. Monsoon Mamma

62. One of the paintings shows some snow has fallen. Which painting looks a bit chilly?

  a. Bali Bumper-Car   b. Manaslu Slammer

  c. Durgas Delight   d. Snow; I don't think so.

63. Treasure Hunt Time! You are almost there. I hope you brought a towel. See how many of these treasures you can find before you are washed away.

  ❑ Peacock feathers
  ❑ Saddle
  ❑ Tape deck
  ❑ Water cooler
  ❑ Cooking wok
  ❑ Bottle of cola
  ❑ Stack of ice chests
  ❑ A boat that is looking at you
  ❑ Purple camera
  ❑ Wooden elephant

❑ First-aid kit
❑ Three-wheeled vehicle
❑ Phone
❑ Rolling pin
❑ A call for help

You're almost there. You might stay dry, or not; probably not. Time to put this book someplace waterproof.

Asia Answers

Expedition Everest: Standby Line

5 bonus points if you guessed that "queueseum" comes from the words "queue" and "museum." _____

1) b. Himalayan Escapes

2) c. A flying yak

3) d. Hiking boots

4) b. Your stamped permits

5) d. "Be Right Back"

6) c. In a fancy wooden box

7) a. Champagne and film

8) Total Treasures found _____

9) e. All these things are there.

10) d. Anandapur Mountaineering Association

11) e. All but a

12) b. The trim

13) Total Treasures found _____

14) c. He is a guardian of the sacred mountain.

15) d. All of the above

16) a. Mountains

17) b. Red paint

18) Total Yeti Treasures found _____

. Looks like yeti again

a. Yeti riding yaks

a. A snake

) Total items collected: bells ___ yeti images___ fruits and vegetables ___

23) e. All except b

24) d. Go through the shop.

25) c. Pick the tea

26) c. A ram's head

27) Yes

28) Total Treasures found _____

29) d. All but of the above

30) d. He proved the yeti is real.

31) e. They are all there.

32) a. To comb the carpet

33) Total Treasures found _____

34) b. Danfe pheasant

35) c. Deer

36) No

37) Yes

38) a. A footprint

39) e. All but a

40) b. Black bear

41) c. 5

42) b. A very big yeti footprint

43) e. Both a and b

44) d. He combines local foods with expedition supplies to create varied meals for months.

45) d. 125 pounds or more

Expedition Everest: FASTPASS Line

1) Total First Room Treasures found _____

2) Total found Outside the First Building _____

3) Total Supply Area Treasures found _____

4) Total Yeti Museum Treasures found _____

Flights of Wonder

1) a. Peacocks

2) Total Treasures found _____

Pop Owl Quiz (Answers 3-7)

3) e. Both a and b

4) b. They can't move in their sockets.

5) False

6) False

7) a. Giraffes have much bigger vertebrae.

8) Number of perches spotted _____

9) Total Treasures found _____

Kali River Rapids

Outside Hike

1) Number of items found:
   Full Statues _____
   Broken pieces of artifacts _____
   Monkeys _____
   Wet People _____
   Total _____

   Museum curator evaluation of your services:
   1-4 artifacts found: Hmmmmm, were you looking?

> *5-9 artifacts found: Thanks for your contribution but don't quit your day job.*
>
> *10-15 artifacts found: A very nice showing; your archaeological skills show much promise.*
>
> *16-20 artifacts found: You are the most promising archaeological talent the curator has ever seen. Welcome aboard as our new professor of archaeology.*
>
> *20-50 artifacts found: Hey, professor, are you the guy who found the Lost Ark?*

Front Porch

2) e. Both a and c

Kali River Queueseum

Statue Room

3) f. All but d

4) c. A cat

5) a. Fruit

6) Total Treasures found _____

7) c. From a bicycle food cart

8) f. He has all but b.

Fountain Room

9) b. A golden cobra

10) a. A heavy metal urn

11) b. The monkey

12) a. He is lifting something on his head.

13) c. The dragon

14) b. A bell

15) b. A human

16) d. Large cauldrons

17) a. A metal barrel containing two watermelons, c. A crate of fruit, d. A large metal jug, g. Several brooms, h. Several mats, j. A handlebar-basket full of bottles, k. A pointy hat, m. A crate full of durian fruit, n. A purple plastic basket

18) Number of platters and bowls found _____

19) d. Locks available on most doors

Duck Room

20) a. The king of the deer

21) b. White

22) d. A monkey

23) c. Because only the foolish pretend to be kings

24) c. Close his mouth

25) a. "The Swan with the Golden Feather"

26) c. "The Swan with the Golden Feather"

27) e. Only b and c

28) b. Lion
29) d. Monkey
Mr. Panika's Shop
  30) a. Looking
  31) c. Dragons
  32) b. 3
  33) Yes
  34) d. At the temple
  35) c. A coupon for ½ off on lunch at the Curry Hut
  36) Total Office Treasures found _____
  37) c. "Private Please No Entry"
  38) Total Treasures found _____
  39) d. Paying in U.S. dollars
  40) b. A brass elephant, c. A horse head, e. A wooden dagger, g. A wooden box, h. A white bowl with a ram's head
  41) c. An urn or vase
  42) d. It's just the head of the goat.
  43) No
  44) No
  45) a. Horse
  46) a. Cash only
  47) d. Horse
  48) e. All of the above and more.
Paddle Room
  49) c. The closure of Sector 8
  50) f. All but c
  51) a. A safe, exciting, and wet trip
  52) c. Logging companies
  53) d. People caring about them
  54) Total Treasures found
In the Office
  55) a. Manaslu Slammer
  56) a. Binoculars, c. Typewriter, d. First-aid kit, f. Film, i. A small basket, j. A weathered old box
River Art Room
  57) d. All of the above
  58) b. 2
  59) a. You hit rocky white-water.
  60) c. The raft takes to the air as it flies over the waterfall.
  61) b. Trisuli Twister
  62) b. Manaslu Slammer
  63) Total Treasures found _____

DinoLand U.S.A.

DINOSAUR

? **POP QUIZ!** It is time to see just how observant you are. Before you get into line, have a look at the sign.

FP 1. **How many dinosaurs did you see on it?**
   a. A whole herd of dinosaurs was running across an open plain.
   b. There were four dinosaurs on the sign: three dining on grass and one planning a meal a bit more meaty.
   c. There was only a half dinosaur on the sign.
   d. Dinosaurs? You saw dinosaurs on that sign?

FP 2. **Something very big was happening on the sign. What was it?**
   a. A Tyrannosaurus was eating the sign.
   b. Something big: well, dinosaurs are pretty big, right?
   c. A Tyrannosaurus rex was attacking a Triceratops.
   d. Is an asteroid explosion big enough for you?

FP 3. **Something was flying off the sign. What was it?**
   a. Small round pieces of asteroid, and one not so small; that dino on the ground better move.
   b. Several Pterodactyls were flying off of the sign.
   c. Broken pieces of the sign were falling off, plus several large dino teeth.
   d. Nothing was coming off the sign.

FP **4. There was a message on the sign. What did it say?**
>   a. Welcome to a time when Dinosaurs Ruled the Earth
>   b. Dinosaurs – Beware!
>   c. It's Fast – It's a Blast – It's in the Past
>   d. Please keep arms and legs outside of the dinosaurs.

FP **5. Did any of the dinosaurs on the sign have wings?**
>   Yes / No

FP **6. Did any of the dinosaurs on the sign have horns?**
>   Yes /No

FP **7. Were any of the dinosaurs on the sign enjoying a good meal?**
>   Yes / No

End of Pop Quiz

FP **8. You are waiting outside a large building. What is the name of the building you are about to enter?**
>   a. College of Archaeology
>   b. Center for Dinosaur Research
>   c. Museum of Prehistoric Times
>   d. The Dino Institute

9. There is one dinosaur pictured on the round seal for this building. Which one is it?
>   a. Stegosaurus
>   b. Tyrannosaurus rex, of course, king of dinosaurs
>   c. Triceratops
>   d. A large purple dinosaur singing about being my friend

10. Four more things are pictured on this seal. What are they?
>   a. A bone, a microscope, calipers, and a shovel
>   b. A microscope, calipers, a tooth, and a shovel
>   c. A shovel, a microscope, a brush, and a tooth
>   d. A bone, a brush, calipers, and a microscope

11. The seal listed three goals, what were they?
>   a. Knowledge, Research, and Exploration
>   b. Exploration, Excavation, and Exultation
>   c. Research, Teaching, and Preserving
>   d. Recreation, Research, Not being eaten

12. Treasure Hunt Time! See how many of these you can unearth before you enter the building.

- ❏ An opportunity to lose your head
- ❏ A dinosaur under attack
- ❏ A broken tooth
- ❏ A dinosaur with horns who's looking very scary
- ❏ A dinosaur who looks like he might make a fine house pet
- ❏ Two Dino Institute seals
- ❏ A dinosaur with a frilly head
- ❏ Dino wrinkles
- ❏ Teeny tiny dino "hands"
- ❏ Back spikes
- ❏ A dino tongue

FP You are about to enter The Dino Institute. As you wait to board your vehicle, you will pass through a beautiful museum filled with treasure. Look around it to answer Questions 13 to 31.

13. Which modern animal is a descendent of *Avitelmessus grapsoides*?

    a. Starfish   b. Crow
    c. Grasshopper   d. Crab

14. Which modern animal can claim a branch on the family tree of *Inoceramus*?

    a. Clam   b. Possum
    c. Dragonfly   d. Fern. Hey wait a minute.
                          That's a plant!

15. How did *Rhacolepis buccalis* **get around?**

    a. Swim   b. Fly
    c. Walk   d. Slither

16. Whose fossil looks very much like the letter "V"?

    a. Prehistoric crow
    b. Prehistoric snail
    c. Prehistoric leafhopper
    d. Looks more like the letter "Z" to me

17. Which of these dragon-like creatures has *Therrophlebia* **for an ancestor?**

    a. Crocodile   b. Dragonfly
    c. Komodo dragon   d. Mushu the dragon

18. What shared the earth with dinosaurs?
a. Plants and animals that are very similar to creatures alive today
b. Vegetation and creatures wildly different from the life on earth today
c. Lots of plants but not much else due to the dinosaurs voracious eating habits
d. Dinosaurs don't share nuthin' with nobody.

19. Check the walls around you. They are embedded with fossilized leaves. You get 1 point for each different type of leaf you find. _____

20. Someone is thirsty. Who needs a drink?
a. A dinosaur   b. A rodent
c. A bird   d. Me; where is a drinking fountain?

21. What is the thirsty creature drinking from?
a. A large wet leaf
b. A volcanic crater lake
c. A dinosaur footprint
d. The fountain; he found it!

22. There's a ex-dinosaur grinning at you. Which is it?
a. Stegosaurus
b. Ankylosaurus
c. Tyrannosaurus rex
d. Albertosaurus
e. None of the above

Everything about this Albertosaurus is smaller than its cousin the Tyrannosaurus rex. That is, everything except one thing.

23. What one thing about Albertosaurus makes the T-rex seem a bit undersized?
a. His long arms
b. His huge saw-like teeth
c. His enormous skull
d. His big heart

24. Treasure Hunt Time! See if you can find these treasures before they go extinct.
❑ Babies taking a ride
❑ Someone with a good hiding spot

❑ Someone who could not hide if he tried
❑ Someone having lunch
❑ A spooky crustacean
❑ A little creature with a scary name
❑ At least six rodents
❑ At least two insects

25. Who hails from Canada?
   a. Anchiceratops
   b. The giant water beetle
   c. Albertosaurus
   d. The box turtle
   e. All of the above
   f. All but c

26. We know that dinosaurs are extinct. For example, you have none living in your hometown, right? Which of these is not a theory about dinosaur extinction?
   a. Egg-eating mammals
   b. A change in the sun's gravitational pull on Earth
   c. Climate change
   d. Asteroid impact
   e. All of the above are theories of dinosaur extinction.

27. The "Theories of Extinction" art piece contains no mammals.
   True or False?

28. There are dinosaur bones in the "Theories of Extinction" art piece.
   True or False?

29. The "Theories of Extinction" art piece includes an asteroid impact.
   True or False?

30. The "Theories of Extinction" art piece shows a flood about to wash away the dinosaurs.
   True or False?

31. There are insects in the "Theories of Extinction" art piece.
   True or False?

In the Main Waiting Gallery

You are now entering the main waiting gallery. It is filled with Treasure for you to unearth.

FP **32. What happened to cause the K-T boundary?**
    a. Volcanic explosions ripped across the Earth covering everything in lava and ash.
    b. Dinosaurs sank deep into the tar creating an excellent fossil record.
    c. An asteroid hit the Earth with devastating effects.
    d. Mammals got tired of all the bullying they had endured from dinosaurs and decided fried dino egg was their favorite treat. The dinos went extinct.

33. Which dinosaur's name means "Swift Running Reptile"?
    a. Roadrunnersaurus
    b. Tyrannosaurus rex
    c. Protostega
    d. Dromaeosaurus

FP **34. Treasure Hunt Time!** It is time for a great big dino-sized treasure hunt. Get out your expedition gear and see how many of the following treasures you can dig up before you board your transport to the past.
- ❑ First Plate
- ❑ Two volcanoes
- ❑ A single piece of dino spine
- ❑ Three insects
- ❑ A bow
- ❑ A dodo having a snack
- ❑ A shell
- ❑ 25,000 miles
- ❑ Clouds
- ❑ A waterfall
- ❑ Lightning
- ❑ A seagull-like bird
- ❑ Desert glass
- ❑ A rib bone
- ❑ A winged-dino skeleton
- ❑ A dino with a head shaped like a hammer
- ❑ A creature with fur

Finding Nemo—The Musical

"Go Fish" Game

OK, it is time to go fishing; who brought their gear?

If you look right in front of you, you will see a large stream of people… er fish… swimming past your location. That is good news, fish being an important component of any successful fishing trip.

To play "Go Fish," you will need to divide up into two teams. (If one team has an extra player then, just to be sportsman like, the other team should receive a 2-point handicap.)

Here is how you fish:

Team 1 must think of something they bet they can find on a "fish" floating by, let's say a red shirt. Team 1 announces its bet, which should sound something like this: "We can find someone wearing a red shirt." Then, Team 2 either chooses to tell Team 1 to "Go fish" or it identifies a new fish to catch – one that's wearing the red shirt Team 1 suggested plus something additional, for example, a ponytail. (Fish love ponytails.) Team 1 can then tell Team 2 to "Go fish" or add yet another element to fish for, say, a teenager. Play goes back and forth between the two teams until one team chooses to tell the other team to "Go fish."

When your team is told to "Go fish," you must spot a fish with all the trappings and characteristics the two teams have decided to fish for up until that point (for example, a teenager with a ponytail wearing a red shirt).

The team that's fishing gets 1 minute of fishing time for each element they are after, in this case 3 minutes total, and they receive 1 point per item caught. So if play went back and forth three times, you'd have a 3-point fish, if you landed it.

Confused? Check the sample round below:

Team 1: "We can find someone wearing a blue shirt."

Team 2: "We can find someone wearing a blue shirt and jeans."

Team 1: "We can find someone wearing a blue shirt and jeans who is also a child."

Team 2, "Go Fish!"

Team 1 now has 3 minutes to find a child dressed in a blue shirt and jeans. If Team 1 makes this big catch, they receive 3 points. Then play starts over, this time with Team 2 making the first bet.

Note: The team that's fishing earns points only if it lands the whole fish, that is, a fish with all of the specified characteristics (in this case, blue shirt, jeans, and child).

Primeval Whirl

FP ❓ **POP QUIZ!** Look at the overhead sign before you enter – or prepare to be a good guesser.

1. How many Dinosaurs were on the sign you just walked under?
    a. 1
    b. 2
    c. 3
    d. No dinosaurs, but there were some really big lizards.

2. There was a dinosaur sitting on something. What was it?
    a. Another dinosaur
    b. An asteroid
    c. A space ship
    d. His head

3. What was that dinosaur doing with his mouth exactly? (I always think it is good to know what a dinosaur's mouth is up to.)
    a. It was open with his tongue hanging out.
    b. It was wide open screaming.
    c. It was open eating a popsicle.
    d. Why is the dinosaur's mouth always open?

4. Could you see any dinosaur teeth in that open mouth of his?
    Yes / No

5. What was floating in space with the dinosaurs?
   a. Parts falling off of the space ship. Hey I don't think that ship is fit to drive.
   b. Clocks. Dinosaurs are very particular about keeping good time.
   c. Books. You can't have too much to read out in space.
   d. Not much. Space is big – very, very big.

6. Were there any stars in space?
   Yes / No

End of Pop Quiz

FP **7. Dinosaurs as we all know are avid collectors. No, it's true. Look around. What collections are the dinos displaying here for you?**
   a. Bumper stickers
   b. Hubcaps
   c. Industrial-size whisks
   d. Alien knickknacks
   e. All of the above
   f. Only b and c

8. Treasure Hunt Time! Can you spot these?
   ❏ A wooly Mammoth in a sash
   ❏ A dino who is showing you his big muscle
   ❏ A dino who is all "pumped" up
   ❏ An alarm clock
   ❏ Cadillac
   ❏ A moon
   ❏ A star
   ❏ Paint
   ❏ A top
   ❏ A set of three initials
   ❏ A silver disk with ten holes in it
   ❏ Two pair of glasses
   ❏ Two red arrows
   ❏ A gas pump
   ❏ An antenna
   ❏ "Yea"
   ❏ A clipboard
   ❏ A tidy dino with a request
   ❏ Earrings not on a guest

FP **9. Do any of the scientists have a book?**
   Yes / No

10. Do any of the gauges or clocks have actual numbers on them?

    Yes / No

FP 11. There is a scientist pulling down on a handle. Which of these things is not true about him?

    a. He is wearing a belt.

    b. He has a pocket protector.

    c. He has gray hair.

    d. He has his glasses.

    e. All are true of him.

FP 12. Are any of the scientists women?

    Yes / No

13. There is a scientist holding a little flag. What's on it?

    a. A picture of a dinosaur

    b. The word "YEA!"

    c. It said "Team Dino"

    d. It said "To the past or bust"

FP 14. Were all of the scientists wearing goggles or glasses?

    Yes / No

15. There was a scientist with a pull-down face shield. What is he doing with his hands?

    a. Holding a clipboard

    b. Holding a coffee mug

    c. Using a calculator

    d. Giving a thumbs-up

    e. Only a and d

    f. Only b and c

FP 16. What is the lady scientist up to?

    a. She is using a calculator.

    b. She is adjusting a knob.

    c. She is writing on a clipboard.

    d. She is waving.

FP 17. Does she have on any jewelry?

    a. Yes, earrings

    b. Yes, a necklace

    c. Yes, a bracelet

    d. All of the above. She's a bit overdressed if you ask me.

e. No, scientists don't wear jewelry.

FP 18. There is a scientist looking over his shoulder at you. What is in his hand?
    a. A chart   b. A ruler
    c. A donut   d. Nothing

FP 19. Are any of the scientists eating?
    Yes / No

FP 20. Do any of the machines have an antenna?
    Yes / No

TriceraTop Spin

The route of this outdoor queue changes depending on the number of people in line, so you many need to skip around a bit to find the questions that work best for where you are standing.

? POP QUIZ! As you walk into the Dino-Rama! area, have a look at the sign you're about to walk under.

1. There were two dinos front and center. One of them held up a welcome sign. What kind of dino was he?
    a. Pterodactyl   b. Brachiosaurus
    c. Triceratops   d. Tyrannosaurus rex
End of Pop Quiz

2. If you have a look around, you will find a dino who intends to do something until he is dizzy. What activity will make this dino's head spin?
    a. Twirling
    b. Shopping
    c. Eating ice cream
    d. Riding TriceraTop Spin

3. Near the dizzy dino, some Pterodactyls are out for a fly. What are they carrying?
    a. Ice cream cones
    b. Shopping bags
    c. Baby Pterodactyls
    d. Now, how would Pterodactyls carry something? They have wings, not hands.

4. How many packages is Dizzy Dino carrying?
    a. 6   b. 7
    c. 8   d. 9

5. What do you do at the Dino Whamma ?
    a. Dance
    b. Pound small dinos on the head as they pop out of holes. Ouch!
    c. Get in bumper dinos and try to wham into other drivers
    d. Hit something really hard to measure your strength and make a bell ring.

6. If someone has achieved the rank of Triceps-A-Tops, what did they do?
    a. They made a bell ring.
    b. They made their spinning TriceraTop fly at the top level.
    c. They lifted a dumbbell that has two small dinos sitting on it.
    d. They hit the most dinos on the head.

7. If you look up high, you will see a dino about to be hit by something. What is going to hit him?
    a. A bowling ball
    b. A red-hot meteorite
    c. A foot belonging to a much larger dino.
    d. A runaway coaster car

8. A dino with two suitcases wants everyone to head for the hills. Why is that?
    a. Because the volcano he is next to is about to blow
    b. Because he is about to be eaten by a very big dinosaur
    c. Because he is about to be crushed by meteors
    d. Because he is packed to go camping

9. Treasure Hunt Time! See how many of these prehistoric treasures you can dig up as you near the front of the line.
    ❑ A pocket watch
    ❑ At least four clocks
    ❑ Lightning
    ❑ An hourglass
    ❑ At least six asteroids

❑ A spinning sun
❑ Two green spheres
❑ A dino using his tail like a hand
❑ A dino tongue
❑ A dino with a hobo stick

10. There are two dinos who are worried that you might be "getting down." What are they holding?
a. Tissues
b. Tools
c. Tops
d. Nothing; their hands are empty.

11. There is a partial dinosaur skeleton. She has something in her hands or, um, claws. What is it?
a. A baby dino skeleton; aw, how cute!
b. A top
c. A corndog
d. A pencil

12. This partial dino skeleton has something between her head and her tail. What is it?
a. A tent top
b. A collection of bones to bang on and make music
c. A collection of balloons for you to try to hit
d. Her ribs, of course

13. What is the posted speed limit on the road running next to the dino area?
a. 5 mph   b. 10 mph
c. 25 mph   d. No faster than the dino chasing you, please!

14. In what year was the Boneyard Fossil Fun Site established?
a. 206 million years ago
b. 1792
c. 1846
d. 1947

15. What is the Boneyard sign made of?
a. A piece of canvas
b. A bone, of course
c. A dinosaur's belly
d. A huge shovel sticking up out of the ground

16. There are two dinos doing battle. What are they fighting with?
   a. Their teeth and claws; they are dinosaurs, after all
   b. They are boxing with gloves off.
   c. They are tail-wrestling.
   d. They are knocking heads. Someone is going to have a bad headache.

17. What color is the biggest dino presiding over the Dino-Rama area?
   a. Blue   b. Green
   c. Yellow   d. Red

18. Treasure Hunt Time! See how many of these treasures you can unearth in the back part of the line.
   ❑ A dino peeking out from behind a sign
   ❑ A big smile way up high
   ❑ People with big heads
   ❑ A pencil
   ❑ Several small plastic toy dinos
   ❑ A Triceratops doing a fancy trick with a ball
   ❑ The find of the day
   ❑ A dino wearing a hard hat
   ❑ Some rib bones
   ❑ A bone with a hole in it
   ❑ A huge dino leg or arm bone standing on end
   ❑ Dino tailbones

DinoLand U.S.A. Answers

DINOSAUR
   1) c. There was only a half dinosaur on the sign.
   2) d. Is an asteroid explosion big enough for you?
   3) a. Small round pieces of asteroid, and one not so small
   4) c. It's Fast – It's a Blast – It's in the Past
   5) No
   6) Yes
   7) No
   8) d. The Dino Institute
   9) c. Triceratops
   10) a. A bone, a microscope, calipers, and a shovel
   11) b. Exploration, Excavation, and Exultation

12) Total Treasures found _____

13) d. Crab

14) a. Clam

15) a. Swim

16) c. Prehistoric leafhopper

17) b. Dragonfly

18) a. Plants and animals that are very similar to creatures alive today

19) Number of different leaf types found _____

20) b. A rodent

21) c. A dinosaur footprint

22) d. Albertosaurus

23) a. His long arms

24) Total Treasures found _____

25) a. Anchiceratops

26) b. A change in the sun's gravitational pull on Earth

27) False

28) True

29) True

30) False

31) True

32) c. An asteroid hit the Earth with devastating effects.

33) d Dromaeosaurus

34) Total Treasures found _____

Finding Nemo—The Musical

Fish landed by Team 1: _____

Fish landed by Team 2: _____

Primeval Whirl

1) a. 1

2) c. A space ship

3) a. It was open with his tongue hanging out.

4) Yes

5) b. Clocks

6) Yes

7) f. Only b and c

8) Total Treasures found _____

9) No

10) Yes

11) b. He has a pocket protector

12) Yes

13) b. "YEA!"

14) Yes
15) e. Only a and d
16) c. She is writing on a clipboard.
17) a. Yes, earrings
18) d. Nothing
19) No
20) Yes

TriceraTop Spin

1) a. Pterodactyl
2) b. Shopping
3) b. Shopping bags
4) c. 8
5) d. Hit something really hard
6) a. They made a bell ring.
7) b. A red-hot meteorite
8) c. Because he is about to be crushed by meteors
9) Total Prehistoric Treasures found _____
10) b. Tools
11) d. A pencil
12) a. A tent top
13) c. 25 mph
14) d. 1947
15) b. A bone
16) d. They are knocking heads.
17) c. Yellow
18) Total Treasures found _____

Disney's Animal Kingdom Scavenger Hunt

You can hunt for the treasure below as you walk from attraction to attraction. Or if you prefer you can devote part of a day to finding these treasures. Either way, keep your eyes open to rack up the points.

Tip: All scavenger hunt items are inanimate unless it says "live."

- ❑ A live babirusa (a pig-like creature with tusks)
- ❑ A pile of rhinos
- ❑ A blue bear tipping a canoe
- ❑ Two chameleons in the mood for pizza
- ❑ A chimpanzee supporting the weight of a zoo on his shoulders
- ❑ Ducks on a hike
- ❑ A well
- ❑ A large stone rat
- ❑ A green-and-yellow butterfly visiting the light
- ❑ A snail climbing a light
- ❑ A seahorse in the rafters
- ❑ A pole that slithers
- ❑ A prayer flag with a butterfly
- ❑ A large fanged mask atop a costume of rags
- ❑ A pink bike
- ❑ A large bell
- ❑ An internet café
- ❑ An elephant with a red head
- ❑ A red rickshaw
- ❑ A tree adorned in rags
- ❑ A giant stone foot
- ❑ A wall of traditional Swahili plaster-carving
- ❑ A building made from tiny stones
- ❑ A drum tree
- ❑ A map of Africa
- ❑ A live colobus monkey
- ❑ A giraffe skull
- ❑ A hippopotamus skull
- ❑ A live gorilla
- ❑ A large stone frog
- ❑ Hummingbird shutters

- ❑ Two zebras back to back
- ❑ A dragon
- ❑ Triceratops' head in stone

Animal Kingdom Scavenger Hunt Tally

Total Treasures found _____

Index

The rides and attractions covered in this book are listed both alphabetically and by "land" or "area" for easy look-up.

The following abbreviations appear in this index:

AK	Disney's Animal Kingdom
MK	Magic Kingdom
E	Epcot
HS	Disney's Hollywood Studios

A

B

C

D

E

F

G

H

I

J

K

L

M